What People Are Saying

"It's been my good fortune to work with Claire L. Hebert-Dow as an adviser and coauthor. She's a consummate professional, with exceptional skills and a steady moral compass. As a writer, she's an inspirational talent embedding innovative thinking with the attention to detail that's so important when conveying a narrative. Claire and I have co-created more than 50 blogs that have enjoyed some 10,000 hits as well as a best-selling book, *Leadership Development: The Next Curve to Flatten!*, a post-pandemic treatise on the need for executives to exhibit empathy, transparency, and accountability.

"Claire's journey is a master class with respect to relentless pursuit of success through purpose-built identity. *Saving Mama* is a must-read for insight and inspiration. It should not go unnoticed that her values are affirmed by her plan to donate the proceeds of *Saving Mama* to training organizations such as the Working Dog Foundation and Hero Pups."

—**Thomas F. Casey**, Managing Principal, Discussion Partner
Collaborative, author of five best-selling books on leadership

"Engrossing read about a single mother trying to make her way, defying the odds to find success and happiness."

—**Katherine Dormody**, Director, Gilford Public Library, Gilford,
New Hampshire

"*Saving Mama* is a window into the private life of a woman as she tackles motherhood, working in a man's world, and discovering who she is, all through the eyes of her beloved felines and one delightful canine. *Saving Mama* shows the real struggles, pain, and happy moments of motherhood and the deep connection between a woman and her pets. I found myself laughing at Claire's sassy attitude, cheering her on during life's difficult moments, and crying for her losses."

    —Amy Southard, author of *Witches of Holy Orchard*

"Claire's memoir is easily relatable on many levels for me: the struggles of a woman in a man's world of business and finding solace in unusual companions. Her kinship with her pets speaks to many of us who have felt that special connection. A worthy and engaging story."

    —**Lauren Lyons**, entrepreneur, Laconia, New Hampshire

"I love how Claire weaves the heart and soul of her beloved pets into this first-person narrative. Well done!"

    —**Rebecca Watson**, teacher, Gilford Elementary School, Gilford, New Hampshire

SAVING MAMA

Claire L. Hebert-Dow

ISBNs: 979-8-218-48902-1—softcover version
        979-8-218-48903-8—eBook version
Library of Congress Control Number: 2024908369

Peter E. Randall Publisher
5 Greenleaf Woods Drive, Suite 102
Portsmouth, NH 03801

Book design by Tim Holtz
Printed in the United States of America

To my beautiful children, Ryan and Sarah,
and to Conan T. Grace, who believed
in me when no one else did

CONTENTS

"Always do what you are afraid to do."

—Ralph Waldo Emerson

PREFACE

"Mama" is what I like to be called.

French was my first language; I didn't speak English until kindergarten, because back in the good ole days, there were many of us here in the heart of the Lakes Region of New Hampshire who came from French Canadian families. Both sides of my family are Quebecois, and I can include Acadian—as Yankee as it gets. I'm proud of my heritage, which harkens back to the mid-1600s.

I'm proud of my parents and grandparents too, for all they did to impart enough tenacity for me to hold on tight as I chased a dream I wasn't sure was attainable. But with every fiber of my being, this dream—to tell the story of my experience as a single mama—needs to catch some sunlight. And in these pages, it does.

I'm grateful for the memories of a carefree childhood, when kids could play in the streets, enjoy hours in a pile of sand with a bag of marbles, or tap into their imaginations with Tonka trucks and teacups. Innocence and simplicity reigned.

Then would come one tsunami after another, domestic and foreign. Their tentacles of restlessness and frustration trickled down to folks like me. I'm a card-carrying baby boomer. We kicked tradition to the curb and we girls went to great lengths to prove our mettle.

Motherhood, on the other hand, has no bounds. Once a mother, always a mother. No matter what decade, no matter what culture. Call it a tattoo on the heart. Just ask any mama bear or mama elephant about the pain that ensues from being separated from a cub or a calf. But what about my pain—mine, that of a mere mortal? Do I shrug off poor decisions and wrong turns and let them go? Or do I find a way to weave my story so that my own precious cubs can begin to understand why this mama still carries such sadness.

I'm lucky not to have been alone through the most challenging years of my life. Five cats and one dog saved me from the despair threatening to unnerve me into a state of paralysis. I won't forget them, but only now am I able to intuit what they must've been thinking as they watched me escape from the reality of my lost motherhood. Meet my Delta Force.

Tia, an abandoned domestic tiger kitty, torn from her mother's teat, taking what solace she could from sucking her tail;

Joey, a cream Persian with a smooshed nose who was sure he'd been king of the jungle in a previous life;

Bailey, the offspring of a Himalayan calendar girl and an absentee father and convinced he'd run the Iditarod;

Casper and *Chloe*, neglected Himalayan siblings from the low-rent district;

Brady, a cocker spaniel–shih tzu–poodle blend who reminded me of . . .

This is our story.

PROLOGUE

I WAS NO YOUNG WIFE when I became a mama. At 28, I was two years younger than my own mother when she gave birth to me. Her marriage to my dad lasted till death do them part—60 years. I didn't make ten. Our vows didn't include those words, but I don't believe that was the cause of our downfall. The marriage was way more complicated than that.

It was already the second for both of us, thanks to the sparks that flew. Our respective spouses didn't stand a chance. We figured the fireworks we were missing would be found in our own union. We were wrong. I'd give anything to fix the potholes we ended up leaving behind for our children. They survived, though, and made matches to the right partners and provided an intact family for their own kids.

Something about growing a miniature human inside my tummy had me shuddering with anxiety. How much pain would there be during delivery? What if my infant emerged damaged in some way?

My fear could well have been rooted in the loss of control. As the firstborn in my family, I was used to concentrating on school to excel and in my working years to be some white shirt's right-hand girl for the minutiae as well as the weighty. But now month after month, the evidence was visible. My body was changing, and I was responsible for keeping this little cub alive.

In the 1970s, Lamaze classes were all the rage. Lamaze is a method of breathing to distract from the turbulence south of the border. Choosing a name for our child offered my husband and me no such assistance, especially if we had a boy. My husband was adamant that a son's name had to be no-bones-about-it masculine. When "Ryan Christopher" came into my mind, it was a win-win. As was the moment after some 22 hours of labor when we had ourselves a not-so-little boy. He was eight pounds, with a full head of hair on his perfectly formed head. He was a sight to behold for my own blue eyes. Just having ten fingers and ten toes would've been enough, but this big boy was gorgeous.

Our joy continued through the fall of 1977. I remember our new trio taking in a football game at Dartmouth College. Made no difference that I didn't understand the sport—it ranks as one of my fondest memories. I wish there could've been more.

By my first Mother's Day, I was facing divorce. I still don't know why. What I do know is that I was reluctant to question my husband's reasoning. That he was an attorney didn't help. I was as much in awe as I was intimidated. How can you present a counterargument against a skilled litigator? But something serious had to have happened to flip the switch on our relationship so soon.

By early fall, Ryan and I had vacated our homestead for an apartment in Laconia, my hometown. I can still remember the turmoil of the move. This baby had been conceived in love and marriage. And now I was about to be a single mother of a one-year-old. Other than my full-time job and my parents nearby to assist, I was like a baby bird who'd fallen out of the nest.

We all know there are two sides to every story, but my impression is that my formal answer to his petition being not as simple as "irreconcilable differences" was instrumental in getting my husband to change his mind. But a dark cloud lingered over me, one that would've benefited from a stiff breeze. I wouldn't be the first one in a marriage to be asked to forgive and forget. But I couldn't do either.

Next came my graduation, at the age of 33, from the University of New Hampshire, bachelor's degree in psychology, summa cum laude. I earned entrance into three national honor societies, including Phi Beta Kappa. Focused and determined, I was a sponge for expanding my mind on an academic level, but that same mind was marinating in anger and resentment. I couldn't let them go.

The next five years were a mix of successes and failures. On the heels of my college graduation, we welcomed another baby, a girl with heart-shaped lips, as dainty as a ballet slipper. Sarah Marie had the look of a pale pink rosebud, but it was her smile that caught your attention—her "Sarah smile." This future mother-daughter duo came to weigh the value of a purchase by that smile alone.

Affection had been ingrained in me from childhood. Coming from a "huggy" family, I enveloped my children at every opportunity. Every night I read each a bedtime story, arms wrapped around one of them as we sat together in a rocking chair. For Ryan it was *Winnie-the-Pooh*, with his favorite stuffies in each fist—Peepers, a yellow chick, and the pale lavender bunny whose name escapes me. For Sarah it was Amy Schwartz's *Begin at the Beginning*. With a main character named Sara (without the *h*), it had a simple message within a complex dilemma. Mother and daughter together would find a solution. Through the many repetitions, my voice danced over the words adding a lyrical quality to the text. One of my finer mama moments. What mother imagines such joy would come to an abrupt halt?

Ryan's babyhood remains more vivid than Sarah's; perhaps that's typical of firstborns. I remember when he looked back at himself while belly-down on the mirror of his geometric black-and-white mat; when he rolled over onto his side with the look of a "whoops" on his face; when he had his first ice-cream cone. During his earliest months, I felt fulfilled and at peace. With Ryan, I embraced my dream.

Married life was complicated, though. Ryan gravitated toward his father's favorite sport, golf, and the Laconia Country Club. Sarah, on the other hand, just wanted to be with me. Shopping was our favorite sport, and the city's Madrigal, an upscale boutique, offered this little girl an opportunity to showcase what worked and didn't work on her mother by her smile alone.

Such memories were my best friend as well as my worst enemy when my status as a wife and mother unraveled. I made many mistakes. It was like the final lap of the Magic Mile at Loudon's Speedway. My tank was running on empty, but I still kept my foot on the accelerator. I wish I'd seen who was coming to overtake me.

In the fall of 1984, a cloud of heartbreaks burst down on me: a special uncle died in his early 50s; my mother dealt with the double whammy of two surgeries, mastectomy and appendectomy; my favorite resident at the nursing home where I worked died; my kitty died.

I was a mess and dropped ten pounds off my 105-pound frame. Coming into the holidays, I knew alcohol would need to be tempered, if not eliminated.

My best friend had asked me to be maid of honor at her late-afternoon wedding on New Year's Eve in Portsmouth, more than an hour's drive. I returned home in time to put the children to bed, but my husband was anything but welcoming. The following morning, with the weatherman's prediction of sleet now coming true, I suited up in full rain gear to run my heart out. I didn't know exactly why, other than that the sadness in my heart was getting harder to bear. There's no telling how far I might've run if I didn't have a midday party to attend at the home of one of my husband's business associates. Kids weren't usually invited, but for some reason my husband insisted we bring the children. They were the only ones there.

Even for brunch, a bar well positioned for easy access was common during these years. All of us hostesses provided pre-prandial cocktails as well as after-brunch drinks and made a show of just the right liqueur or bubbly thanks to a nearby specialty wine store.

The host in this case decided to whip up a batch of Bloody Mary's. I leaned more toward champagne or a mimosa for the occasional midday get-together, but I certainly wasn't averse to tomato juice, vodka, and whatever else he added. He seemed proud of his mixture and insisted I have one. After I'd finished the first, he handed me a second. To say that my reduced frame could manage one would be stretching the truth, and two should have been out of the question. Should've been. I wish the alcohol wiped out the memory of what happened next. It didn't.

Who knows why, but there was a tug within me that Ryan and Sarah were in some kind of danger. I reached for my little girl—and promptly fell before the entire assembly. She rolled on top of me, but there's no ladylike pose for an inebriated woman laid out like a mackerel. I also remember locking lips with a male guest when he made a late entrance. I was blotto.

Two days later, a sheriff was at the door, with a second petition for divorce, again irreconcilable differences. The marriage had managed to stay upright on parched ground, but I recalled no decision to proceed with the finality of a divorce. What I discovered just before our hearing, set for the 17th, one week after Sarah's third birthday, was that my husband had already secured one of New Hampshire's top attorneys and alerted the principal of Ryan's school that he was going to be the solo contact on behalf of our son.

Just the tip of the iceberg of the surprises on the day I walked into Superior Court. The details will emerge in what I hope will be my second book, but suffice it to say that on the first day of the year 1985 I wasn't just a full-time mama; I was a mother with benefits. By the end of January, I had moved out, advised by my attorney to cede primary physical custody to my husband. I couldn't support them on my part-time salary.

And so began my life as a minnow.

PART ONE

"Oh, Mama," Sarah pleaded with eyes that could melt an ice cap. "She's so soft, so sweet. Can we get her? Pulleeze. I want *herrr*."

It was a Saturday morning in the spring of 1987. Sarah was five years old and I was Play-Doh in her hands. My daughter. She gave me the look, the voice, and I was like a popsicle on a hot summer day. "*Herrr*" was a little puffball, all of five pounds, who carried the power of a neutron bomb and rearranged my life story better than anything I could've done on my own. But one thing was crystal clear: Going for a "look" at the Humane Society for available kitties with my little girl was a non sequitur.

At our animal shelter, kitties were on one side of the building, doggies on the other. We walked into the room where two small gray domestic kittens were settled in a cage on the second level of some kind of staging. We *oohed* and *aahed* as we peered from one to the other through the grates. But only one of them looked down at us, and that's all it took for Sarah to fall in love. The contrast of the white around her nose and neck against alternating gray and black made this kitty irresistible. Not like I was in the position to say: "Why don't we get both of them?" I'd never done *that* before. I was a stickler for tradition. Sometimes.

Tia was a bit of a lost soul—really, a wounded soul. Coming to live on the second floor of a high-ceilinged oak-floor apartment, she probably wished she had a scrip for Xanax.

Tia: *Why? Why me? Why couldn't they have picked my sister or maybe brought both of us to this "forever home"? Does this mean I'll always be by myself? Why couldn't they have moved on and left us alone? I've never been without my sister. Since when are families broken up as if it's no big deal? It's a huge deal. I'm too young to understand these humans, but I understand my feelings. How else can I be but sad when I can't see a way out of this mess, this mess of not being with my best friend, my family. At least I can console myself. I may not have nails to chew, but I've got a tail.*

The Humane Society had failed to tell us that we were adopting a kitten removed from its mother well before the minimum eight weeks of nursing. Mother cats, like all other mothers, need time to nurture their young. Through no fault of her own, Tia was maimed for life. But she'd offer us all the love she could muster, and we'd provide her with the forever home she deserved.

My previous kitties, Beauty (from my childhood) and Tanya and Tigger (from my two earlier marriages), never had to deal with the second floor of anything. They all lived on the main floor of a real house. The good ole days. "Now" looked a lot different—now being my new life as a single mom with two children on part-time visitation. As if that made any sense.

Mothers are attached to their young: the animal kingdom is proof positive. Has anyone ever seen a mother duck without her ducklings in lock-web behind her? How about Mama lion? She's the one in charge of her cubs. No one would dare argue. Good grief, I once had an encounter with a mama turkey. Oopsie! How could I know an innocent walk in the woods might entail getting a wee bit too close to her precious chicks. Almost got pecked to death!

MEANWHILE, I WAS FORCED to reinvent myself. If I couldn't be the mama I was groomed to be—to follow in the steps of my own mama and the mama before her ("Mémère," French for grandmother)— then what were my options? For the first 18 months I'd been living out a movie scene, proving that life does imitate art. Consider *The Martian*: the actor Matt Damon marooned on Mars with no Plan B.

That was me on January 17, 1985, when in 17 days, from start to finish, my nine-year marriage went *poof*. As did my motherhood. Sort of. Some folks might say I had it coming. A few too many miscues on my part to be dismissed. I'll admit I'd become a shadow of my former "little Laconia girl" self. Thirteen years of Sacred Heart School had been kicked to the curb. The nuns would say I was going straight to hell, but I thought I'd already been there.

Like Matt Damon's character, I had to devise a means of communicating with the world and a way to re-up my own food supply via dollars and cents. I may not have landed on another planet, but I sure felt like a lone star circling the Milky Way looking for a place to hide, a place to call home. When I was a kid, there was a granite boulder the size of an airplane hangar in our backyard. In response to any blip on my screen, I could tuck myself behind it and come up with a viable answer. That was then; this was now. Matt was getting paid to act; I was the real deal, and I was no Sally Ride.

I'D STARTED OUT with a Suzy Homemaker mother with a direct feed to Betty Crocker and a Cracker Jack dad with a mind like a steel trap. In two languages. I figured I'd inherit enough of their virtuosity to start my own Cinderella story. Let's just say I wasn't there yet, but I thought I was holding an ace. I couldn't see it but I could sense it. Or her. That was my sister, Yvette, and she was, and is, an angel. Somehow, together, we'd figure out my next adventure.

But how many of my readers believe in angels, especially if their lives are sane? Angels don't need to be draped in white with wings attached to their shoulders so they can hover about like a humming-bird. No, they're spirits. And I'd bet there're many spirits wafting over Mother Earth keeping an eye on loved ones.

In the Catholic religion, we believe in angels. Period. It's how we manage our grief when we lose a child before the age of seven, the age of reasoning. If a child hadn't learned to choose between right and wrong, then no sin had been committed. Angel material. That was Yvette.

She lived long enough for me to remember her—a lovely, doe-eyed blonde with hair like silken thread. Her cerebral palsy kept her bedridden, but she loved music. She was living at Mémère's house because our mom had her hands full when she and dad introduced a new family member, my little brother, Dan. Of course, my grandmother wouldn't hesitate to step in and help her daughter. Mothers ruled the roost.

I'm thankful I can still envision Yvette's sweet face. When I was old enough to visit her after school, I'd walk into what Mémère called the front room, which today would be called a den. Music came through what sounded like a juke box jammed into a bureau. With her baby blues and her head tilted toward me, lying on her hospital bed, she was a beauty. I'd sit by her side and hold her hand. Even without conversation, the love between us was palpable. Two sisters. I wasn't there when she died, but Mom told me when I came home from school. In those days, a wake was two days and then a funeral mass plus a burial. Seeing my dad tear up for the first time was tough. I didn't know Superman could cry.

Through adolescence, my life was like a plop of vanilla ice cream in a plain cone. Only in my 20s would a variety of flavors and sprinkles be impossible to resist. We girls of the boomer generation pined to reinvent ourselves, cut loose, burn our bras, expand our consciousness, and let's not forget what the Pill did for our freedom. We were rebels with a cause and supported by the queen bees themselves: Betty Friedan, Gloria Steinem, and Helen Gurley Brown, who'd tell us "You can have it all!"

"Okay," we said. "Let's roll."

WHEN I LEFt 13 years of Catholic school and headed for a two-year all-girls business college, I envisioned my life as an interstate highway. As long as I had enough gas, I was good to go: secretary—marriage—children. But life provides no road map. Now I was forced to look in the rearview mirror and ask myself: Who am I? What am I? Where am I going?

On the bright side, there were two perfectly formed human beings on a branch of my family tree. They were healthy, smart, super good-looking—every mama's dream. But they lived with their dad under primary physical custody and visited me on alternating three nights a week. If I could find an apartment nearby, their transitions would be easier. So I thought.

Having lived in Laconia almost all my life, few streets bring to mind a Cinderella existence quite like Pleasant Street, aptly named for this stretch of three-decker mansions with round and octagonal turrets, widow's walks, eyebrow windows, ornamental cornices, and wrought-iron balustrades on upper floors and with tricolored, scalloped-shaped shingles, mansard roofs, arched terraces, entrances with Roman or Greek columns, stained-glass enhancements, beveled-glass windows in any combination of size and shape, and a patchwork of pastel shades separating one stunner from another. Move over San Francisco, "Lil L.A." (my nickname for my hometown) prides itself on its own beauties. And it was just a ten-minute walk between these two disconnected parents.

Offered the front-facing unit on the second floor of what was once a wealthy family's private home, I could reimagine a child's make-believe world. Pretend I was okay to figure out a new life plan. But I was not okay. How could I be okay with memories of my children as babies holding me together as much as they were tearing me apart? Four part-time jobs and enrollment in an MSW program seemed the best way to cover my $700/month rent and dull my senses at the same time.

Had my morning position as activities director at a nursing home morphed into full-time employment, I'm convinced there'd have been no *Saving Mama*. How I loved that job. Some 34 ladies and one gentleman looked to me for joy, and I delivered. I couldn't be everywhere at once, so I started a volunteer corps from the board of directors. I then organized a stenciling group, which yielded theme place mats for restaurants and note cards with a creative Hallmark-type insignia I'd designed myself, with sales directed to Community Health & Hospice; expanded the nursing home's monthly newsletter to an outside audience and included articles written by the residents themselves; developed rotating art exhibits, each with a wine-and-cheese reception to introduce the artist. I couldn't seem to do anything wrong.

Despite how well suited I was to this position, returning home to an empty apartment sapped the spirit I showed the world. It was impossible to ignore the tug of love and the pang of guilt affixed to motherhood. The more time I had on my hands, the more chance I had to dwell on lost opportunities—like imparting my French heritage and my belief in God to my children. And what about the backyard badminton games I'd enjoyed with Ryan or the shopping days with Sarah? Were they lost forever?

Never would I ever feel so alone as I did during this first year. Like I didn't fit in anywhere as a mother, though I was within walking distance of two schools. In the mid-1980s, there was one car that boomed "Married with Kids," and that was the gray Volvo station wagon. Plain as a paper bag, but my neighborhood was teeming with them. Made me feel like a lone wolf looking at a sheep pasture through a mile-high fence.

All these mothers, as nice as they continued to be to me, had no idea what it was like for a gale force wind to blow across their family with the mother left on one side of the street and the dad and the kids on the other. Would it have made any difference in my adjustment had our breakup been planned together? Would I have been able to work out the pangs of not having my children to bed down every night and cuddle with bedtime stories? Being a single mom was a mind crusher.

In November 1985, I spied a want ad in the paper: LOCAL REPRESENTATIVE NEEDED. FLEXIBLE HOURS. UNLIMITED INCOME. Sounded good. I submitted my résumé. Some days later the phone rang during dinner with the kids. It was the Bedford office of Mutual of Omaha. Insurance sales. Conan Grace, district manager, kept me on the phone for an hour and a half using his own brand of psychology to convince me to take an aptitude test. He wouldn't let me go.

I never understood insurance, but I appreciated its importance. I'd already purchased tenant insurance for my meager possessions and a $25,000 life insurance policy—just because. Buying, yes; sales, though, were not my forte. But there was one particular thing in the conversation that caught my attention: "My wife, Kathy," said Con Grace, "made $28,000 last year, and it's just her second year in the business."

What? Here I was working four jobs and making $12,000, and she more than doubled me with one job? Okay. Why not? I took the test. I failed the test, with a score of 12 out of 20. Needed a 16. Psychology guided me on what I felt were the best responses but apparently not what a salesman would say or do. However, Con was convinced I could prosper despite not being the perfect candidate. He made it clear he wanted to hire me and would go to bat for me.

"Claire," he said, "I don't believe you can't succeed in this business. And I promise that if you follow the outlines of our sales process, you'll be making more money than your ex-husband in five years." *Five years? My ex was an attorney!*

Now I had a decision to make. I was due for an annual review with Mr. Administrator at the nursing home. After all I'd accomplished in less than a year, I expected him to be quite pleased, maybe even proud. The offer of a full-time position might've tempted me to stay.

"Are you kidding?" I asked. "A ten-cent raise? As it is, I'm working three other jobs."

"Not my problem," he said, with not a hint of compassion. "There's nothing more I can do for you."

"Well, then, you leave me with no choice," I said. "I love working here, but I'm accepting an offer to work for Mutual of Omaha. I'll leave the first of April, providing you ample time to find a replacement."

"I've never heard of anyone making money selling insurance," he said. "Good luck."

In the interim, I sought out every one of the residents for a personal goodbye. On my final day, there was a reception for me. Tears spilled as I read notes from each resident telling me how much she'd (he'd) miss me and to thank me for everything I'd done. Mrs. Bartlett, part of my stencil group and a regular contributor to the monthly newsletter, penciled an image of me holding my children's hands and framed it. It's still in my bedroom.

I then addressed each of my volunteers with an eight-line poem in appreciation for her dedication and looped it around her unique relationship with her resident. The joy I found working with these residents presented a side of myself I hadn't known existed. An offer of a full-time position would've kept me there.

Having been booted out of a partnership that had run on ruts for far too long, I was sensitive to pretending all was well when it wasn't. I was more than ready to validate my worth, but I needed a partner. It doesn't always take a village—sometimes just one person to have your back. I believed I'd found my wingman in Con Grace.

Tia

WHY DID HUMANS bring a kitty into their home if they were too busy to pay her any attention?

I didn't know how long I was here all by myself, hiding here and there, sucking my tail, feeling sorry for myself. But it was too long. Too long in cat years. If I couldn't have my sister, then at least be kind and get me a pal—someone to talk to and maybe even make me laugh.

I was a kitty with no family, no friends. And that's not fair. Mama seemed to fly in and out of here, always in a rush. Only when her children visited did I get some attention, especially from Mama Sarah. But just as soon as we snuggled and got used to each other, she was gone again. I don't know why. I bet if my sister was here, she'd know.

A WINGMAN IS NO COPILOT. I'd still need to learn how to steer my way through this beast of an adventure by myself. But was I really alone or was my angel sister pulling a few wings to help navigate me through the finer points of insurance jargon and then embolden me to extract money from strangers? It's like I was whacked upside the head to take this leap, to quit flitting from one job to another spinning a web of nickels and dimes.

But it was more than about money. It was about pride. Although I remained proud of having earned a BA in psychology, it didn't go anywhere. Moving through an advanced degree at Boston University for a career as a clinical psychologist had to be scrubbed. But would a career as an insurance lady make my kids proud of me some day?

But no matter how deep into the particulars I was as a budding agent, my mamahood was sensitive to the smallest setback. I swallowed hard when Sarah returned from a weekend with her father with her nails painted by his first lady friend. That was just the beginning. Whether a big deal or a small token, a mother's connection to her child is so engrained that not being able to oversee the who, what, when, and where can never be digestible.

Given that I'd never understood insurance and was now attaching my livelihood, my character, my legacy to it, I'd need to concentrate on the essentials, not on the what-ifs of my life. To my relief I'd have a buddy: Another recruit found himself on the same path. His name was Jeff and he was 18 years younger than I. Although we lived an hour apart, we'd meet at the Bedford office and test each other on specifics ahead of our state licensing boards.

Once we passed our tests, Con invited us to attend the agency's annual meeting for an official introduction. Formal attire wasn't required for us, but we nonetheless dolled up as each other's date for the night. Here was our first peek at the recognition and awards bestowed on those who followed the Omaha code for success. Broken down by product, each agent was called to the podium to be acknowledged and photographed. I couldn't help but note that one of the agents in the unit to which I was to be assigned, Billy, was doing quite well. I'd have to keep my eye on him.

There'd be no way to predict how a sales career in a man's world would upend my life story—my own dash between birth and the dirt nap—and begs the question of whether I'd do it all again. The answer is a resounding yes but not without securing a moment of silence: a pause to reflect on the balance of wins and losses. A woman in outside insurance sales in 1986 was an anomaly for a reason. We were invited to the table not with open arms but rather with a sneer and an eye roll.

June 25, 1986

THE FIRST DAY OF MY REINVENTION. As in America's favorite sport, it was my turn at bat. Suiting up like I'd be live on ESPN, I knew the importance of first impressions. Where else to go for a briefcase but to the cobbler, where I chose a dark brown leather beauty with a lock. It needed a three-digit code: 371—I was 37 years old, and I was vying for a grand slam.

I'm not sure I ever saw *Wild Kingdom*, Mutual of Omaha's hit TV series. America had become fixated on host Marlin Perkins and sidekick Jim Fowler up to their galoshes in alligators. Or maybe just Jim. That's what I'd be told time and again. What I soon learned was that Marlin Perkins, this spokesperson and beloved pack leader, had but two weeks earlier departed this world for safer ground. He'd never be forgotten: he'd put Mutual of Omaha's *Wild Kingdom* on the world map.

What company can top a dynamic duo bringing to light the plight of endangered and forgotten species? Good that Jim Fowler could pick up the reins and go on to expanded broadcasting with links to the *Today Show* and Johnny Carson. This kingpin of late-night TV couldn't wait to match wits with Jim and his latest partner, some unique breed of jungle madness with zero interest in adhering to protocol. The audience never failed to roar.

Back in my own jungle, Tia was acclimating to life on a sliding scale: either there was plenty of activity when the kids visited or nothing at all when I was squirreling away my nuts of insurance minutiae for a long-term residence. But kitties don't care, right? It didn't help that Tia was shy. She never slept with me but gravitated toward Sarah when she visited.

Tia

MY NEW HOME made no sense. Is this what life was like as a human? I had no one to talk to. I was so lonely. Why couldn't Mama go back for my sister?

With the children on a set visitation schedule, I planned appointments around my free nights. Monday nights were always free for fun cold calls. Every other Saturday morning for these same calls was the best I could do. It dawned on me that following up on every lead and learning bit by bit how to evaluate success for a completed appointment was tantamount to the skills of a fly fisherman. Pull on your hip boots, select your location, cast your line, balance yourself, and hope for a bite.

Jeff, who'd been assigned to a different unit, pursued his own approach to success. At 19 he was in a better position to "try" insurance sales. Free of parental responsibilities and with plenty of time to stretch his wings, he had no reason to reach for the stars. But we stayed in touch and planned a dinner once a month to review the good, the bad, and the ugly of our freshman initiatives (always D'Angelo's on Second Street in Manchester; always tuna sub, small chip, Diet Coke for me).

"Claire, you have any idea what you're doing? Your turn-in sheets are full every week!"

"I pay no attention. I make the calls, see the people, and try to sell them something before I leave. I don't care if it's our $10/month accident policy—anything to get me back in the door. My goal is five policies in every household."

"Talk about driven," Jeff said, teasing.

All our business was evaluated at the agency's monthly meeting. Coffee and Dunkin' Donuts were a welcome break as we all learned of the newest products and discussed any concerns. But the big kahuna meeting took place every May. Meanwhile, Billy and I had developed a friendly rivalry. Tall, dark, and handsome with a boyish grin that would force an ID well past the age of 21, he was confident in his predictions as my own level of business crept closer to his. "I'm not worried about her" was his standard statement. What guy in 1987 ever heard of a top female producer?

I WAS NOW FIVE MONTHS into my first official full year in the business. Jeff and I went to the annual awards banquet as bona fide members of the agency. As required, we fell into place with formal wear. The finale always came with the announcement of who would be Agent of the Year. No surprise it was my archrival, Billy. I couldn't resist whispering to Jeff:

"You watch. That'll be me next year." Spoken with all the confidence of a woman tanked up on rocket fuel.

"Yep, no doubt about it, partner. I can see it now."

A DEVOTED READER of my local newspaper, right around the same time my attention was on the FOR SALE pages. I saw that a litter of Persian kittens would soon be available for adoption. Having had nothing but a domestic tiger as a child and again through my early adult years, I never gave thought to a pedigreed feline. They cost money, but at least now my tank wasn't running on empty. During one of Sarah's visits, I asked her to accompany me.

"Oh, Mama. Can we? Can we *puulleeze* get another kitty? Maybe Tia would come out and play more . . . maybe she wouldn't be so shy. Maybe she'd let me hold her longer. Please, please. Can we goooo?"

I knew better than to bring up this subject without having already made that decision.

"I was thinking the same thing, sweetheart. We had no idea this little girl would be so timid and want to hide all the time. Maybe having a pal will make all the difference. Let me call the number. Let's see if we can visit Saturday afternoon."

The house was on the south end of town and positioned diagonal to Sacred Heart Cemetery. I'd never noticed its proximity to the Hebert family plot, where my sister and now my parents rested in peace. Although neither Sarah nor I can remember the exact number of kittens, we do remember on which one we'd both locked eyes: a tiny, charcoal gray female with a smooshed-in face. We held her, cuddled her. Then I asked how much.

"I charge $200 for each of my kitties," said the breeder. "They're pure bred and both parents are on premises. I've been in this business long enough to feel justified in saying that all my customers say it's the best kitty they've ever had."

"Gee. That's quite a bit of money. I'm sorry, but I can't commit at this time. But I'm working hard to save up and maybe by your next litter, we'll be able to take one of your kitties."

Sarah and I departed feeling very sad. But $200 just wasn't manageable. Kitties at the Humane Society were one notch above free, just a token contribution for inoculations. We soon learned that our chosen girl was adopted by a family who'd head for Texas. We pictured her, a forlorn little munchkin, looking out the back window, wishing the mother with her little girl had been the ones to provide her with her forever home.

As most of us cat aficionados know, mother cats can have more than one litter in a year. Now that I knew how much money I needed, it was simply a matter of time for a few cases to close and my bills to be paid. I'd catch the ad: FOR SALE. PERSIAN KITTENS. This time I decided to visit alone, not chancing having the pressure of Sarah bearing down on me. Same house, corner lot, two hops and across the street from

Sacred Heart Cemetery. The breeder remembered me and brought me into the kitchen. There to my right, one o'clock, was a family of cream-colored kittens and one single redhead. I was hooked.

Joey

ROUND ABOUT JUNE 1987, a star was born. That would be me—cute, intuitive, and quite full of myself, A pussycat with cattitude. Not just any pussycat but one destined to be king of the jungle. Someday I'd be sitting high on a mountaintop and able to gaze down on all my subjects. By then I'd be used to the call of the wild, this ear-piercing racket of one pack against another foraging and hunting for food.

But now as a wee cub I had no worries. My mama took care of me. Me and my brother—the pesky sibling I inherited. It seemed whenever I was hungry, so was he. When it was time for a walk around the den, there he was, at my heels. Mama let us feast on her whenever we wanted. Soon we started tagging along, leaving the safety of the den to begin our journey to follow in dad's pawprints. But one day we heard a loud C R A C K, and our mama fell in a heap. My brother and I had no idea where to go, what to do. But then we heard sounds we'd never heard before. Heavy boots were heading our way. They were close. I scrunched up in a ball and shut my eyes . . .

August 1987

I AWOKE WITH A START. My heart was pounding. Wait . . . just . . . a . . . minute. Where was I? I looked around. I couldn't see. Snooze. Zzzzz

What-da? I looked at myself. A midget? Who was I, what was I, and where was my brother? I was crushed by the weight of squirming furballs who looked just like me, except for one. Holy cats! I was nothing but a house cat. A Persian, though, with three identical brothers. And just my luck—we were cream! Not even a color. Not white, not tan. Something in between. Ugh. Maybe I was invisible.

But wait . . . wasn't I supposed to grow up to be king? King of the jungle? What happened to that story? Was I hallucinating? There appeared to be one odd duck among us who somehow got dipped in a can of red paint and was missing a set of balls. What was with that one? Oh, she was a girl. Good luck with that.

Oh, no. Our noses looked like they had been stomped on. Did that happen in the jungle? Were we trampled by a herd of elephants? Why else were our noses darn near flat against our cheeks? At least I lucked out with another loving mama. But would I lose her too? Our new dad lived with us, but he was no king lion. He was more of a lazy bum soaking up the sun's rays off the living room window like he didn't have a care in the world. No interest in saving the day.

Another thing bothered me. You could hear a pin drop around the house. Like, dead quiet. I overheard that our neighbors had all passed on. Guess they're not likely to throw a party anytime soon to welcome me to the neighborhood. Yawn. Guess this life will be spent on my back contemplating all I could've been. But soon enough, my own ears were ringing. What now?

Maybe we were being invaded and what happened before would happen again. Mama would die. And we'd be alone. And scared. What would we do? Where would we go? I exhausted myself. Needed sleep. Zzzzz

One day, a lady showed up. Alone. She knelt to get a good look at us. Never one to shirk my responsibilities, I took the lead and walked right up to her, tail high. While my brothers were wrestling and chasing Red, I introduced myself.

There was something about her. I looked at her. She looked at me. I froze. I couldn't move forward. I couldn't move back. For some reason, I was drawn to her. Like she needed me. Like maybe I'd get another shot at being king of the jungle.

In no time, I found myself scooped up in her hands as if I was putty. She looked me square in the eye and said over her shoulder "I'll take him," as if she didn't even have to think about it. And why would she? I was adorable, even as a midget.

I was tagged with this bright green marker on the bottom of my left front paw to set me apart from my brothers. The next time the woman came, a little girl named Sarah was with her. I didn't get a chance to say goodbye to the boys or to Red. Mama

Sarah scooped me up and away I went, off to another adventure. I thought. Maybe this one would last longer.

They named me Joey (Joseph when I was naughty). Although I was still in the same city, I now lived on the second floor of what seemed like a rooming house in bad need of a paintbrush. I couldn't even look up without getting dizzy. Maybe giraffes used to live here.

No one told me I'd have to learn to hold my balance on a wood staircase. How was a wild young 'un supposed to remain vertical with no dirt to grip? Where the heck was the cushy stuff we had in our last rooming house? If I'd paid for this transfer, I'd want my money back. After all, I was just past eight weeks old. I felt lost and basically lay low, already homesick for my bros and even Red. I found my voice. A teeny-tiny meow . . . pathetic.

Soon though, I was feeling a bit frisky and wandered about, exploring this new landscape, and realized that I now live way up high—kind of fun to live atop a mountain. I pretended "King Joey." As I peered down between the railings, darned if I didn't lose my balance and topple head over paws, land hard, and poo myself! Really? Mama came running and cuddled me and checked me all over to see if I was broken or bruised.

"Joey. Joey. Sweetheart. Honey. Are you okay? Are you hurt?"

Was I too young to have an ego? Mama carried me back up the stairs like I was some kind of hapless creature, grabbed some tissues, wiped my butt, then placed me ever so gently on the floor, probably praying I could move under my own power. Of course I could. She didn't have a clue who she was dealing with. Not yet.

Still, I wanted to hide, but I couldn't. While I was searching for something that resembled a bush, I spied a bigger furball, who must've come from some other reservation. Gray striped, short fur, white-tipped nose. Why couldn't I have had a nose like that?

"Who are you?" I asked. "And what's wrong with you? What's going on with your tail?"

Tia: *They named me Tia. Not even a real name, because I'm a nobody. I was born in a dark, dingy barn in the back of a hay wagon. My mom was the village tramp. She kept having kittens and couldn't take care of them. One day a police officer came by and saw me and my sister and carted us off to a shelter. At least they put us in a cage together. Sis and I needed to be fed from a bottle because we were orphans. At least that's what I heard them call us. We needed our mother, but she was gone. And no one wanted us. We were safe but still so lonely for our mom.*

Joey: Gee, Tia. Hey, is it okay if I call you Tee? That's a tough break, Tee.

Tia: Mama and Mama Sarah came by one day and stopped at our cage. I barely looked up because they kinda scared me. But I made a mistake. I dunno. Maybe. I did look back at them. I didn't think I'd get picked up, just me. My sister never even got a chance. I was told it would be my forever home, but I didn't wanna go. I didn't wanna leave my sister. And now I don't know where she is. And I'm still scared. And I don't know what to do. And I can't stop sucking my tail.

Joey: Well, fear no more, little sister. You're not alone now. King Joey is here to protect you. And you're not a nobody. At least you've got a nose. You've got all kinds of color—black, gray, white. Look at me: a colorless blob with no nose. But Tee, it's all about cattitude.

Joey

Not surprisingly, I was a whole lot more mischievous than Tia. But one day it was Tia's turn. She was a proper lady, always going potty in the litter box. For whatever reason, though, she decided to sniff out a new potted plant Mama had brought home.

Tia: Oh, Joe-Joe. You won't believe how cozy-squishy it is to scooch down in some dirt instead of that grainy litter.

Joey

And right in front of my eyes, she pooed! Well, Mama was never too far away, and when she detected an odor, she caught Tia in the act. She grabbed a broom and started chasing Tia all over the living room, looking to give her a good swat on the behind. "Bad girl," Mama yelled.

But holy cat, could Tia run! Mama never did catch her, as Tia tucked herself away in one of her many cubbies until Mama simmered down. Mama Sarah just watched on the sidelines and laughed.

Life was pretty good. I had a shy but sweet sister for a pal. Mama Sarah and Big Brother Ryan played with me and gave me treats when they visited. But I was still too young to know: Nothing. Ever. Stays. The. Same.

I was back in a crate (um . . . what's that for again?) and Mama and I went for a ride. I recognized Dr. David's office, but I was clueless. Wasn't I just there for shots? I'm not stupid, but huh?

"Oh, my. He's soooo handsome," cooed the woman behind the desk. "Could I bring him home at lunchtime and get him together with my Marshmallow? They'd make beautiful babies."

"No way," I said. "I'm sorry. He's here for a procedure."

Joey

Procedure? What was going to happen to me? Oh, no. Now I was shaking in my paws. Was I gonna die? Was I going to—

Dr. David picked me up and . . . poof! I was frolicking in a meadow. The faster I moved, the more flowers sprang up. Now I was running and I saw her. I stopped in my tracks. She was soooo beautiful. I'd never seen a kitty like her. She was all white and sparkly and had enormous blue eyes and a cute upturned nose. She was looking my way and then started walking toward me. My heart was bursting out of my chest, my body temperature soared, and I wanted to . . .

I woke up fuzzy in the head, dizzy. I couldn't even walk straight. Someone, something had just happened. Did they know who I was? Wait . . . my loins were . . . yikes! . . . they were gone! Where did they go? Oh no, I was a girl—no, I was still Joey but not the same. I needed a good cat-to-Mama talk, but later. Now, I couldn't keep my eyes open.

I got home and slumped onto my bed. When I got around to functioning again, I realized my strut was at half-mast and Mama was nowhere in sight. I found Tee.

Tia: *What's the matter, little brother? You don't seem like yourself.*

Joey: *I'm in a foul mood, Tee. I've lost my manhood. Hiss, spit (no offense).*

Tia: *Oh, for crying out loud, get a grip. I had my own dissection; it's just that mine doesn't show. Tee-hee. I can't have babies but I'm good with that. I didn't have a good role model. I know I'm better off free of responsibilities.*

Joey: *You need to know we boys are defined by our . . . um . . . er . . . private parts. Besides, you didn't almost meet the love of your life, like I did with Marshmallow.*

Tia: *You're hallucinating. Go back to bed. Soon you'll be your strapping self again.*

Joey: *What's done is done, but Mama will soon learn there's a price to pay for lopping off my manhood. From then on, every morning at about four o'clock I'll walk all over her pillow and purr at high volume and of course—my purpose—wake her up. She knows. Tit for tat. As for the loss of my progeny, I figure I'm smart enough to come up with an alternative. Even if it means reinventing myself.*

PART-TIME MOTHERHOOD is like high blood pressure: a silent killer. Unlike blood pressure, though, there's no instrument to measure vital signs. For example, when I watched my children walk to school from my apartment—Ryan, a full head taller than his sister, who was strapped to the world's tiniest backpack—no one saw me as anything but a mother. But you can't be a mom if you have no say in your children's lives.

Here I was betting the farm on a career soaked in testosterone when for my whole life my goal had been to be a mother. Only now can I better appreciate my meteoric rise in the land of suits—a chance to mummify my broken heart and force its ticking. Still, the *what ifs* continue to stick to my rear window regardless of how many Reiki washes I have.

For example—*what if* I'd brought Ryan back in the spring of '87 along with his sister to what would be her first musical, *Evita*. Would he enjoy theater today as much as she does? She'd been the only child in the two-story Palace Theatre in Manchester, New Hampshire. Seated between my insurance buddy Jeff and me, she whimpered through that first gloomy dirge of Evita's death but then sat up with what had become "the Sarah smile." Even losing one of her red Jellies (hard plastic shiny ballet slippers) between the seats didn't dim her enjoyment of the show. As wonderful as that memory is for me, not introducing Ryan to a potential lasting "first" carries the weight of a missed opportunity.

My own "first" was just around the corner: securities training. Such a license would stretch me long and thin in a man's world—in more ways than one. But an all-expense-paid week at the home office struck me as exciting with a dash of sexy, especially when I entered its glass rotunda with a ticker tape showing the number of claims being paid *by the second* around the globe.

With the addition of financial-planning options, an agent could walk into any home and expand a client's Income Protection plan (or his wheel of fortune, as I came to view it). Our fact-finding folders were highlighted with what looked like a Ferris wheel wherein each "seat" was labeled: HEALTH. DISABILITY. LIFE, RETIREMENT. In time, Long-Term Care would have a seat. Sales could work only if one of those seats was empty.

Like Sarah's initial experience with the theater, my memory of this intro to the home office stuck with me long past my years of employment. Not too many financial newbies got to dip their toe in finance on Black Monday, October 19, 1987, when stocks fell off a cliff, sending shivers down the spines of investors worldwide and stock pickers out of windows on Wall Street. At week's end, approximately 25 of us novice agents returned to our respective home bases to be tracked over the next 12 months. Whoever captured the highest sales would be awarded the coveted gold mantel clock, engraved for the world to recognize the leader of the pack.

FALL, WITH ITS PAINT-SPLATTERED LEAVES sashaying against a brisk breeze, provides a whiff of fresh air to assess options ahead of the arrival of Old Man Winter. My apartment was already suffocating under the weight of a home office in just shy of 18 months. Tucked as it was into an alcove (more like an attic) on the third floor, I could barely navigate around the stacks of files. A bigger apartment might've made sense if it weren't for a client base of self-employed contractors. I consulted Andy, in custom carpentry, for his thoughts on the viability of a home I'd seen with one of my clients in the real estate business.

"Claire," he said, "I had no idea you were interested in buying a house. You need to see the one I'm building on Province Street. It's in the beginning stages but come take a peek."

Never in my wildest dreams had I imagined that inside of three years my reinvention would include my first home purchase—in my name only!

Just like I lived in when I was growing up was my first thought upon entering this stick-built skeleton of a Saltbox. "It reminds me of my childhood, Andy, not only for its design but also for the backyard—woods for the kids to explore and enjoy with neighborhood friends, just like I did."

At approximately 1,500 square feet, the similarities were striking. Entry was through the kitchen, which opened to a dining/living room combination. Half bath with small bedroom (Ryan's future room) off the kitchen. Back-deck slider off the kitchen. Upstairs had two bedrooms with a double-sink full bath. Full basement capable of being subdivided.

Although my kids showed little interest in these backyard woods, I was mesmerized. But a bank loan was a formidable hurdle.

Affordability was based on a ratio of income to expenses. I was still in possession of that CD from my half of the marital homestead, earning a hefty interest. Whereas I'd need to take a penalty for early withdrawal, it would provide a decent down payment. But not enough. Andy would have to save the day.

"Here's what I can do," he said. "I'll take a second mortgage with you for $10,000. That, in addition to your CD, should support the 10 percent down payment. You can pay me back at no interest over the next ten years."

I was facing an $845/month payment based on a variable rate of 9.5 percent to a cap of 11.5 percent for 30 years. Such a commitment. I knew there was no golden goose in my basement—a metaphor used by us intrepid agents selling disability insurance. In other words, as a means of identifying the importance of protecting your income against sickness or accident, you're asked to ponder that if there *were* such a goose, would you insure it? Of course! In effect, a self-employed individual *is* the goose.

For the past two years I'd tapped into my mother's approach to budgeting and gotten myself one of those envelope kits: each one labeled according to weekly budget for rent, food, utilities, insurance, clothes, entertainment, miscellaneous. If the money wasn't in the envelope, it didn't get spent. I was determined not to carry any credit-card debt. Thus far this approach had served me well. What took time to assess was the taxable component of being self-employed. Not only did I now need to separate quarterly tax payments, but I also had to open a retirement account and, naturally, buy my own disability insurance. I needed another pack of envelopes.

Now I had even less time to feel sorry for myself. But I was fortunate to work for a company that not only was a household name, but also offered a slew of products within the average person's budget. My success was dependent on numbers—how many calls to secure how many appointments to make the number of sales that would carry an 85 percent rate of insurability. Only then would I be able to pay my bills.

Joey: *HEY, TEE. Have you noticed Mama's got boxes everywhere? Looks like we're on the move. Yippee! Another adventure!*

Tia: *Yeah, I see, but change scares me. Where do you think we're going?*

Joey: *Tee, get a grip. Never mind about that. Follow me. Watch me.*

Tia: *I can't leap like that. I . . . I . . . I . . .*

Joey: *Tee, trust me. Do it!*

LITTLE BY LITTLE, those boxes disappeared, and by early February 1988, we were settled into our own home. Joey was a bundle of energy, bopping from one room to another, quite unlike Tia, who most of the time remained tucked away.

Joey: *Tee, look here. See this . . . it's called a rug. We didn't have one before. Now we can scratch and sharpen our claws whenever we feel like it. No more slick floors. It's like being in the jungle again.*

Tia: *You and your jungle. I don't even know what a jungle looks like. Are there any places to hide?*

Joey: *Tons. But the jungle is no place for you, Tee. You stay right here where I can keep an eye on you. The jungle is for big boys like me. But look, Tee. Look outside this window. See those trees? Imagine climbing up, up, and away and then looking down on everyone and being able to . . . ROAR!*

Tia: *Sure, bro, whatever you say. But I'm headed for the nearest closet. That's where I belong.*

YOU MIGHT WONDER just how I managed to crack the code of insurance sales. Simple, my dear Watsons. I mixed psychology with heart—and threw in some grit with burning the midnight oil. I remembered the insurance man of my youth who'd come to collect the premiums. Never liked him. Perhaps it was his dour expression or his lack of enthusiasm at seeing a kid in the house.

In my career, my first line of offense was to put myself in a potential client's shoes. How could I convince anyone I was deserving of his trust if I didn't own it myself. (Who tries to sell a prospect a line of protection from both sides of the mouth?)

Because I was self-employed, as were almost all the folks I visited, I too had to budget for life and disability protection. In time, I bought juvenile life insurance for both my children as well as all available mutual funds for all of us. In that way, I had my own portfolio to prove I was safeguarding the American Dream. Work your buns off till retirement, protect yourself along the way in case of a setback, and keep your eye on the future.

It seemed to come naturally for me to enter a home not as a salesperson, but rather as a technician there to address a problem. Like any electrician, plumber, or handyman, I had a tool kit. A potential client had a problem; I had a solution. Another strategy was to adjust how I would approach each prospect. Eye contact, body language, tone of voice, vocabulary—all came into play. First impressions matter.

I also evaluated where my appointments were located for appropriate attire. Would I be on Governor's Island on a million-dollar property the same day I'd be at a third-floor walkup in one of the city's most run-down tenements? Or how about the time I had an appointment in one of the shabbiest trailer parks in the area only to knock on the door and enter what looked like the den of a wild man obsessed with wolf wall throws. Having to squeeze in as many sales opportunities as possible, I had to set up a 6 a.m. meeting or three appointments after 5 p.m.

How sure would I be of not being stood up? I did my homework. Was there a real need within the family? And just as important, were there any preexisting conditions? It didn't take a PhD to recognize that the best product to begin my career was disability insurance. So why not put DSBLTY on my license plate? My eyes still lock onto a license plate or the writing across the side of a truck. All that was missing now was my ten-year-old son with paper and pencil eager to assist. Home construction was brisk and self-employed contractors were everywhere, and I often had Ryan busy at every intersection.

In time, he became just as interested when I introduced the concept of saving for the future through mutual funds. I was putting the minimum of $25 a month into the two main Omaha funds for both him and his sister as UGMA accounts (Uniform Gift to Minors Act). Identified under a child's Social Security number, an adult was the custodian to protect its disbursement until the child turned 21. On the Sundays the kids were with me, I asked Ryan to look up how their funds had done for the week. He already understood the difference between the NAV (Net Asset Value) and the POP (Popular Offering Price). Because I was licensed in securities, my family could purchase at NAV and save the 8 percent sales charge.

"Ryan, let's take a peek. What did they do this week?" He was intrigued by the idea of saving money.

But sometimes the best of intentions become dismal failures. These savings were destined for a fate like that of the pine trees surrounding my home. But in this instance, I'd be the one getting the ax. And I never saw it coming.

I'D BEEN CO-OWNER of four houses since leaving the nest, but at no time had I given thought to a home in my name only. It just wasn't done—at least not in my social circles. Not in the 1980s. Being a trailblazer was laughable given my affectation for being a "sheep," as my mother had warned. To switch metaphors, sometimes you learn to swim by being nudged overboard. Sink or . . .

Keep in mind that I was in my late 30s—not considered over the hill. When my client Michael offered to introduce me to his best friend, I figured why not? "B-Bear," as the friend was known, burst into my life glowing with spirit and joy. Raised on the North Shore of Massachusetts, his ancestry sowed the seeds for academic excellence, encouraging him to set the bar high for his own stamp on humanity.

He had already made a name for himself in the Lakes Region, having leapt onto the nascent wave of alternative home-heating appliances. His business degree afforded him the knowledge to merge quality, quantity, price point, and market availability. His personal side carried few exclusions. Whether on water or on land, in summer or in winter, this New Englander grabbed the throttle of what this four-season area placed at his fingertips. There seemed to be nothing he wouldn't do for the thrill of adventure—quite different from my play-it-safe self. He embodied energy and laughter wrapped in an insatiably curious mind. Being in his orbit was intoxicating. It was the beginning of a few months jam-packed with once-in-a-lifetime experiences.

B-Bear lived on Governor's Island, so named to set its residents apart for a combination of privacy and luxury. As was true of most of these residences, B-Bear's home hugged the shoreline of Lake Winnipesaukee. A sprawling ranch, it had many luxuries, including an indoor hot tub. When I noticed a pink bathrobe hanging from a hook, I sensed our chapter might already be closing. What I didn't know was the degree of affection he had for this woman.

But before reality set in, two amazing adventures lay in wait. First, B-Bear pulled together three couples for a ski trip to Jackson Hole, Wyoming, a popular destination for the U.S. Ski Team, and invited me along as a birthday gift. The powder conditions and the altitude were a major adjustment for me, but being amid the rugged beauty of the snowcapped Tetons was worth every discomfort. Our next trip was my treat, based on having earned a high enough sales production to achieve President's Club, second tier in Mutual of Omaha's honor clubs. We went to Miami for a stay at the luxurious Fontainebleau hotel, right on the beach—how wonderful in the middle of March.

Perhaps taking a page from upstate Disney or maybe Cirque de Soleil, on our first evening costumed performers on seven-foot platforms danced among us. At another social it didn't surprise me to have B-Bear grab the microphone for a solo karaoke rendition of a classic rock song and thrill the audience. But in a few short weeks, I had my own chance for the spotlight.

Joey: *HEY, TEE. I don't know about you, but I'm getting smarter by the day.*

Tia: *How so, lil bro?*

Joey: *It's Mama. I know I haven't known her for too long, but it doesn't take a wizard to notice how giggly she's been lately. She's flitting around here more like a butterfly than a bull moose rushing in and out of the house.*

Tia: *Gee, I hope she's okay. I'm so confused. Some days we have Brother Ryan and Mama Sarah and some days we don't. Sometimes we see this roly-poly guy come and go and sometimes we don't. Then we have Pépère, who comes to take care of us and makes all these squeaky sounds and cleans our litter boxes and freshens up our water and food bowls.*

Joey: *Yeah. I've gotten to know him. He's Mama's daddy. He sure does love us kitties. When Mama packs her bags, I know Pépère will be here. He gets all googly handing us treats, like he's doing something behind Mama's back. If I wanted the whole bag, I think he'd let me have it.*

Tia: *He seems nice and I like his squeaky voice. But I'm not ready for someone new. Maybe someday I won't be so scared.*

Joey: *Listen, lil sis. I'm in charge here and nothing and no one is ever gonna hurt you. So stop sucking your tail! Next time Pépère comes for a visit, get yourself out here in full view for a pet and a treat.*

May 1988

CON'S ANNUAL AWARDS NIGHT, an evening never to be duplicated. B-Bear was in a black tux enhanced with a white silk scarf and I wore a stunning dress. White with spaghetti straps, it wrapped around my waist in layers and draped down my leg with a split. White lace stockings and white high heels. My hair arranged in curls. It was a beautiful late-spring evening when B-Bear's friend Michael greeted us at B-Bear's house with a bottle of champagne. B-Bear had just added a baby blue BMW convertible to his collection, and off we headed to Bedford for an evening for the record books.

Con designed this night to mimic the Academy Awards and spared no expense to bring the glitz and glam for those agents who'd given their all for the company. It took time to parade some 25 agents onto the stage for their respective pin or ring (based on years of service) or any number of ancillary recognitions. Formal pictures followed. Ahead of the equivalent of "Best Picture," aka Agent of the Year for overall production, specific products were identified. I'd nailed them all—me, a tadpole in a sea of bullfrogs.

Top Disability. Top Life. Top Health. Top Mutual Funds. And now in possession of the engraved gold mantel clock, having surpassed my classmates from around the country. At most sales calls, I discussed saving for the future. Who couldn't afford to set aside $25/month, $5.81/week? I'd written more minimum-level accounts than anyone before me. As I recall, the monthly commission was along the lines of $.67. Con never forgot that he'd had to talk me into taking that aptitude test and was convinced I'd succeed despite my failing grade. He nicknamed me "Star"—Agent of the Year, 1988.

It was perhaps the following weekend that B-Bear suggested we go to Ogunquit for a walk on the beach. Time to address the lady with the pink bathrobe.

She was his business partner and had been integral to the success of a secondary enterprise. B-Bear had long ago fallen in love with her, but she'd been unavailable. Recently widowed, she'd had a change of heart, and B-Bear couldn't dismiss the love he still felt for her, regardless of the fun he was having with me.

But B-Bear shined more than a light on my life: he made me laugh like I hadn't in a very long time. Whether learning the art of a poker face during a game of Balderdash, skiing far away from the comfort of nearby Gunstock, or letting loose on the dance floor, everything was over the top. I missed his joie de vivre. I cried in front of the children, which I eventually learned didn't sit well with Ryan.

Equally troubling were the incessant rumblings of my being a gold digger. Why? Because I didn't live on the gold coast? Because my father wasn't a self-made man whom everybody knew? Because I was a girl? Such a cruel label.

It took time for me to realize that no one gains ground by leaning on someone else. I was too raw from my divorce and too young in the business to understand that I needed to find the laughter and the joy within myself. I needed to find my own roar. It wouldn't happen overnight.

Tia: *HEY, BRO. Why so sad? I've gotten used to you poking my heinie to distract me from my tail. Where's my Mr. Know-It-All?*

Joey: *Grrrrr. When Mama is sad, I'm sad. I can't help myself. I dunno why. There's just something about her that makes me want to make her happy, to see that I'm here in this house under her wing as an extra son and you as an extra daughter. Why can't she see that?*

Tia: *I don't claim to have any kind of royal pedigree, like you have, so I'm just guessing. But I'm thinking it has something to do with the chubby guy with the big laugh not being around anymore. Mama was all ga-ga goo-goo over him.*

Joey: *Darn him. If I'd known he wasn't going to stick around, I'd have worked my magic (which I'm still in the process of developing) to boot him out before Mama fell in love. Look at us—we love each other and we're the real deal. We're not going anywhere.*

Tia: *Yup. So go ahead, give me a boot and let's grab ourselves some chow. When Mama comes home, we'll wind ourselves around her ankles and she won't feel so alone.*

FEW IN THE 1980s had a home-based business. My brother, a banker, told me he could never work from home. (Never say never, Dan.) Too distracting with TV, refrigerator, laundry all vying for attention. I couldn't afford that luxury, but I could take a day off. When my home phone was also my business phone, there was no getting away from the "office." No Friday-afternoon card games with the boys. But I could drive to Concord, hop aboard a Trailways bus to South Station in Boston, take the subway's Red Line two stops to the Green Line, then walk a few blocks into a shopper's paradise. Imagine the freedom of being unhinged from anyone or anything, a relic tossed onto the heap of past indulgences, never to be seen again.

One weekend I had the children and made plans for a two-night stay in the heart of Copley Plaza. I wasn't accustomed to driving into

Beantown, and Massachusetts drivers had earned a reputation when they assaulted the Lakes Region every summer. By the time I rolled into the front entrance to the Westin, my eyes were glazed; and I was sweating. Couldn't wait to hand the doorman a five and get out of the car. *Take her!*

The kids and I lucked out with a room on the 11th floor with a view of the city as well as the first snowflakes of the season. Having their own vending machine in the room was a treat, as was the pool on the lowest level. But seeing the wonder in Ryan's eyes as we navigated the underground on the subway brought me immense joy in providing him with his own "first."

On our last night, I brought the kids to TGI Friday's: its bustling pub atmosphere was quite unlike anything in our hometown. I ordered a margarita, which toppled onto the table from a miscalculation by our waitress, but no harm done. Like the early photo of the kids walking to school, after dinner I took a picture of Ryan carrying Sarah on his shoulders back to the hotel. Her feet were tired, but those Jellies held fast.

SELLING A PRODUCT no one wants or trusts was easier than figuring out how to assess the viability of a lasting relationship. Even as I started regaining my balance, deep within me I didn't feel complete without a man. Could I find a way to keep one at arm's length but still *have* one? Why couldn't I just leave them alone and say no thanks? Because I had children. Because children belong with a mother and a father. I'd never known anything else my whole childhood. Dads earned the money; moms handled the money and the kids. It worked. Now not only was I earning the money to maintain a house by myself, but I had two children who visited in what I considered to be half a household.

But: *what if? What if I'd meet one prospect who'd complete the missing piece? Would I be able to slow down long enough to recognize him?* One such prospect proved to be the biggest mistake of these single years. When a man gets creative to make you smile without asking anything in return and oozes affection, why in hell wouldn't I hogtie him and thank my lucky stars?

I'll call him Griffin. He was the administrative assistant for one of the area's most prolific landlords. Although our introduction through a business lead never resulted in a sale, the spark between us was difficult to ignore. He drove a small red truck, probably a Chevy S-10, and asked me for a date to attend a church social. He too had graduated from the University of New Hampshire, with a degree in accounting. A blond cutie, with a receding hairline and a beard that covered severe acne scars, he was like a grown-up version of my childhood teddy bear—warm and cuddly. He was nine years younger than I. He came to enjoy my kids, and it was obvious he had the makings of a natural father. What neither of us realized was that this budding relationship was competing against two powerful forces, neither of them another person.

He came into my life at a crossroad, when I had a shot at making enough money in one job. Never mind how many hoops prevailed on a daily basis. But I couldn't shake off the feeling that he deserved to be a father in his own right. I couldn't have us marry and not have another child. In my early 40s, it was now or never. I had wanted a third child even during my crumbling marriage. I asked and was rejected. Now it was either/or: a baby or a high-octane career. I already had two beautiful children. Now I wanted money.

Griff had no desire to prove anything to anyone. He was satisfied with his bachelor's degree and had no interest in moving up the food chain of business enterprise. Working for this landlord suited him just fine. Why couldn't I have left him alone instead of encouraging him to pursue a CPA license? Does everyone I associate with have to be a B-Bear or a hungry caterpillar of an insurance agent? And who am I to decide that someone should be given the chance to father a child?

Griff was much more low-key than B-Bear, and we settled into cozy outings at what grew into a passion for the Maine coast, especially Kennebunkport and Ogunquit. We would meander hand in hand, peeking in shop windows. One I found irresistible: a baby and toddler boutique on Main Street, just past the bridge in Kennebunkport. On display were garments in bright colors and unique embroidered designs. I could see the wistful look on Griff's face mirroring mine. Having Sarah every other weekend didn't warrant a considerable sum for something that might get worn once or twice. I had no crystal ball to appreciate that the day would come when I'd indeed be able to make the most of this boutique.

Other weekends we spent sitting on park benches in Alton Bay, at the southernmost tip of Lake Winnipesaukee. Leaning into Griff, I could break away from the frenzy of my work week and let myself dream of a future I didn't know was possible. Evenings, we watched families stroll along with their fur buddies.

It didn't matter whether they were big, small, or in between: There was something about a dog—tail up in the air, content to be matching stride with its owners. One of my clients raised German shepherds and trained them for police work. The one he chose for himself could understand commands in English and German. I pined for such an intelligent, loyal companion. And then there was the breeder in New Hampton who had a reputation for the gentlest chocolate Labs, a great family addition. But how could I provide any kind of exercise for a dog if I worked day and night?

The strongest tug on my heart, though, was linked to a golden retriever named Nicole. During our marriage, my ex and I had chosen her out of two remaining pups from a nearby breeder. Nicole was clearly the frontrunner on energy. With two full-time jobs plus a baby, we had no time for her. No time for walks along the shore or even training. It was a disastrous experience and she constantly escaped. My ex told me he had found her a different forever home with a large yard. But I never forgot her.

Griff had a sixth sense when it came to what I was thinking. He noticed which breeds caught my eye. Soon, on his own, he made the decision to add a furry friend: a buff-colored cocker spaniel he named Maggie. He couldn't do enough for me and looked for opportunities to put a smile on my face. In another show of affection, he envisioned a tire swing for the kids and knew just the tree for the job. For the swing to hang so many inches off the ground, yet be accessible to both Sarah and Ryan, the height of its attachment was key. All he had to do was shinny up some ten feet. How he scaled the tree with a tire strung over his shoulder remains a mystery. Perhaps a beer or two helped him unleash his inner Boy Scout.

As I've said, neither of my children became enamored of our woodsy backyard, and the swing remained still. The rope in time choked off whatever nutrients the limb needed and one winter the branch crashed from the weight of the snow. In fact, the whole tree required removal, which in turn required the presence of a skidder angled across my 90-degree-pitched driveway with a most adventuresome tree surgeon scaling its height and taking it down limb by limb. It took an entire day.

Joey seemed to have his own issues with the backyard.

Joey

BUMMER. I WAS TRAPPED inside these four walls with my poor-excuse-for-a-nose flat up against a windowpane. Me, head cheese of the animal kingdom . . . One day I got lucky—a chance to escape when the back slider was left open. But then what? With no plan for attack, I figured I'd slip under the deck and ponder my options. But ugh, ants and spiders were everywhere. Miserable little wretches. Shoo! Shoo! Now I'm confused. I thought it'd be a blast to be outdoors, run through the grass, roll on my back, pretend Lion King. But frankly, sitting in dirt surrounded by creepy-crawly gremlins didn't much appeal to me. Oh, no! What if I'm domesticated?

Ka-bang! There was Mama on her hands and knees yanking me out. She carried me back inside and gave me the usual "Joseph" lecture. If she knew I was done playing mind games with myself and thinking how brave I'd be out in the wild, she could've saved the sermon for another time.

But some things didn't change: When I'd see other felines walking across my property, I'd lose all sense of refinement and out would come my inner lion. I'd climb the screen door hissing at full volume. Much to my embarrassment, I'd end up looking like a fool, with my claws stuck in the screen. Mama loved me too much to leave me hanging, but I never could let go of playing King.

One night I scared a guy who was looking to break in. I was convinced of it.

Tee, you won't believe what happened last night while you were sleeping.

Tia: Weren't you sleeping too?

Joey: I sleep with one eye open. I have to. Someone needs to keep a lookout while Mama is gone. Remember when we were all alone except for when Pépère came to feed us and change our water?

Tia: Yeah.

Joey: Well, last night there was this guy with a moonbeam in his hand looking in our front windows. I got up on the back of the couch and stared right back at him and scared him away.

Tia: Wow! My hero!

Joey: I even saw his name on a shiny thing on his shirt. I kept repeating it to myself just in case someday I'd find a way to tell Mama how brave I was.

Tia: What did it say?

Joey: M O Y E R.

SOME WEEKS INTO MY RECOVERY (read my next memoir to learn what I put myself through for the sake of vanity), Griff and I were having a conversation that would reverberate long after our chat. As usual, Joey was perched on the back of the couch, keeping an eye on us.

"Have you noticed how much this cat loves you?" Griff asked.

"No. Um . . . I don't know. I've never given it any thought. What makes you say that?"

"It's the way he looks at you. He stares, like he's watching over you. I've never seen that look in an animal."

"As far as I know, cats spend more than 90 percent of their day studying the inside of their eyelids. Living among us, not much stirs them up. Of course, when their motors run, I know they're content. He seems like an ordinary cat to me."

"Well, I'm telling you Joey is no typical cat. It's as if he's trying to communicate. Fascinating."

"Funny you should say that. When I was at the home office for a week, Dad took care of the kitties, and I had the police checking my house every night. When I returned, I ran into one of my clients who's on the police force and had been on patrol that week. Everything was fine, but Corporal Moyer commented on the cat 'with the smooshed-in nose' peering out the window. He was looking back at the officer like he was a burglar!"

"I'm telling you, there's something different about Joey. He's not just a cat."

Griff, as humble as they came, was unlikely to gloat regarding how life with Joey would play out. Unfortunately, he never got to see it for himself. During these early years of my career, my intensity was directed far more on building my client base than on the tumult my kids were experiencing from the switch of houses every few days, let alone picking up on any nuances from the animal kingdom.

IT WAS QUITE the coincidence that my ex-husband and I were in home construction within a year of each other's separation, as if we were excavating our mistakes and creating a new life from the ground up. That was the only similarity, though. Along with location and square footage, the biggest change for my children was their father's remarriage and the addition of a stepfamily, including a sibling, grandparents, and aunts and uncles. I saw it as a win-win for their father and for my children to be surrounded by an intact family. But how did I fare against their Currier & Ives household?

I buried myself in work. If I could build my own castle, then I could also prove I didn't need a man. I was hallucinating. The reality was that I felt like half of nothing—regardless of awards and commendations. Living in a small city rife with couples and families, I felt like a sandwich with no middle.

My appointment book kept me sane. The angst of being separated not only from my kids physically but also from participating in their development was a lot to bear. I can't speak for a man, a father, but a woman who is a nurturer through the better part of a year is never not a mother. She can pretend and tie herself up in knots of distraction, but she'll never not be a mother.

Thanksgiving Weekend 1988

MUCH TO MY DISMAY, an innocent introduction through Con created a crucible of catastrophic proportions. Given the dastardly consequences emanating from this union, its content has been slashed to ward off any relapse of my current state of good humor.

Con happened to be entertaining an out-of-town guest, a friend made through home office connections. Let's call him Stephen, also a general manager but in Orange County, California. Why not suggest a double date with his "star"?

Allow me to cast some blame for my lapse in judgment on the fact that I was in the early stages of my sole proprietorship. Let's just say I might as well have been raised during the Depression for how starstruck I remained at seeing a man in a suit. Made no difference whether I found him attractive; and because I'd been taught not to say anything if it wasn't complimentary, let's move on.

Experienced in interviewing budding agents, Stephen noticed immediately the fire in my eyes. The look of hunger. He'd no sooner returned to California when he took stock of how to woo me from across the country. Before the internet was ubiquitous, he was forced to take pen to paper for a detailed backstory, overnight the letter, and send along a dozen roses "just because."

Being chased by a suit was one thing, but Christmas with Griff set the bar for devotion. For whatever reason, three presents were typical in a gift exchange within a relationship. It was not my year for the Christmas morning with the kids, so I visited Griff at his home. Christmas is for children—unless your diamond-in-the-rough boyfriend is a flesh-and-blood Santa.

The sight of Griffin's tree soaring with presents for me underneath left me speechless. And there I stood, with just my three gifts for him. He knew he'd taken me by surprise and was enjoying the look on my face. But it was that teeny, tiny box, wrapped in blue felt Caspari "coupons" and tucked into the base of the tree, that should've slapped me silly:

"One gourmet dinner."

"Flowers and wine and romance."

"One surprise but coupon must be presented 24 hours before surprise will be received."

"Anything within reason."

"Lots of hugs and kisses and nibbles and . . ."

Perhaps if these coupons weren't still in my possession, I wouldn't beat myself up. But ingenuity wrapped in affection within the soul of a man has GOAT written all over it.

Stephen, on the other hand, played the insurance card by inviting me to George Herbert Walker Bush's inauguration. Geez Louise—a chance to hang out with the Omaha brass. But my own place in the spotlight soon followed, when I earned my first Chairman's Council, Omaha's highest honor club, an achievement held by fewer than 5 percent of its agents.

Desert Springs, California, was this year's treat for its top agents. Less than a two-hour drive from Stephen's office, it was no surprise he'd invited himself to accompany me to various functions. Omaha was adamant that no "friends" were allowed unless the relationship was sanctioned by the church, state, or both but his status within the company allowed for an exception. Given the discomfort of being solo amid 500 couples, I didn't argue. But this temporary comfort paled in comparison to the distress that lay ahead.

Cross-country relationships stretch the patience of a lonely bachelor, and Stephen decided to move east and join ranks with the Bedford office—not as a manager but as an agent. Most familiar with employee-based group sales, he jumped headfirst into cold calls and made the entire state his territory. He concentrated, however, on one line of business. The rest of us followed the wheel-of-fortune strategy. He became the hare to my turtle home-based sales—one policy at a time. His sales aptitude for group business would by design lead to bigger premiums.

For what little personal time I had, I was now squeezed between two men who couldn't have been more different. Griffin, soft spoken and thoughtful, was a calming influence against my appointment book. Steph worked on feeding my hunger for dollars. If I'd been able to look at my dilemma as a chess game with me as the queen, then I might have believed I'd nothing to lose. I knew neither man would walk away. But I felt anything but powerful. The push and pull of my ego against my heart was set for a day of reckoning.

I thought a weekend getaway to New York City with my mother might clear up any ambiguity. It was the morning after our dinner at the revolving restaurant on the 48th floor of the Marriott Marquis Hotel. Mom and I were awake in our beds but I was quiet. She looked over at me.

"What are you thinking?"

"I don't know what to do, Mom. I've got two good men but I have to choose one. What if I get it wrong? Dinner last night is just the type of experience I enjoy now—a chance to get dressed up for a more formal dinner. Stephen is fine in this situation, but Griff . . . he'd be uncomfortable. What should I do?"

Mom, married to the love of her life, didn't have any advice. I don't even think she asked if I was in love. I hope she didn't. It would've been embarrassing to admit it was all about money. In my new work environment, with Stephen now involved in my budding small-group business, Griff didn't stand a chance, regardless of how compatible we were. Nothing could compete with my need to remain at the top of the leaderboard, but how naïve to believe Stephen was key to that goal. A hapless hamster on the wheel of fortune has a pea-sized brain for analyzing facts.

As transparent as I'd become about my love of jewelry, Stephen soon recognized he had the equivalent of a pair of aces in his hand—a chance to get an unengaged friend out of a jam while tapping into the metaphor of Eve with the apple. A diamond ring nestled between the front seats of his car as we worked our way through one afternoon after another of cold-calling was tantamount to dangling a bone in front of a hungry rottie.

Stephen figured any sparkler would do and paid cash for a ring designed for a full-figured woman with fingers the size of piano keys. An experienced poker player, he played his hand. Of course, a one-carat diamond wrapped in layers of yellow gold is quite lovely. All it needed was a yes. Like a deer in the headlights, I crashed headfirst into this temptation and was forced to break the news to Griff. We met over lunch.

"You don't even *like* him," he said, shooting me his best withering look.

"I know, but . . ."

The "but" had everything to do with Stephen's ability to match my exuberance for success—to be the best in my field. It didn't hurt that he played golf and would provide the missing link for Ryan. Now I too could have my own complete family, without having a baby. Sort of. So what if I wasn't in love. If I could be a success in a man's world, I would *be* somebody. Finally.

But why add a husband when I was already on track for independence? Because making money wasn't enough? Because my kids were now balanced with a full family with their father's recent marriage but weren't with me?

Because I needed to compete.

I think Griff was aware that our age difference was a factor. Like I'd rob him of the opportunity to marry a woman his own age and have children with her. Like somebody this sensitive, kind, and affectionate should be free to procreate. Like I knew if we were a couple, I'd never reach the stars and shine on my own. I'd want another baby and have another go at creating a full family. I wouldn't be relegated to the nosebleed section of at least this child's life. The sad reality was that I felt it was too late to grab hold of that dream, and I was too busy to pause for what I had. That was the last time Griff and I spoke.

As it happens, some years later I was volunteering at an art auction and in walked Griff with his wife—the woman he dated after our breakup, a woman with a daughter even older than Sarah. He wrote the check for the paintings they purchased. I was told they had moved to Maine. I soon realized I'd made a grave mistake letting go of this gem. He was no diamond in the rough. I was the one knee-deep in a bunker with with my second chip in the LOSS column.

In March 1990, Stephen gave up his apartment and moved in with me, bringing, I might add, his 50-inch television. I had the ring on my finger (no recollection of how it got there from the bucket seats). Eager to make our union official, we married in the fall.

Joey: *HEY, TEE. Get a load of this monstrosity of a TV. This is no jungle gym. How come we weren't consulted about where we wanted it?*

Tia: *I'm sad it got moved in front of the window. It's not safe for us. What if some boogeyman peeks in? What if he breaks through the window? What if he steals our safe zone? What if he kidnaps us?*

Joey: *I think it has something to do with the big guy. He never pets or feeds us— he just sits there on the couch like a lump watching this . . . this . . . this jumbotron.*

Tia: *I miss Griffin. He was kind and gentle. He got down on the floor to give us treats. I even let him pet me a little.*

Joey: *I miss him too. I don't like this guy. I don't like his laugh. I don't like his belly. I don't like this TV set. Cuts our playroom in half. And Mama has too much taste to like it either.*

Tia: *How long do you think he'll be around?*

Joey: *No idea, but I'll tell you this—I'll be the first to know. Mama doesn't get it yet, but I know stuff before she does.*

Tia: *How so, big bro?*

Joey: *When you've got the call of the wild in your blood, you don't wait for something to happen. You troll the woodlands and get your bearings on who's friend and who's foe. My ancestors were rulers of the animal kingdom for a reason—we've got brawn and brains.*

Tia: *I think if Mama were a cat, she'd be chasing her tail, like I suck mine. She's always on the phone or out the door. At least when Mama Sarah visits, we get cuddles.*

Joey: *If Mama were a cat in the backwoods, she'd spend her life jumping from one bush to the next like a jackrabbit. I think that's why the big guy is here with us. Mama thinks he'll protect her. Never a good idea to show weakness. I'll have to keep an eye on him.*

THE WEDDING TOOK PLACE on September 25 in the sleepy town of Sandwich, which wakes up once a year for a fair over Columbus Day weekend that draws thousands. A little white church in the heart of the village had a short aisle, perfect for my updated Cinderella story. I wore a full-length white dress with lace overlay, a bit bouffant, with matching V-shaped see-through front and back lace panels with delicate workmanship. No matter that it was my third walk down the aisle.

Sarah, as my flower girl, wore the classic Cinderella dress in miniature. Ryan stunned in a black tuxedo and carried the same air of purpose he had at the age of three as the ring bearer at a friend's wedding. Judy, my best friend, in peach tones, was my maid of honor. Con stood up for Stephen.

In less than five years, I'd secured a healthy cache of clients from all walks of life. One was a star in his own right, having made quite a name for himself in real estate. He drove a Rolls-Royce and offered to escort the wedding party to the church. My very own coach with a formally dressed horseman.

My parents were already seated in church, as were Stephen's two kids from California and a small group of friends and business associates. Even my cousin Ray, from Georgia, was there, as an usher. But there was also a close friend with whom I'd shared many stories of angst about being in the company of men who were absent.

"I can't watch you do this," Faye announced when we'd sat side by side at a seminar. She knew I'd sold my soul to the devil.

Just before we prepared to walk down the aisle, Sarah leading the way, followed by Judy, then Ryan with me, I whispered to Judy:

"If he's not the real deal, I'm in trouble" (or something less delicate).

We had a touching moment at the Unity Candle where Steph's two children and mine circled around as we each held a candle to light one in symbolic representation of our new family. Tears filled my eyes as I recognized that I alone hadn't been enough.

With seven marquis-cut stones as my wedding band now complementing my bulbous engagement ring, I had enough weight on my left hand to readjust my center of gravity. No one would mistake my marital state. I was no longer a one-winged albatross.

My euphoria had a short shelf life. Two months later, we brought Ryan and Sarah to Disney World and stayed on the grounds. With two double beds in our room, I found myself relieved to sleep with Sarah. In March, Steph and I went to New Orleans, thanks to my second Chairman's Council honors trip. In the Big Easy, music is everywhere, and 5:00 starts early. For us, it was the calm before the storm.

There wasn't any one episode to jettison this marriage—just a boatload of unanswered questions. It didn't take long for that 50-inch TV to become more than an anomaly to my country theme. Stephen's preference for group work meant he stuck to a 9-to-5 schedule. Most of my business, though, was in individual sales. While I was in my basement office making phone calls, Stephen was plunked in front of his TV set with a jumbo screwdriver in his hand. And then another. Did he think his future was secure with his buddy's star agent at the helm?

But he knew if I was plied with enough wine, I'd settle down, especially if we went to Ogunquit. The movie *War of the Roses* often came to mind during this phase of my life. Its two stars gave spine-tingling performances as a couple on a slow burn to a cliff dive. Although Stephen and I never got physical with each other, I found my voice, as did he, and it happened when we were at a restaurant. As if our getaway wasn't fraught with enough challenges, we no sooner returned home when I was looking everywhere for Tia.

Her food and water bowls were still full . . .

"Teee-aaahh. Tia. Where are you? *Tee-aaah!*"

Couldn't find her anywhere—not in Sarah's closet (where she'd been one weekend when we'd gone to Maine), not under her bed, not behind the couch. Where was she?

I headed downstairs to do a load of laundry, opened the cellar door, and out came Tia.

"Tia, sweetheart. I'm so sorry. Honeybun. All weekend? You poor thing."

Of course, I looked to see if she'd peed. Couldn't find anything. No food or water for two days.

Joey: *TEE, TEE. Dang it! You know I did my best—scratching at the door all hours of the day and night. I stretched to my full height and still couldn't grab the knob.*

Tia: *I know, lil bro. I could hear you. I knew I wasn't alone. But you know me, I like to hide anyway. I can't help myself. It's like I was born on the dark side and can't shake it off.*

Joey: *It makes me sad. And mad. I want you to be more like me. Maybe not like king of the jungle—that's my gig—but you know, just being my sister out in the open roaming the halls of our house like we're in the real jungle.*

Tia: *I know. Hey, listen, I'm starving. Let's get some chow.*

WE WERE NO LONGER a small-group team. Along the way, Stephen had befriended a gentleman from outside the company, and now they were the ones writing small-group business with competing companies as brokers. Con's buddy had gone rogue. Because of my high Omaha production, Con stepped out of his comfort zone and agreed to my own application for a broker's license, but only if the clients' needs were better served. He trusted me to keep Omaha in the mix with ancillary products.

Married less than a year and already our relationship was unraveling. One night, as I tucked Sarah into bed, she said:

"Mom, why do you look so sad?"

Aaargh! Every night I'd find myself going to bed when I thought Stephen was asleep. I'd pancake myself to create the least impact on the sheets and blanket, praying he wouldn't stir. But all he had to do was extend his left foot toward me and I'd turn into a block of ice. The full realization of my mistake seemed to come all at once. I was stuck in a trap of my own making.

March 1992

VARIOUS INTERNATIONAL INCIDENTS had forced the home office to admit that foreign travel wasn't safe for its top agents at the next Chairman's Council. San Francisco might not have had the allure of Paris, but I was good with it. I was set to be a speaker on group health insurance, of all things. When national events are held in large metropolitan hotels, meeting rooms are expansive. Stephen, instead of being proud of me, told me he planned to be in the back of the room and taunt me with questions he knew I'd have trouble answering.

To make matters worse, the night before this engagement, the company brought us onto a boat for a cocktail cruise, followed by a five-course dinner at one of the city's renowned Russian Hill restaurants. When a fine bottle of red is about to be served, someone is asked to do the honor of sniffing the cork, swirling the wine, peering into the glass, and rolling the wine around the tongue to determine if it should be drunk or tossed. The last thing I wanted was to be the focus of attention at a table of ten filled with home office personnel.

Steph stood up and pointed to me: "She'll do it!"

I wanted to wring his neck. The overnight would be a screamer with my eyes the size of golf balls the following morning, hours before I was to stand at a podium. Stephen never did show, but he'd sealed his fate with me. We'd be married just 18 months by the time the divorce was final. I saw no reason to hire a lawyer. I could handle this separation pro se, meaning on my own. Save a few dollars. He'd have no claim on my house.

He wanted the engagement ring back—take it. He wanted the Christmas gifts he'd given me, a set of copper pots and various CDs— no problem. He got to keep the full closet of L.L. Bean fall and winter clothes I'd gifted him. And let's not forget the 50-inch TV. There were plenty of awkward moments with the two of us in mandatory Bedford meetings. Men continued to far outnumber women in the office. Steph retained his friendships, including with Billy. As for me, I had no time for gossip.

Joey: *Tee, you see what just happened?*

Tia: *Yeah! Mama got rid of the monstrosity and put back our jungle gym, and now it's away from those scary windows. You think he's gone for good?*

Joey: *Oh yeah. We've got our old mama back. No more sad mama.*

Tia: *Do you think Griffin might visit us again?*

Joey: *I think we've lost him. Mama is a busy bee, but we're back as a family. We're good just as we are. We don't need anybody else. I wish Mama knew we're all she'll ever need.*

WHEREAS GROUP BUSINESS did have the advantage of daytime work, I still had to maintain my Omaha honor club status through evening appointments. I was now working toward my fourth Chairman's Council. My individual and group business had now melded thanks to part-time support staff. When I earned another honors trip, to Nashville, it was the inclusion into the exclusive club known as the Million-Dollar Round Table that had me beaming with pride. As an international consortium of the top 1 percent of all insurance producers, mostly men, how else could I be?

This year's convention was held in Las Vegas. You can't appreciate an assembly of thousands in a city as distracting as Las Vegas until you've gone solo. Housed in the Paris complex, the accommodations couldn't have been better. But whether participating in a company-sponsored reception or alone for dinner in June's 100-plus-degree heat, the lack of companionship took its toll. Fortunately, the Paris's patios, overlooking the Bellagio's timed fountains, took the sting out of taking up a single seat at a table. I earned this same distinction in the years ahead but always took a pass. Once was enough.

IN THE FALL OF 1992, the winds of change were again upon me. Permit me to paint a picture: I was Tom Hanks adrift in *Cast Away* but with no Winston. I'd just finished playing tennis when I arrived home, just in time to meet my ex-husband. Memories are tricky little rascals. Beyond color coded, when they ignite a firestorm hot enough to upend your parenthood, you remember only what you can handle.

The visit cast a long shadow. He wanted to keep Ryan in private school and have him complete his high school education at Bishop Brady, in Concord. But for some reason he needed money from me to execute his plan. This jolted me back to the day I received a call from the principal's office at Memorial (the city's public middle school):

"It's about Ryan. Why isn't he in school today?"

"Huh? He's not there? I have no idea."

My ex had transferred Ryan from Memorial's eighth grade to Holy Trinity's *seventh* grade without discussing it with me. A double whammy of my invisibility. No need to revisit the terms of our divorce, whereby issues such as healthcare and education were to be decided between the parties. Now I was being asked to pay half of Ryan's tuition, at the time approximately $3,000 (my half). After the fact.

The sum itself wasn't insurmountable. It wasn't the money. It was the principle. For eight years I'd swallowed the terms of a divorce decree that stated I'd support myself and their father would support the children. Period. My attorney assured me it was the right decision based on the difference in our incomes. Only after I'd confirmed that he'd pay *all* the children's expenses did I agree to forgo any alimony or child support.

I'd been too dumbstruck at the time to demand more specificity. Disagreements on who paid for what depending on which days of the month the children visited surfaced before the ink was dry. But how many mothers know that a school will recognize only the parent with primary custody? How crippling to have given life but be dismissed during a child's formative years if the marriage ends. Motherhood was now relegated to the mercy of the machinations of bureaucrats.

I had ignored his previous written requests because I found it implausible that an attorney with an office the size of his and a home with lake access would need *my* money to send Ryan to Bishop Brady. I was so caught up in the past that I overlooked the emotional content brewing within the request. It was a huge mistake. Only in hindsight is it clear that my refusal wouldn't sit well with Ryan. Like why wouldn't I support his education? Is private school a privilege or a right? I was in a no-win situation. I'd never said it before and would never do so again, but "No" came forth like a dam had burst. My ex got up, shot daggers at me, and pointed his finger:

"You'll be sorry!"

As he was backing down the driveway, I stood and stared into space. *What did I just do?* Years of beating myself up for never saying no or asking why had come to an end. Lord knows I was surprised, though pleased, that my son would continue to have at least a modicum of Catholic instruction, but my bubble of excitement at standing my ground was punctured by reality. My nerves were coiled tight, the tips of my fingers prickled, as if they knew something I didn't. Joey caught a scent.

Joey: *Hey! What just happened? Tee, get over here.*

Tia: *What? What is it, bro?*

Joey: *We've got trouble. Big trouble. When have we ever seen Mama stand still?*

Tia: *Um, never. She's always on the move.*

Joey: *Right. Well, that guy who was just here is Brother Ryan and Mama Sarah's dad. He sucker-punched her, sure as heck.*

Tia: *How can you tell?*

Joey: *She always pets me when she walks by. Instead, she looked like she'd just seen a ghost. If I hadn't gotten out of the way, I think she would've tripped over me. Her eyes were open, but she looked like she'd been fried.*

Tia: *What can we do? I'm scared.*

Joey: *Prepare for battle, sis.*

IT WAS A BLESSING that my life was a blur, as I was straddling the line between an Omaha agent and a broker for employee benefits, and I couldn't dwell on the consequences of that visit. Gravitating toward the group market required a boatload of spreadsheets and analysis unnecessary in home-based sales. Never mind I'd soon learn that group sales were for the most part sealed by a male bastion of low handicaps. Few women dared enter the room. And for those of us who eschewed convention, we stuck to the small-group market, usually ignored by the big boys.

Like women in the courtroom, it behooved us to mimic our male counterparts in appearance. Whereas the courthouse seemed to require that ladies be in pant suits, at least I could carry off a more casual look in khakis, tweed jacket, button-down, cleaner-starched oxford shirt with initial cuffs, bow tie or scarf, Cole Hann loafers. From a distance, I even looked like a guy. Only for the occasional white-shirt prospect would I don a navy blue suit with matching heels.

But that tiger in my tank, the one who showed up when I entered the business, was no longer a cub. An eye-blink marriage in front of family and coworkers kicked me into a higher gear. Now I needed a part-time assistant to manage all the moving parts, one trustworthy enough to have a key to my house. Over the years, a revolving door of part-timers got me through spreadsheets and the technicalities of broker sales, forcing me to consider whether I wanted to continue working out of my home. It's one thing to hold fast to one company; it's another to attempt to cover all bases for potential business so as not to leave any money on the table.

One of my friends in the business, and the father of one of Sarah's classmates, had started his own insurance practice. More focused on financial planning, Ted asked me to partner with him to create more of a full-service agency. He was based in the historic Belknap Mill in the heart of downtown Laconia, a location more professional for meeting clients than my cellar office. With three failed marriages in my wake, even a business connection with a trusted ally could give me the heebie-jeebies, regardless of the benefits of separating home and business. As much as I'd appreciate a partner, I was apprehensive about the additional expense despite the potential for increased revenue. I was dubbed an independent producer, but I was just shy of Jell-O inside. My last name could've been Walenda for my sense of having to retain my balance across a high wire with no net. What I didn't know was that this wire was about to go live.

WHAT'S THE DEFINITION of *success*? Is it working day and night to be a top gun? Is it being an average producer with perhaps a penchant for running marathons or scaling mountains on days off? Or is it making sure you never miss a child's basketball game or track meet? Ryan's basketball games were either in the evening or on Saturday morning, and I made many of them. While at Holy Trinity, he'd established quite a reputation as a point guard. I had the chance to video several of his games thanks to the residuals of an agency contest with a video camera as the prize. Although I was a first-timer with this type of camera, I managed to keep it still as I followed him around the court. While I was forced to remain quiet and let the action speak for itself, I could let 'er rip later, when he played for Brady. I dipped into my high school roots as cheerleader. Ryan always knew when I was in the stands.

Sarah's cross-country meets, on the other hand, took place in the middle of the afternoon and not once did I attend. Made no difference how many trips or shows we'd come to enjoy together. Mama Bear should've been there. I was starving for validation and allowed my business numbers to determine my sense of success. Adding the broker side was akin to managing quicksand—the deeper I got involved, the more I understood the need to have access to as many health companies as possible to match my competition. Soon there'd be more than a dozen for me to juggle. It was within this fog that I lost sight of the importance of family.

But being an agent did offer some unique adventures, which only when I look back can be viewed with a chuckle. I always found Omaha to be the people's guardian for its straightforward products, anything from my favorite \$10-a-month accident policies (\$9.46 to be exact) to disability, Medicare supplement, long-term care, and variations on life insurance (\$14.60 for 20-year, \$100,000-term non-smoker). Who wouldn't protect his family for under \$4 a week? One appointment long stuck in my craw because I came home empty-handed, something I could ill afford after I'd done hours of homework. Insurability and affordability were the only variables.

The *why* in this case would have to be left to the gods of missed sales. One evening I entered a home consisting of a mom, dad, and seven children. With no discernible medical conditions and what I considered a clear need, I couldn't believe the dad wouldn't agree to cover the mortgage for less than 50 cents a day. Always thought I should've backed the hearse to the rear door.

But that one-night stand paled in comparison to the evening I set out for Governor's Island for a lead interested in life insurance. It was my first time back on the island since the breakup with B-Bear and my first for a business-related issue. The appointment was set for seven o'clock, which happens to be the pause that refreshes for a couple who'd just awakened from a nap following multiple rounds of drinks ahead of their chef-prepared dinner mid-afternoon.

Dressed in silk pajamas, this couple introduced themselves through a summary of a lifestyle of splitting time between this lake house and a home in Mexico. Sitting upright on their damask-covered Queen Anne loveseat, I held myself with as much dignity and sophistication as I could muster. I had to have made a good impression because not only did they purchase insurance, but eventually they also asked Sarah and me for a "light" supper, prepared especially for a young girl: a hamburger with all the fixings. I should've left it at that.

Instead, I accepted the family's invitation to visit them in Mexico in January, the coldest month in the Northeast. I flew out of Manchester to Chicago, only to have the airport shut down because of weather. Once it reopened, I flew into Fort Worth/Dallas and landed at 12:30 a.m. Even though their driver would be waiting for me, I had to wade through signs in Spanish to find him. I figure my angel sister sat me next to a young lady familiar with the layout. But being alone in the backseat with a stranger at the wheel for a two-hour drive in the dark was an unsettling finale to a long day's journey.

My hostess rose to the occasion and greeted me at 2:45 a.m. But her charm toward me soon wore thin. Her home, like most of the others in this enclave, was hidden behind a high fence and managed by a staff of servants. She and her husband had their own tennis court. I played tennis, but never with a spoiled brat from Belgium who would rather walk on a bed of nails than speak French with a Canadian. Midday meals required the consumption of cocktails with an air of gentility long before it was 5:00 anywhere. Wine was served with each course, followed by cordials. Napping was a necessity.

My hostess needed to find something for me to do. One day she sent me off with her driver, the same gentleman who'd picked me up at the airport, to give me the lay of the land. She trusted him, but he had other ideas about what *lay* meant. The guy had six kids! But my last day before departure was *la pièce de la résistance*.

My hostess's inner circle was friendly with the Houston Bush clan—impressive, considering who was occupying the White House. One of these friends was my next tour guide. She was quite down-to-earth, even though her husband owned a string of hotels. We drove through the better part of town, and she introduced me to local merchants. She discovered my love for jewelry and made sure to include a stop at my client's favorite haunt. I felt I should buy something, and chose a chunk of metal shaped into a heavy bracelet. Bulky, with a pair of cheetahs facing each other and grappling with a ring of rubies, it was hardly appropriate for my pint-sized self.

The real hit to my sense of self came at the next shop. In its window was an exquisite handmade white lace dress. At least it seemed more typical—something I'd wear to a nice restaurant. But at $945, I took a pass.

My hosts and I were invited to the home of one of the city's most esteemed citizens. When the woman opened the door, she took stock of my outfit: a knockoff Hermès top, matching skirt, gold flats, and a fake gold purse, all picked up at a flea market. My top had the designer's name stamped diagonally across my chest. As we entered her sumptuous villa, with the courtyard open to the stars, this thrice-widowed woman (who, I was told, became wealthier through each husband) said, "Oh, Hermezzzzz. Even I can't afford Hermezzzzz."

And what was she wearing? The very dress I'd admired in that boutique window . . .

Ooof. It was a tough night. Everybody seemed to shrink at the sight of me. Even my client ignored me. With all the women in glittering cocktail dresses and dripping in diamonds, I was *way* out of my element. Too bad my client hadn't suggested I pack one "nice" outfit "just in case." I drank Dewars on the rocks, with the glass held across my chest to prevent other guests from seeing my faux pas. When dinner was announced, a sumptuous buffet awaited us. Seconds were apparently unheard of, but I was so discombobulated that I returned to the table, plate in hand, and dumped more food onto it. Take that.

I left in the middle of the night. My client decided not to see me off. Rather, Mr. Can-I-Possibly-Get-Lucky drove me to the airport. At the departure gate, I grabbed my bags, threw him a hefty tip, and found my way to my flight. No shutdowns at O'Hare. I arrived in Manchester, where my brother was waiting for me. I came *this* close to kissing the floor before kissing Dan. I'd never been so grateful to be home.

It wouldn't take a genius to ascertain that I wasn't doing a bang-up job of reinventing myself. A single mom dabbling in the world of the rich and famous was a recipe for humble pie. Cracks in my veneer of confidence were widening by the day. Booted out of motherhood to reestablish myself in a different role was beginning to look like mission impossible.

As THE KIDS GOT OLDER, I found myself more involved with Sarah than with Ryan when it came to recreational activities. My son now showed considerable talent for golf and in time became a member of his school's golf team. But it wasn't like I could accompany him to the links. Sarah, on the other hand, was free to gravitate toward whatever outing I suggested. Disney movies, the annual Elks Carnival, summer weekends when I brought her and a girlfriend for a two-night stay in Ogunquit, fall fairs where we focused on the horse- and ox-pulling demonstrations. Then there were Sunday afternoons when we headed up to Weirs Beach and set ourselves up by the channel, where boats of all sizes cruised by at wake speed. For years I'd visited this same spot and mentally aligned these dream boats on a scale of 1 to 10. Usually, Sarah and I agreed that certain two-deckers with the right canvas color would come in at an 8 or a 9. She was my mini-me and reached for my hand wherever we went. One day, she introduced a new topic.

"Mom, I want to live with you."

Just like that. But how? What could I do? She and her stepsister seemed to get along fine, but Sunday-night returns were the issue.

"Mama, I don't want to go back tonight. Why can't I stay with you?"

With no communication between her parents, a compromise seemed out of the question. But our schism was more complicated. Her father had a different perspective. Word got back to me that he thought I was brainwashing Sarah into saying such a thing. He decided we'd seek counseling with a school psychologist to assess the merits. The doctor soon determined there was no evidence of such influence, but nothing changed. One setback followed another. Sarah and her stepsister got their ears pierced. My little girl! I was crushed. Sarah was too young to ask if her mother could come along. It stung to be treated like a stranger, unattached to this blended family.

Whenever the kids had a school or a sports event, there'd be me on one side and "the family" on the other. Ryan seemed especially uncomfortable at his eighth-grade graduation when my parents—his grandparents—accompanied me. I couldn't bring myself to stand tall, as I did in my business life. Rather, I felt like a piece of wood on a toddler's peg board, as if a hammer pounded me down inch by inch. I hoped my misery wasn't obvious.

Ryan had always been somewhat of a challenge, but I reached for every opportunity to find something he'd enjoy outside of golf. Like the trip to Storyland, a watered-down version of Disney World, for him and a friend for a day of fun when he was a young boy. For one of his birthdays, I surprised him with a 21-speed Schwinn bike right out of the showroom. But times were changing. Although I believe he may have used it for his paper route in his father's neighborhood, I never got wind if he biked apart from his route. Soccer moms were the new thing; kids were being driven to wherever they needed to go. Bikes were vintage and so, too, were paper routes.

For another birthday I brought him school shopping at Steeple-gate Mall, in Concord. Men's clothes were far more basic than women's, perhaps because men had no patience for matchy-matchy. But I reveled in what was available: pants, shirt, tie. Ryan rocked the khaki look for school. Of course, with those eyes he could rock anything.

One evening, with Sarah in bed early, I put the Jiffy Pop to work and cranked up the VCR for us to watch *Silence of the Lambs*, a psychological thriller I knew Ryan could handle. Side by side on the couch and glued to the screen with our fingers in the bowl, it was one of the few opportunities since our badminton matches that were time for just us. We also took in a Red Sox game at Fenway. Trips to Beantown meant fresh seafood. Around Faneuil Hall I often gravitated toward Marshall's Bar for its jumbo shrimp cocktail. Like many pubs in the area, it opens to the street. Still remember the two of us at a high-top.

Another image of my son is fixed in my mind's eye. I was driving by the Laconia Country Club on my way to an appointment and in my peripheral vision caught sight of Ryan at the putting green. At perhaps 35 mph, I whipped the wheel around and screeched to a stop, inches from the flagpole, beet red from not only creating such a racket, but also laying a good amount of tire tread. Some folks might say my parasympathetic nervous system kicked in, stripping me of control. But I see it differently—Mama Bear couldn't resist her cub.

Wish there were more memories than could be counted. The term "quality over quantity" never made me feel any better, but every memory is precious in its own way, like the comment I remember him making on our last Christmas morning together upon going through his stocking:

"Where do you *find* all these things?"

March 1993

FOR FOUR CONSECUTIVE YEARS, I'd earned the coveted position of Omaha's top club, Chairman's Council. Now I was headed to Hawaii and the Waikoloa Beach Resort and Spa on the Big Island. The sights and sounds and aromas of a luau with its fire and music in the balmy night air brought this Yankee right out of her flip-flops. And how many hotels transport guests via a man-made canal into suites half the size of my house? With sky-high pillars in the lobby and a dolphin pool nearby, Omaha had outdone itself.

I had the opportunity for a side trip to Maui. Without obligatory meetings and company meals, enjoying the beauty of a setting sun over the ocean with what I think of as banana boats moving slowly in the distance was worth every hour of travel.

It was the calm before the Category-5 storm that made a joke of all previous blizzards.

Joey: *TEE-TEE. Come here.*

Tia: *What's up, bro?*

Joey: *You remember when Mama was rattled enough to spill our water after the father left?*

Tia: *Sure. How could I forget? She'd never done that before.*

Joey: *Well, I heard him tell her she'd be sorry—that's not good. Something, I don't know what, something is gonna happen. I'm picking up a scent, and it ain't from no rosebush.*

Tia: *So, all we can do is wait?*

Joey: *We can hope whatever he's gonna do to make Mama "sorry" won't be as bad as it sounds.*

Tia: *What if it is? We're helpless. We're trapped in our wee bodies.*

Joey: *Tell me something I don't know. It's true we're stuck in this world of hapless humans. Their lives are more complicated than being in the jungle, where you can duke it out once and for all, especially if you're head cheese. I picture the father as a panther hunkered down in the bush waiting to strike. I know I could overcome him with my brute strength. Sure, I'd suffer a few whacks from his claws, but I'd survive. He, on the other hand, would be toast.*

Tia: *But we can't fight this guy. He's no cat.*

Joey: *What we can do is rev up our motors, curl our tails high in the air, weave between her legs, and show Mama we're together in this battle—whatever it is.*

Tia: *You're my hero, bro. What would I do without you? What would Mama do without you?*

SIX MONTHS HAD GONE BY and not a peep from my ex.

Although I'd been duly warned, nothing prepared me for what awaited one afternoon in the mailbox shortly after I got back from my trip: a letter from his new attorney. In just over two pages, it outlined the process by which he had chosen to pursue my cooperation with Ryan's education. The original $3,000 was now off the table. Based on my most recent financial affidavit, filed at the time of my pro se divorce hearing from Stephen, it was evident I was now making more money since the divorce from the children's father. Understandable, given I'd earned every conceivable award year after year and was considered one of the top women with Mutual of Omaha.

Apparently, what with changes in family law, it was now routine for the custodial parent to be entitled to one-third of the noncustodial parent's income based on two children—money nontaxable to the custodial parent but taxable for me. In other words, to provide these dollars I had to earn an additional 20 percent. My jaw dropped. I didn't reread the letter. My windpipe seemed to narrow to a slit. I couldn't breathe. This can't be happening. *I'm going to pay him?*

I'd thought that terminating my marriage to Stephen was too simple to warrant a JD's imprint (an attorney). Besides, my last experience was anything but satisfying. But would a professional have alerted me as to what constitutes "earnings" when you're self-employed? How ironic to have been puffed up like a peacock when filling in my last year's gross income, not adjusted by deducting expenses, and now be crushed into a pile of feathers.

Would a professional have advised me to protect my privacy from outside intervention? Did I give any thought to my financial affidavit being public information? How else could a decision on child support be made without such specifics? It behooves anyone trying to compete against a legal eagle to know the parameters of their power. Then I got a call from my childhood best friend, Cecile, my first maid of honor.

"Claire, I've got some bad news to tell you."

"Oh, no. Well, I have some bad news too. You first."

"I've just been diagnosed with ovarian cancer."

"Good Lord! No! Oh, Cees. I don't know what to say. When we had dinner in November, you told me you were having a few digestive problems. But you didn't seem concerned."

"I just found out. Now, what's your bad news?"

"I just got a letter from my ex's attorney and he's suing me for child support!"

"What? How can he do that? He's a lawyer himself. Doesn't he make more money?"

"It doesn't matter if he makes more. He can take advantage of a change in the law and be linked to one-third of my income based solely on having primary physical custody."

"That's incredible. What are you going to do?"

"I don't know. I guess I need a lawyer. But I don't know where to turn. I'm scared, Cees. I can't believe I'm going back to Superior Court."

"I'll pray for you, my friend."

"And I'll pray for you."

Cecile's illness must have been advanced. The last time I saw her was in her home; she was weak and vomiting and had to excuse herself. Within 90 days, just short of her 43rd birthday, she was laid to rest. She was the first in our graduating class of 26 to die as an adult, and we honored her with a heart-shaped shrub planted on the front lawn of the church. Her parents, three children, and six siblings, among them her twin brother, were left to pick up the pieces of their lives.

As for me, I could never return to C J Avery's, the site of our last dinner together, without my eyes darting to the booth we had shared. Same thing with a Roxette song that brought me back to *Pretty Woman* and the video I'd rented for us. Thirty years later, I'm still heartbroken.

"MOM, DO SOMETHING! Joey is peeing in my suitcase!"

"Okay, Sarah, I'll talk to him."

"Joseph, no peeing in Sarah's suitcase. Do you understand?"

Joey: *Sure, Mama. I get it. No peeing in Mama Sarah's suitcase. Pssst.*

I reprimanded him as much as anyone can reprimand a cat, using my stern "Joseph" voice. It wasn't as if he'd let me catch him in the act, but this act of aggression was unmistakable in its intent. Sarah was understandably frustrated, leaving me no choice but to bring Joey to Dr. Mike to assess if there was something that would ward off a repeat performance.

"We'll put him on Buspar, an antianxiety medicine. It's available only through regular pharmacies, but it should take him down a bit."

"You mean my cat will now be on a human dose for what appears to be an anxiety-induced situation?"

"It's the only solution we have. It's not like we can reason with him or take him to a counselor. We can alter the amount to suit his ten-pound frame."

Joey: *HISSSSS, MIAOW.*

Tia: *What's going on with you, little brother? You're moping around like you've lost your best friend. Don't I count? I'm still here.*

Joey: *Mama Sarah is mad at me because I left a little pee in her suitcase. She doesn't get it.*

Tia: *Doesn't get why you're peeing in her suitcase?*

Joey: *Argh. Humans are so dense. They'd never survive in the wild. You know why I'm doing this, right?*

Tia: *It's a guy thing—you're marking your territory, which in this case is Mama Sarah.*

Joey: *You betcha. Doggone it! She keeps telling Mama she wants to live here, but nothing ever changes. Back and forth. Back and forth. So I decided to take matters into my own paws. If I leave a pee in her suitcase, at least my scent goes along with her. That way she can't forget us while she's at the father's house.*

Tia: *I miss her too. I sleep with her when she's here. She pets me and tells me how soft I am. She makes me feel safe.*

Joey: *That pill Mama gave me about took my head off. I was dizzy and couldn't think straight. If I was a human, I might be puking all over myself. Good thing Mama doesn't believe in drugs cuz she stopped giving it to me. It didn't make sense to her. And I just got bored anyway. I made my case. I figure the only way Mama Sarah will get rid of my scent is to get a new bag. Tee-hee.*

I ROARED WHEN A LETTER from a law firm came addressed to Joey, informing him he was now part of a class-action suit for having taken this prescription. Eventually, he got a check for $1.83.

Author with sister Yvette. (1956)

Mama and her cubs, Ryan and Sarah. (1985)

Tia snuggling in Ryan's arms as Sarah awaits her turn. (1987)

Ryan standing guard as Joey gets a king-size squeeze from Sarah. (1987)

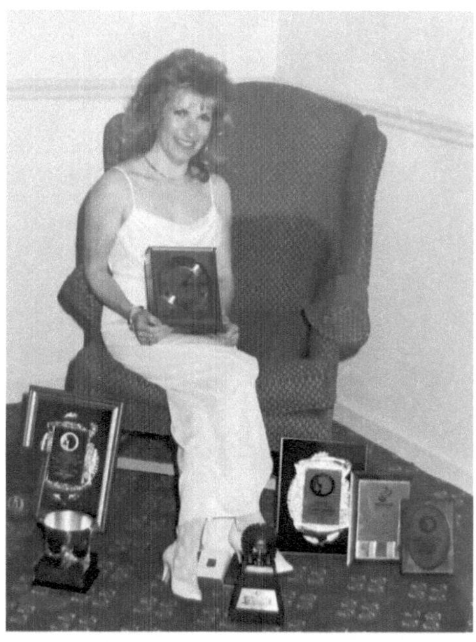

Hebert Named Firm's Agent of Year

LACONIA — Agent of the year for Mutual of Omaha is Claire L. Hebert, the insurance firm's Lakes Region representative.

This honor was based on her outstanding sales performance after attending the company's career sales-institute, a year ago.

She will receive an engraved gold anniversary clock and will be featured in the February issue of Focus magazine, a monthly Mutual of Omaha publication, which will outline Hebert's accomplishments and "share her insights on prospecting."

Hebert completed her first year as Mutual's top freshman disability agent.

Since achieving veteran status, this August, she has been in the top-10 of all agents for both health and disability production and among the company's top-15 female agents.

She will begin working for the company's fund-management company, shortly, with the securities license she acquired in November.

A Laconia native, Hebert has been affiliated with the Con Grace Division office in Bedford since July, 1986, after being licensed with Mutual of Omaha, largest individual- and family-health insurance company in America, and its life insurance affiliate, United of Omaha.

In April, she plans to attend her first company-sponsored seminar, in Florida, where she will learn, first-hand, the latest in Mutual's investment and insurance products.

Claire L. Hebert

1987 Agent of the Year, Bedford, New Hampshire (1988)

"Life is not a matter of holding good cards,
but of playing a poor hand well."

—Robert Louis Stevenson

PART TWO

TALKING TO PROSPECTS some 20 times a week about the *what ifs* had left its mark. Few people think ahead. Much easier to kick the proverbial can down the road. It was my job to readjust their perspective. But what if a person has no time to plan? What if the best-laid plans go awry, simply from a single man-made piece of kryptonite wrapped in a court document—for the third time? I had no intention of leaning on Big Pharma. I had a business to run, three with securities and group health business separated from basic Omaha production. But just as troubling to me were our two children thrown into the middle of this brouhaha. No longer ages three and seven.

Returning to the Brotherhood is like sleeping with the enemy. Mainstream folks have no training to comprehend the intricate underpinnings of our legal system, let alone assess any underlying prejudices. I learned that the Petitioner (ex-husband) gets to address the court first and summarize the reasons for this hearing through his attorney, who would begin his monologue on my refusal to support Ryan's private high school education, ending with this bombshell:

"And she sells health insurance and doesn't even provide it for her own children!"

The English language is rife with words to communicate, and less is more when applied with such pinpoint accuracy. (*Frankly, it was brilliant.*) I came right off my chair, my eyes bugging out of my head. A quick jab from my attorney sat me down. Why would I provide health insurance when their stepmother's employee benefits package offered family coverage? To include my children wouldn't up her premium. And never had I been asked what was available through me, a sole proprietor. My attorney remained mute.

Move over, peg board, make room for the pincushion. I was up against another power hitter with my attorney in the minor leagues. Why didn't he caution me to remain calm despite any innuendoes and falsehoods I might hear? And why wouldn't he realign the narrative on a home-based business vs. a law firm?

I'd been too afraid to partner with my friend in his financial business for one reason: increased expenses. Working out of my home kept those at a minimum, which by design provided a greater taxable income. A little backstory on the details of the 17-day divorce in 1985 could've also shed light on why the parties found themselves back in court.

The Master ruled that effective immediately, I was to pay my ex-husband a lower figure than requested because the children were domiciled with me half the month minus two days. For the second time, I walked into a courtroom having done no research into potential land mines.

Tucked amid cuff links and three-piece suits was a lion waiting to pounce. He could roar either for me or against me, regardless of whether he was presiding at the front of the courtroom or sitting by my side. But one thing was for sure: Billing was by the quarter hour, and payment in full followed the verdict—regardless of whose favor it was in.

Interesting how payment for goods and services is a typical amenable exchange of needs—except when it comes to what appears to be an aberration of justice. I was trapped; I just didn't know it. Like a wounded cat, I scratched back at the Brotherhood seeking a review in more ways than one, hoping for relief. All for naught.

Joey: *YOU'RE THE ONLY ONE I can talk to, Tee. What da heck? Mama walks around like we're invisible. I'm lucky to get my treat in the afternoon. Now Brother Ryan*

slams down his books and mopes around and won't even look at me. Me, King Pooh-bah—like I don't exist.

Tia: Yeah. I feel safe with Mama Sarah and stick by her and hide in her closet, so I don't see Brother Ryan very much. But what happened last night?

Joey: Best I can figure is his team lost the game and he was upset. When he got home, he slammed the door to his room and that was it. He never came out. I know, cuz I walk the halls at night. But you know what?

Tia: What?

Joey: Mama felt so bad that she put out a peanut butter and jelly sandwich for him and placed it by his door. Lucky for him it wasn't tuna. You snooze, you lose. But he never came out and it was still there this morning.

Tia: Our house is so sad. No one said anything at breakfast. I think Mama was crying. What else is gonna happen? What if Mama gets sick and goes to the hospital and no one takes care of us? What if we never see Mama Sarah again? What if—

Joey: Pulleeze, Tee. Get a grip. I don't know what the heck is gonna happen. But I'm not leaving this house. And neither are you. We must be strong for Mama. If she forgets our treats, don't complain. If she doesn't change our water, let it go. But if she doesn't feed us, hmmm, then doggone it—pee in Mama Sarah's suitcase. That gets results!

TEMPORARY INSANITY. What other state is there for a waif beaten down yet again by the good old boys club and facing the reality of writing a check every week based on bloated income figures. Forget that I'd been raised to believe in the concept of hard work to support myself. Now we entered an era when it's who you know and how you play the game. Left unchecked, this child-support figure was greater than my two mortgage payments.

Fire and ice. I was burning up from my ex's full-frontal assault on my integrity as a professional and frozen in place for having to write that first check. In one sweep of the pen, my will to succeed was squashed. I let a week go by, two weeks, a month, another month. I was stuck in neutral with my foot on the brake. A hearing on a Motion for Contempt showed up in my mailbox.

Joey: *IT'S WORSE THAN I THOUGHT, Tee. I've never seen Mama like this before. In the jungle, when there's gonna be a fight, you can smell fear from the one who's going down. That's Mama right now.*

Tia: *Is that why she's talking to herself? There's no one there, and sometimes she's screaming. That scares me.*

Joey: *Well, the good news is that the more she says, the more I learn and the more I can try to figure out what da heck to do. I mean, Mama is like a wounded cat who took a roundhouse in the belly. She's all hunched over either crying or saying bad words.*

Tia: *Sucking my tail always made me feel better, but not so much anymore. She's our mama. What if we lose her? What if she dies? What if we can't live here anymore?*

Joey: *Now, Tee. Try to calm down. We're not going anywhere. Mama loves this house too much. She loves us and her kids. She's a smart lady. She'll figure it out. But you remember what I told you, right?*

Tia: *Yeah. I know. You want my tail up as high as it goes and my motor to run as loud as possible. But I don't think I can do it now.*

Joey: *Yes, you can. Don't you give me any girly-whirly excuse. I need your help. We're in this together. We're family. And nobody's gonna take that away from us.*

THE THOUGHT OF JAIL haunted me. Like *what if?* What if I stood my ground and screamed: *You win! I'm done! Take me, take my house! But I'm not paying you! Now leave me alone!* How would that play out with the kids, with Mutual of Omaha, with my clients, with my parents? Why did the thought of someone sneaking me brownies laced with THC have me in stitches? It wasn't just a fleeting thought. I was coming unglued.

If only it were that easy. How could I light a match to seven years of concentrated effort to prove my mettle in a man's world? And what about Con's motto, "Attitude Determines Altitude"? I was the personification of the Hindenburg—I couldn't hold on; I couldn't let go.

I MADE APPOINTMENTS with two attorneys in Concord experienced in domestic issues. One was a queen pin in the field but I had two problems with her: She required a five-digit retainer and she had litigated cases with my ex. The other attorney, who viewed himself as an expert in family law, left me cold. I knew I was face-to-face with a rerun. Eventually, I fell back on the support of a former police detective who was now working in the private sector as an investigator/paralegal. For the time being, he was the glue I needed.

"Child support" seems self-explanatory, but I felt uneasy for a host of reasons. Not until I wrote my first check, which by then had crept to more than $1,000, was there some clarification. A Caribbean vacation for my ex and his wife, leaving Ryan in charge of the house and both 11-year-old girls, was another arrow to the heart. In a boxing match, a referee decides when an opponent has taken enough of a beating. But life doesn't give you a referee. I knew I was brushing up against a meltdown.

One of my friends suggested an attorney in Manchester. Referrals hadn't done me any favors, but I went to see him. Bill had a different air about him—like he was a regular guy with a head full of details unavailable to the average Joanne. He must've been a rock star for me to trust him. I hired him even though he was based in yet another county, which by necessity drove up the fee. Money is meaningless when you're stripped of free will.

Now I felt motivated to address Sarah's request to live with me. We filed a petition for primary custody, which would require a guardian ad litem. Having already been baptized in the power of this position, I was adamant that the role not to be held by another attorney. We proposed the Green Group in Manchester, a clinical counseling center with a staff of seasoned therapists. A hearing would determine whether our choice of a clinician or the attorney proposed by my ex was better suited. At least now I was at the table, and I was in full Mama Bear mode. We were awarded our choice of guardian, but it came at a miserable price: Ryan, at the age 16, found himself at his wits' end.

"I can't take it anymore. I'm leaving."

Joey: *TEE, TEE, WHERE ARE YOU? Wake up. Wake up! Wake up!!*

Tia: *Huh? Okay. It's late. I was dreaming . . . I thought I heard Mama and Brother Ryan but their words seemed kind of loud, and I just wanted to . . . Well, you know me. I can't handle the tough stuff.*

Joey: *My paws are in a crimp. I wish I could stand up and talk to Brother Ryan man to man. "Why are you leaving?" I'd ask him. "Why are you doing this to us? When will we see you again? We're your family." Yes, Tee, I'd say all that, and more. This isn't right. I'll never understand why humans make life so difficult. In the jungle it's simple. You're either pack leader or you're not. The leader makes the rules; the pack follows the rules. No second-guessing, no arguments, no mutiny.*

Tia: *So, do you think he'll change his mind and we'll be a family again?*

Joey: *How can I think straight when what I need right now is a shot of tuna water . . .*

Tia: *Oh, bro, what would tuna water do?*

Joey: *It'd take the edge off my nerves. I'd feel better.*

Tia: *Too late. Mama has already turned off the lights. I'll sleep with Mama Sarah; you go with Mama. Maybe tomorrow this will all go away, and Brother Ryan will be back.*

RYAN'S DEPARTURE WAS UNDERSTANDABLE. No child should be weighed down by contentious marital litigation, especially a teenager—no longer a child, not yet an adult. I could say it was out of my control, but it wasn't, sort of. If I'd simply let go of the past and agreed to his father's request to split the cost when first approached, we might not be in this mess. Now look what I've done.

Once a battle of this nature began, no motions from one attorney to the other to compromise, to find a middle ground, changed the trajectory of what was a lengthy, torturous war for supremacy—and each lawyer reaped the financial rewards of additional hurdles. It was Hell's Kitchen without sustenance and a 24-hour OPEN sign.

"If this hearing were held in California, Claire, you'd be seen in a different light," my attorney told me, "but here in New Hampshire, a woman as driven at work as you are isn't the norm."

I soon discovered that Stephen had jumped at the opportunity to discredit me, hell-bent on testifying that my need for success was stronger than my love for my daughter. And then there was the Grim Reaper card I drew at a tarot reading. This card suggests a tough battle ahead. Now I wanted a peek into the future of the mother–son connection and headed to Ogunquit to see a fortune teller. Joey took note.

Joey: *TEE, CAN YOU BELIEVE THIS? I heard Mama tell Mama Sarah that she visited some wannabe genie who took her hand, looked into her eyes, and said she knew she was in deep sorrow over a child—a son. Now Mama is convinced this woman knows everything and plans to see her again soon.*

Tia: *That sounds creepy. What's happening to our mama?*

Joey: *Far as I can tell, she's falling apart. She's crushed about Ryan and can't think about anything else. If you'd come out of your closet, you'd hear her crying.*

Tia: *I do hear her. It scares me when she cries. Do you think that genie-wannabe just made a lucky guess?*

Joey: *You betcha. When a wizard—and in the jungle a wizard is always a male— sees a mama walk in, he figures it's either a husband, a boyfriend, or a child who's breaking her heart.*

Tia: *I'm timid, but if Mama needs us . . . what can we do?*

Joey: *Not a darn thing cuz humans are wacky. Like I've told you, this would never happen in the jungle. Mother lion would grab her son by the scruff of the neck and give him a good swat on the behind. Family is for life. No one walks out.*

"WILL MY SON COME BACK?" I asked the fortune teller.

"Yes, he will. It'll never be what you want it to be, but it will be better than it is now."

MY NEXT MOVE was far more devastating to my relationship with Ryan than any combination of stressors that had caused him to leave in the first place. I was struggling under the weight of two mortgages, household expenses, child support, counseling, and attorney's fees. And my business had fallen off a cliff. Most Chairman's Council agents remain top tier the rest of their careers. By early November

1993, Con was forced to break some news I'd never expected to hear: I was nearing the downgrade to Builder's Club and in jeopardy of falling away from even that half-pint position.

How could I go from cream to sediment within ten months? I was now an inkblot on a squeaky-clean white board. Let me count the ways: trips to Manchester for conferences with Bill; trips to Manchester for analysis with the Green Group; miscellaneous issues relating to interrogatories and various other legal maneuverings to delay or get to the heart of the matter.

Never had I asked my parents for financial help, and I wasn't going to start now. I had one choice: tap into my children's mutual funds.

A Uniform Gift to Minors under a Declaration of Trust—Revocable calls for a parent or guardian to be custodian of the funds until a child reaches age 21. I'd been putting in a total of $100/month for some six years across two funds for each child. It was "for the benefit of the child." *Isn't that the definition of child support?* With my back against the wall, I made the call.

"Mutual of Omaha Investor Services. You are on a recorded line. Jane speaking."

I was sobbing. "This is Claire, Claire, Claire Hebbbbbbbe . . ."

"I'm sorry. I can't understand you. Can you repeat that?"

"This is Claire . . . Hebbbbbee . . ."

"I'm sorry. I still didn't get your name."

This went on for some seconds as I tried to compose myself. I'm surprised she didn't hang up. I was crushed to have to redeem Sarah's and Ryan's funds and couldn't stop crying.

It didn't take long for my ex's attorney to alert the court that I was "stealing" the children's money. Bill told me it wasn't kosher, but I saw it for what it was: child support. I hadn't even thought to run it by him.

If it was my money providing these funds as gifts for the kids at age 21, why couldn't I borrow against it under the excruciating circumstances I found myself in? It's not as if I was buying myself a car or adding a wing onto the house. I'd replace the money long before Ryan and Sarah became eligible for ownership. But this court battle I was embroiled in had nothing to do with logic or good intentions. The law was the law was the law.

If Google had been available, I could've searched for an exception to parental withdrawal for child support of a minor. It hadn't crossed my mind that Ryan had given me a portion of his paper-route earnings. Much to my chagrin, I'd forgotten. Otherwise, there's no way I would've touched those dollars. I believed I was using "mine."

Parental mistakes breed catastrophic consequences when the law is involved. Bill referred to it as a "mistake in judgment." As worn down as I was from all sides fighting a losing battle against working for a living and apparently pretending to be a good mother, I took the news like another beating. This mistake manifested itself in a tornado of resentment that didn't do its damage and move out—instead, it hovered over my relationship with my son and stuck around.

If I were a balloon capable of fending off pinpricks, this setback was more like trying to escape a cleaver. I was seeping in more ways than one. I did my best to calculate what the market had done since the first withdrawal, added a generous bonus, and wrote Ryan a check, along with a letter apologizing all over myself. It didn't matter. Guilty.

June 5, 1995

THE FINAL CHAPTER on the Battle of the Parents. For 116 weeks I'd been living in a vapor of fumes assaulting me from every conceivable angle of motherhood. "Child support" payments were now replaced by college costs split between us based on *any* state system—not on the University of New Hampshire's, which would've made sense to me. I also thought having the children involved in a 1/3 split as an incentive for maintaining good study habits was appropriate, but that offer was rejected, proving that once a marriage is terminated, academic decisions are no longer within the noncustodial parent's prerogative.

But my ex threw one last surprise. He'd interviewed with a nationally recognized insurance company and agreed to become an agent in Laconia. This decision made front-page news. A noted attorney choosing to leave the practice of law for direct sales was pretty much unheard of. He was burned out. He would now compete with me.

His wife informed me in a letter that she'd be relaying each expense incurred by the children. Stripped of communication with Ryan, I was now relegated to a walking checkbook. I was accustomed to being on the sidelines when it came to academic details, but upcoming college info was based on the student's choice.

Meanwhile, I missed catching another family reset button. During these court years, Sarah had morphed from hand-holding Mama's girl to budding free spirit. My Sweetpea was growing up. Graduating from elementary to middle school brought changes. Big changes. She and her new friends talked incessantly about sex and music. Thank you, MTV.

When Sarah was in seventh grade, I became nervous about her choice of friends. A mother's intuition is important, but I knew that—especially without any support from her father—I wouldn't have an impact on her behavior. Sarah managed to navigate this tumultuous stretch unscathed (to my knowledge), despite the petri dish of dissension percolating from two households poles apart.

One Sunday night, as we approached her father's driveway, I experienced a heart-tugging moment when I lamented what I believed was our mutual distress that she wasn't able to remain with me overnight. She turned to me and said:

"Mom. Why can't you just be happy for me?"

Good Lord, why is being a mother so tough? It was a challenge to keep my frustrations to myself and not load them onto Sarah, but I did. Because there'd never been a dismissive word between us, I was stunned. I kissed her goodbye with the usual "Love you," but my eyes filled with tears before she even got to her father's door. The train had already left the station.

PERHAPS MY ANGEL SISTER realigned the weather. But after more than two years of fighting and rage, I accepted what the forces of nature had sent my way. It wasn't as if I was in control. In late June, on a Sunday morning, my mind pole-vaulted over the sermon during mass right into a pair of cowboy boots. Why such an item, no idea. Maybe a consolation prize for surviving the chaos. I already owned a pair of Frye's. I headed to a boot store in Weirs Beach before going home. I entered the shop only to recognize the clerk at the counter as a previous prospect in insurance. An attractive blonde with a welcoming smile, she oversaw a comfortable space in which I could peruse the aisles.

Soon, her boss came in. When he saw me at the counter with two boxes of boots and a credit card in hand, a Cheshire grin spread over his face. "So, what's a cutie like you doing in a place like this?" *Chuckle.*

"Truth is, I was at mass, and the idea of getting a new pair of boots just came to me."

"Aha! I knew it. It's divine intervention. We're destined to be together! How about I bring you to Boston for lunch next weekend?"

Big Al turned out to be one of the good guys in my life—a towering man with a rambunctious spirit ready to motor through life with a wink and a nod. He was intoxicating, like B-Bear, with his own unique blend of mischief and humor. He grew up outside of Boston and knew his way around the city with his eyes closed. We had lunch in the North End, an opportunity to soak in the friendliness of the Italian culture. Family extends beyond genetics—all I needed to belong was a good appetite for food, drink, and laughter.

Al was Jewish, a similar culture for conviviality. We attended two lavish Jewish weddings that left nothing to the imagination. With soaring floral centerpieces cascading in bursts of color, five-course meals sandwiched between hours of alcohol consumption, and guests attired in formal wear over a string of days, it was an eye-popping experience for this girl. One nuptial even took a page from the final scene in the movie *When Harry Met Sally*—held in the Skylight Ballroom in Lower Manhattan's SoHo district.

He convinced me to accompany him on a 17-day trip later in the year. He had chosen Egypt and assured me I'd gain a new perspective on life in America. He was like a kid with a new friend, eager to show me the sights and give me a chance to taste *real* coffee—in tiny cups with enough caffeine to hold a spoon upright. Our trip was set for late October, when the heat would be manageable.

But something far more potent was brewing right under my nose.

Joey: *TEE-TEE. What's going on with you? You seem more tuckered out than usual. I know Mama sends us mixed signals. Sometimes she's like her old self and sometimes she sits on the couch in a daze. I don't have to worry about you too, do I?*

Tia: *To be honest, bro, I didn't want to say anything, but I don't feel so good. I have no energy and don't even feel like catching a few rays with you.*

Joey: *Oh, come on, Tee. Things are getting better with Mama. I know we still don't have Brother Ryan back, but Mama Sarah shows us the love when she visits.*

Tia: *Okay, I'll hang around a bit tonight and show Mama some love.*

SOMETIMES LIFE IS LESS A ROLL of the dice and more a screeching ride over potholes. Tia was never one to be held, although Sarah was occasionally successful. But on this night Tia stayed by my side as I sat in my usual living room chair. Then she looked up at me like she wanted to be picked up, and then she jumped on my lap. Never before had she done that! My goodness, she was a bag of bones. When did she become so emaciated? Is this what she wanted me to know? She'd been fine at her last checkup. When was that? Surely within the year, but she was way too thin. I'd have to call her doctor in the morning and get her in for an emergency visit.

That evening, as I prepared for bed, I stopped by Sarah's room to ponder the oil painting I had commissioned from one of my clients. An established artist, she had captured the sweet faces of both Tia and Joey through a composite of pictures I had taken of them while they lay on my bed. Only later did I recognize the subtle tap of my intuition preparing for heartbreak.

Sarah was in her father's custody, but I called her on my way to the vet to see if she wanted to come with me.

"No, Mom, I don't think so. Gee, what's wrong with her? She was so cuddly last weekend and even let me hold her. I hope she's okay."

I had gotten used to being alone, but there are times when "alone" morphs into lonely, and this was one of them. Even though I was unsettled about Tia's frame, I was unprepared for what Dr. David had to say.

"I'm sorry, Miss Hebert. I'm afraid Tia is suffering from leukemia. There's no cure, and there's nothing I can do for her."

"I can't believe this! I had no idea she was sick. She's always been shy and doesn't like being held. I didn't notice anything unusual with her eating. How can this happen?"

"Her immune system may have been weak from the beginning, and she was unable to fight off this virus. As an indoor kitty, we know she didn't catch it from another animal."

I thought back to when we first chose Tia. We'd never been told she was a preemie and needed to be bottle-fed, and now our time together was over. I called Sarah from the waiting room. Tia was her first official kitty; and teenager or no teenager, this one was going to hurt. I bent down and hugged Tia's little body. "Goodbye, sweet girl. We're going to miss you. You'll always have a special place in our hearts."

I watched, numb, as the doctor carried Tia out of the exam room. There was never any conversation about my being present. Frankly, I'm not sure I could've handled it. I was a little fragile myself. Instead, I returned to the car and let myself soak in this loss. I felt responsible. I wept.

That evening, Al and I had plans to have dinner with two other couples. I felt it might be better than staying home. Besides, what was I supposed to say to Joey? How do you explain the Rainbow Bridge to a pet? There's supposed to be some solace with that image, but my eyes told a different story. They were bloodshot and swollen; even my glasses couldn't hide my pain. I was far from my outgoing self. Al provided companionship, but he wasn't one for sentimentality. And I needed to be held.

For eight years this shy little girl had been part of our household. Like in any other family, some members are more outgoing than others. She was the quiet one, never interested in finding her inner tiger. Still, her presence was comforting, especially to Sarah, with whom she'd often settle in for some cuddling. Sarah, unlike her mother, wasn't a fly on the wall trying to be everything to everyone.

Joey

Wouldn't you think Mama would scoop me up, give me an extra cuddle, maybe even tell me everything was going to be all right? Nada. Humans. They bragged about having five senses, but a lot of good that was without the call of the wild in their blood. Like being able to detect changes in air quality. When two felines troll the same space and one of them goes missing, it's like being lost in the desert. I needed to find my bearings—a kind of watering hole where I could take in some nourishment after all the adventures Tia and I went on.

Two weeks later

It seemed like forever since Tia was gone. And as if that wasn't enough, now I saw that Mama had her suitcase out. She got to escape while I stayed back and sniveled. But I had to control my temper and remember why I was in this house with this mama in the first place. She needed me. She just didn't know it yet.

If I'd thought back to Griff's comment about Joey not being "just a cat," I might've handled the loss of Tia differently. But what? Sit down on the couch and chat with him about feline diseases? He'd be in good hands with Pépère, who was coming over twice a day and would be spoiling him rotten with treats. But I was being selfish. I had a business to rebuild and a trip taking me far away from my heartbreak.

A Trafalgar Tours brochure teased the mysteries embedded in the Valley of the Kings. Getting there was brutal: a car trip to Boston, a motorcoach to New York's JFK airport, an overnight flight to London's Heathrow with an all-day layover, then on to Cairo, landing just after midnight. By the third day, I was this close to being among the walking dead. Being greeted by militia jolted me into rearranging my stooped posture.

We were bused to one of three hotels: ours was the one closest to the pyramids and farthest from the city. We got into our room at 2:30 a.m. Pick-up time for our first tourist attraction was in two hours.

My beau had chosen a five-star hotel, one frequented by dignitaries and even royalty. It boasted an attached game room straight out of *Casino Royale*. It's embarrassing to admit that yet again I found myself out of my element. If there had been even a hint of coquette in me, I could've tried to fake it, but lacking cleavage as well as a shimmering crimson sheath, I returned to the room while Al went to the tables.

Although I was nowhere near as attached to my pillow and bed as I am now, two days of travel with a pittance of sleep doesn't make for a happy camper. But there's nothing like a step back in time to appreciate the availability of modern conveniences. And that was long before I'd be placed atop a grumpy, snorting camel with scant tolerance for tourists and resentful of every click of the camera. Al had experienced other Third World countries and was as comfortable in the desert as he was at a formal dinner. As for me, I just never got my sea legs.

Air quality was terrible, what with odors from camel dung, gasoline, horse manure, rotting vegetables, and shirtless bodies wafting about. And five lanes of BMW motorcycles, Mercedes sedans (always silver), donkey-drawn carts, limousines, buses, bicycles, rusted-out vans, and ambulances navigating the main traffic circle was unlike anything I'd ever witnessed.

The two-week-plus "vacation" was divided by a Nile River cruise. The puddle-jumper we boarded should've been relegated to the used-parts hangar a long, long time ago. White knuckles and multiple prayers saved me, and that was just for lift-off. The engines were screaming for mercy, trying to get the hunk of junk off the ground. Really, enough said.

Lest I give you the impression that the trip was an all-out disaster, let me tell you about a couple I met. At our first lunch onboard the boat, Al and I found ourselves at a table with four others, two women and two men, traveling together from San Diego. These folks were outgoing, funny, and enjoying the heck out of their adventure. They were already world-class travelers and loved Third World countries. My naivete was once again on display when I whispered to Al: "So, which ones are a couple? In other words, who belongs to who? I can't figure it out. They blend like they're all the best of friends."

I give Al credit for his patience. "Oh, Claire," he said, "the boys are the couple."

My jaw dropped; I'd never seen a gay couple—certainly not in Laconia. They looked just like any other couple, especially given that they traveled with two women. Robert and Lyman became dear friends of mine—it's been more than 25 years now (details in my next book, and yep, I'm working on it).

For seven days our boat went from one village to another. One day we'd be deep below ground exploring tombs with an occasional light-bulb providing a glimmer of the next step; on another we'd be strolling the remnants of a village seemingly abandoned by civilization.

In one port, a young woman came up to me with something hand-made. She looked at me as if I were a goddess. I was ready to give her the clothes off my back. Al informed me that any souvenir from an American would be considered a gift of high value. I parted with my favorite lipstick. She stared at me with wonder. I can't imagine she knew what to do with it.

As is often the case on cruise ships, the final night offered a special party. This one was a costume gala, Arabian style. Dressed in our multicolored kaftans, with sashes at our waists, we joined our new friends from San Diego. It was Lyman who grabbed the spotlight and never let go. Garbed as King Tutankhamen, he led a conga line of us peasants. Strutting bare chested, with the fruits of a serious workout regimen in evidence, he was a natural magnet for this crowd of amateurs. Adorned with gleaming gold bracelets, earrings, pantaloons, and a headdress, he raised the bar for our farewell banquet.

As our vacation wound down, a video camera emerged from one of our travel mates, a honeymooning couple from Washington state. I had nothing to hide. It was almost over. I mouthed the words: "I. Want. To. Go. Home."

But not before a trip to the Cairo Museum, which boasts the largest collection of pharaonic antiquities. Maybe it was my mood, but its appeal was lost on me. I was ready to leave far sooner than was Al, but I was still capable of being a good doobie and followed the crowd. "Following the crowd" takes on a whole new meaning, however, if you're dropped off in the heart of Cairo's shopping district. Merchants abound in every direction—far beyond what the eye can see. Only one other time in my travel life did I find myself in a setting in which I could be elbowed down an alley and no one, I mean no one, would ever find me.

Lucky for me to have a big American man by my side, a pro in the art of negotiation. Nothing like a seasoned frequent flyer to whittle down a trinket's price to the quick. I still treasure the result: an 18k gold hieroglyphic-etched bangle bracelet. It sits patiently in a safe place, awaiting the maturity of one of my two granddaughters to take up ownership and spin a yarn about how Mimi once risked life and limb to travel far and wide.

As we headed back to the hotel for the last time, I was convinced I was destined for Lakes Region General Hospital, to see if the pollution had caused any permanent damage. Even 19 miles outside the city, the air spat out sawdust like from a chainsaw.

In the morning, as we approached our bus for departure, all activity in the plaza came to a screeching halt: no cars allowed in or out. We learned that this was a common occurrence when the royal family spent the night at the tables. As we waited in suspense to see who would emerge, only one person caught my eye—the saucy siren accompanying the prince, some second cousin to the king. Just as I had imagined, like in a Bond movie, this knockout brunette was poured into a low-cut, floor-length silk sheath and hugged by a red mink wrap. She was a stunner.

When I got home, I was happy to see Joey, but he seemed like he had a chip on his shoulder or something. He was puffed up and walking back and forth. At one point, I swear he shook his paw at something.

Joey

WHAT WAS I? Chopped liver? Did Mama not think my opinion mattered? Did she think Tia's disappearance was some sort of magic trick? I knew my sister was toast as soon as Mama said she was "a bag of bones." Not good.

I wasn't not all that sure about a Rainbow Bridge since I hadn't seen it for myself, but I wanted to believe. It sounded like a blast—leapfrogging through fields of daisies and dandelions with other kitties and even dogs because they all love each other. No more fights. No shots out of the blue. Maybe I'd even catch up with my real mama and brother. Maybe even that cutie-patootie Marshmallow, who I could've had all to myself before my boyhood got rearranged.

Sometimes I found myself staring into space and then realized Mama was looking at me. I hoped she wasn't getting any ideas. Although I missed Tee-Tee, I had a lot on my paws just keeping an eye on Mama—and these big guys she kept bringing home. When she disappeared with one of these strangers, how was I supposed to protect her? What if she got into trouble and learned he was useless? MEOW!

Maybe because I was one of the chosen few to lead the whole jungle, I couldn't imagine being vulnerable to everything and anything that crossed my path. Me, King Leo in miniature, was afraid of nothing. But being left alone with nothing to do is a waste of my talent. I'll give Mama the cold shoulder for a while. Maybe she'll get the hint.

I may be in good paws with Pépère, but to be able to feast on treats is not my mission. I need her in earshot to figure out what in the dickens is my next assignment. Big Al didn't cause me any concern. I could tell that this time he was the goo-goo ga-ga half of the couple: He pretty much slobbered whenever he looked at Mama.

Still, it ain't easy being Mama's sole protector. I can only do so much. Humans make life too complicated. I dunno if Big Al will stick around or vamoose like the rest of her guy friends. Maybe my mission is to make her realize that all she needs is ME!

BIG AL AND I REMAINED TOGETHER through year's end, but we weren't a match, although his family welcomed me warmly. He walked out of my life with no animosity—and into the arms of his forever woman.

IN ONE OF MY GROUP HEALTH APPOINTMENTS, I saw a photograph of a gorgeous, pure white kitty in a picture frame on the desk, apparently a blue-point Himalayan. I wanted details.

"There's a breeder in Old Orchard, Maine, who is well known throughout the state," my client told me. "She's been breeding Himalayans for 20 years. I think she may have one left from her current litter."

Joey seemed lonely. Just the other day, I caught what seemed like a dazed look on his face. Who knows what goes through a cat's mind? I figured he was missing Tia. Even though she spent most of the day tucked into one of her hideaways, I bet they roamed the halls while I was asleep. I know they visited their food dishes and litter box. I contacted the breeder—one kitten left, a male.

I waited until the weekend of Sarah's visit, then grabbed a girlfriend and the three of us headed north for the two-hour drive. We parked in front of a Cape, knocked on the door, and were gestured to enter the living room. The breeder, who was old enough to be my mother, greeted us with Maine hospitality: short and to the point. She went into the basement and came back with an oversized cotton ball with not a hint of color beyond its crystal blue eyes. As she placed him on the floor, I couldn't help but notice that he had a bit of an unusual gait.

"What's wrong with his hips?" I asked. "He walks as if he has two peg legs."

With a snap like a pull on an elastic band, she said, "I don't think you can love this little boy."

Whoa! Wait just a minute. Slow down, lady. Can't I make an observation?

"No, no. That's not true," I said, pleading. "I just . . . I was just wondering why his back legs seem stiff. I know we can love this little boy."

She simmered down, and we completed the transaction. His mother was on the premises but kept out of sight; Dad was, apparently, a hired gun. This kitty missed the mark as a show cat; his strut would never pass muster with the Cat Fanciers Association. Well, their loss.

Sarah settled into the backseat with our little guy wrapped in a blanket. But we were hungry, and when we stopped for a late lunch, we discussed a proper name. Sarah had been watching the TV show *Party of Five*, and one of the characters, a boy, was named Bailey. And that's how our Bailey was named, never mind he looked nothing like Baileys Irish Cream. Joey wasn't impressed.

Joey: OKAY, I ADMIT IT ain't easy being King of the Hill when there's no one to give you an "atta-boy." I was just getting used to my single status when with no warning, my life took an about-face. Mama and Mama Sarah left for the day—a long day—and came back with a "friend" for me. And to add insult to injury, without consulting me they'd named him Bailey.

I heard them say he was a blue-point Himalayan, which told me he was a hill cat always looking down on others. Harumph! That's my gig. So, maybe we're from the same neighborhood, eh? We'll see about that. Damn those eyes of his—outsized, crystal blues—and a fur coat meant for the North Pole. But he still walks like a duck.

This surprise didn't sit well with me. It was the principle of the thing. It was done behind my back. Me, top cat. I puffed myself up, stared into his baby blues, and threw him a long hiss. He needed to know up front who's the boss.

"Who do you think you are, you little mongrel? This is **my** house!"

Bailey: Hey, take it easy, mate. This sure wasn't my idea. I was quite liking my life with Nana and my mum when three strangers showed up. And now, look here, matey, I'm no mongrel! My mum, Sara—no h, how's that for class?—was on the front cover of last year's Maine's Best Breeders calendar. She and my dad, Pogo, are world famous for their posh litters, as in yours truly.

Joey: Oh, brother. Give me a break. With a name like Pogo, I get why you walk with your butt in the air. On the other hand, this "yours truly" is the product of Miss Rajah and Mr. Eukariah. Top that, Mr. FluffnBuff, or Mr. Posh, or whoever the heck you are.

Bailey: What a load of balderdash! Strikes me as your family is on the carnival circuit. When you were strutting like a miniature King Leo, you got your nose bloody smashed for trying to be someone you're not. And, by the way, I almost didn't get allowed into this household because of your mother's catty comment about my hips. Imagine the look on Nana's face when your mum questioned my gait. "What's wrong with his hips?" Bah. Nana came to my defense and questioned whether she was capable of loving me. "Oh, yes, of course," she replied, or some such rubbish.

Joey: Do you think I believe that cockamamie story—that with parents named Sara and Pogo you were groomed to be a high-end purebred? Hahahahahahaha.

I SOUGHT OUT MAMA for some clarification. "Why wasn't I consulted?" I asked, as she tried to cajole me with an overdue treat.

"You seemed so dejected, Joey."

"Hogwash. Maybe I was studying the inside of my eyelids. Maybe I was adjusting to being man of the house. Aw, forget about it." I meow. "I'm mad at you."

"Come on, Joey, be nice to your little brother."

"No way. I'll hiss and I'll spit, and now I'll go sulk on my bed."

I figured I'd wake up the next morning and realize this was all just a bad dream. But not a chance. There he was in all his self-important glory—all white fluff. Boy, what I'd give to roll him in the dirt. Then he wouldn't look so . . . so perfect. He didn't seem afraid of me, like I was wasting my energy. To heck with him. But with Mama working so much, we had to spend a lot of time together.

For example, Mama opened a can of tuna, and I scooted over as usual to lap the dish clean. Now here was Mr. Show Cat for a sample. Mama put out a dish for him, and now I had to share. I finished ahead of him and went to nudge him away, but Mama wouldn't let me. But okay, life was good again—he was letting me be king—and now I'd have an audience when I climbed the screen.

Joey

MAYBE I'VE BEEN LUCKY. Or maybe just spoiled. But I've been a brilliant but full-of-mischief cat, proud of my heritage. Until now. I have no idea what came over me, but it didn't take long for Mama to notice I was a bit slow on the uptake. Maybe house cats show their malaise in their attitude. When we're hot, we're hot; and when we're not, we hurt.

I couldn't seem to get out of my own way. A centipede could've overcome me. Sure enough, I was headed for a doctor's appointment. Not my favorite thing, but, hey, once a year a few pokes and a nail clip weren't all that bad.

Not this time. Dr. David gave me a head-to-tail exam, then told Mama he needed some blood work. I had no idea what he was talking about. But I sure found out! Got my paw shaved, and a quick jab of pain told me that if I got my paws on this doc—well . . .

Soon I was back in Mama's arms and on my way home to my cozy bed, where I could sleep off this miserable day.

I didn't hear the conversation between Mama and Dr. David about the test results, but I could tell Mama was upset. But back we went on the road for what ended up being a second opinion. Now I found myself with someone called Dr. Mike, and I listened to Mama giving him a summary of my blood work. Even though I'm a near wizard, this medical mumbo-jumbo made my tail curl. This nonsense would never take place in the jungle. You're either up on your back paws ready to duke it out or spreadeagled doing a face plant. I hate to admit I might now be reduced to a dang domestic.

But Dr. Mike seemed to have a solution that changed Mama's mood from sad to hopeful. I noticed that my food was different. Little by little, it was switching from tasty tidbits of meat and fish to a dry mixture of veggies and chicken. Proud as I was of my physique, I figured if this is what the doc ordered and I got back to feeling like my strong, handsome, fabulous self, then bring it on.

Meanwhile, Bailey and I decided we were brothers from another mother. We fed off each other's antics. Bailey was first to figure out how much fun to have on laundry day when Mama stripped her bed and then tried to remake it. He'd dive onto the mattress pad and leap from side to side like a jackrabbit as she tried to stretch the fitted sheet. It always took her longer, but she didn't mind. Not with that smile on her face. Not one to miss out on fun and games, of course I joined in. Now we added hide-and-seek and anxiously awaited our favorite blanket so we could knead to our heart's content.

Bailey may have led the charge to the bedroom, but he took my lead in sitting at the kitchen counter. Good thing there were two stools—one for each of us. Bailey appreciated this new vantage point as we could track so much more activity, not to mention get handed a few more treats while Mama fixed dinner. The picture of brotherly love.

WHENEVER I NEEDED ENCOURAGEMENT to pursue a career that would stretch my talents, I headed for the Swiss hills with our resident Olympian, Penny Pitou. Away from the madding crowd, unsupportive of my venture into the world of finance, I pined for space to think. Now, I needed space to regroup. Like a car with 100,000 miles on it, I required more than a tune-up. For my tenth anniversary in the business, I chose Austria, again with Miss Pitou for a full-service overhaul of my beat-up engine.

On the first day, humming "The hills are alive with the sound of music" came naturally. The Alps will do that to you as you wander through fields of wildflowers overlooking breathtaking vistas. By the middle of the week, Penny offered us a "hump-day" break to spend in Innsbruck to soak up its charm. Baskets of blossoms hung from first- and second-floor windows in chalets as far as the eye could see. The village was awe-inspiring—kind of like listening to a violin concerto: serene and languid. But it was the sight of man's best friend that shook me. My roommate caught the same vibe.

"Karen, can you believe this afternoon? Here we are with nothing to do but kick back with a carafe of chilled Riesling and puff pastries."

"It's a welcome break. Hey, have you noticed that everyone seems to have a dog?"

"How could I not? I try not to stare—a dog but no babies, no children anywhere. Where are they?"

"And these dogs don't look familiar. They must be breeds specific to the Alps."

"Right. This is no place for a Cavalier King Charles or a Maltese tucked inside a jeweled pouch. These hardy pooches are built for endurance, almost like workhorses."

Canines, not kids, accompanied their owners to restaurants—a twist on being seen but not heard.

Even as our muscles acclimated to daylong hikes, the elevation was taking its toll—the rarefied air was rougher, meaner, and without mercy. One adventure had ten of us in single file across the side of a cliff. Peering below wasn't an option. I took nothing for granted as I placed one foot in front of the other, untethered to this behemoth. Gave me pause.

In such a setting, it's impossible not to feel the power within each of us to control our destiny, and I was grateful for such breathtaking moments when I understood how good it was to be whole, to manage setbacks and heartaches and then move on. When this trip came to an end, I returned home invigorated, ready to make the most of my life and focus on what I had and not on what I was missing.

I'D BEGUN SEEING a certain gentleman. With an outgoing personality and a girth to match, Big Ben was full of life. Perhaps because of my diminutive size, I seemed to gravitate toward hulking giants like they'd protect me. I had high hopes that I'd chosen well for this next chapter of my life with men, but it appeared I hadn't done so well in the pet-sitting department. Given the amount of time I'd be away from home on that trip to the Alps, my boys needed more attention than what my father could provide.

What I needed was a house sitter. Perhaps because my choices were few, I agreed to the daughter of a business acquaintance without knowing her. One weekday, on a whim, Big Ben stopped by the house, unannounced, and peeked in the windows. He didn't want to ruin my vacation and decided not to get in touch with me about what he'd seen via the bathroom window.

When I came home, I had no sooner set down my bags when I spied a countertop encased in grease and remnants of a meal gone bad, not to mention a floor with all shades of new colors. Rounding the corner, I saw that the litter box was overflowing. In the living room, I noticed candle wax smeared across the coffee table. So, there I was, going from blissful escapade to a perfect storm of fury-regret-heartache?

Bailey: *I KNOW I'VE BEEN TWITCHY, but it's about time Mum got back. One more day with that lazy bum and I was prepared for a hunger strike.*

Joey: *Hey, take it down a notch, bro. Quit acting like a spoiled brat. Since you've been part of this household, we haven't suffered any setback. I'm sure Mama thought this biped would take good care of us. No way would she have gone away thinking we'd be ignored.*

Bailey: *Rubbish! I was bred to be fluffed and buffed and I'm chuffed about our mistreatment. I have a mind to teach Mum a lesson about just what happens when she abandons her precious boys and leaves us in the hands of an incompetent.*

THIS TRASH BIN of a setting hit me hard. I took no time in contacting the mother of this young woman and laid out the facts:

"Hello, Mrs. Mac. I've just walked into my home, having left it and my two precious animals in your daughter's care. Your husband assured me she was trustworthy. The countertops, stovetop, and kitchen floor are covered in spills and shriveled-up food. Dried candle wax covers half my coffee table. And worse, the litter boxes and pet placemats show blatant disregard for the animals' care. Did she live here or just stop in and add more food without emptying the bits that remained at the bottom of their bowls? You're welcome to come by and note the state of their litter boxes. I'm not paying for this fiasco."

No argument from the mother, but there was plenty from my white fluff ball. Bailey developed the habit of pooping outside the litter box. I even found myself scolding him:

"Bailey! No! Bad boy! No pooping on the floor. Poop in the litter box."

Ha!

He knew exactly what I was saying, but he cast a passing glance at me, then walked away. It took months for me to give up, to allow him to do his thing. Too bad I couldn't teach him to use the toilet.

Big Ben had done more than keep an eye on my house. He had spied a FOR SALE ad tacked to the bulletin board of one of his retail stores: "Himalayan kittens for sale." Would I want to take a peek? Adding to my menagerie was just another stretch, but yes, I did want to check them out.

The address was in a remote location, so I brought my neighbor Jack with me. If my memory serves me right, there were at least five kittens nearing their eighth week. I had already had a female with a male, and now two males. Which sex would better complement this pair of brothers? Once I got home, I called Dr. Mike for a professional opinion. Which one?

"Get one of each."

What? I'd need to think about it. I was leaning toward a female, a touch of yin and yang. I returned with Jack in tow. Now I picked up the male I'd been ogling, a ringer for an albino mouse. He looked at me with hazy blue eyes that seemed to dissolve into a murky shade of gray.

"Look at this little guy," Jack said. "He fits perfectly in the palm of your hand."

"I know. I don't think I've ever held this tiny a kitty, certainly not one looking back at me."

I couldn't take my eyes off him. His sister had also grabbed my attention because she reminded me of my earlier domestic tigers. If I was going to get two, these were my picks. Names like Casper and Chloe came to mind. The breeder hovered and offered a discount if I took both of them.

One of my girlfriends offered to come with me when it was time to pick them up. Because Dr. Mike's office was between where the kittens were and my house, I thought it'd be a good idea for him to get a quick look at my new additions.

"Are you *sure* you want these two kitties?" he asked. "They're covered in fleas, have ear mites, and their eyes are infected."

How can this be? I asked myself. The seller called herself a breeder of Himalayans, yet she was selling these little tykes loaded with health issues. I was furious, in part because of what these kitties had endured but also because I was already in love with them. I mean, how could I return them to this poor excuse of a human being?

We loaded up on all the medicines and creams necessary to straighten out the kitties. Although the eye and ear infections would resolve themselves with treatment, there was no way around the vermin issue other than a sudsy bath. One at a time, my friend and I soaked the little guys in my kitchen sink and watched the "dots" disappear down the drain, unable to scurry fast enough from our capable eyes and hands. Then came the hair dryer. A standard hair dryer must have seemed like a fire-breathing dragon to these tiny tots.

As most animal lovers know, introducing a new pet requires due diligence, based on existing personalities and intuition. I decided to squirrel these two siblings into Sarah's room until she returned for her visit. But here comes Mr. FluffnBuff to investigate these new smells. I was aghast at Bailey, who seemed to morph into the

Abominable Snowman, hissing and growling like he had a vendetta to settle.

Joey

WHAT IN THE NAME of King Leo was Bailey doing? Was there a Monster Cat beneath that posh exterior? Sure, I wasn't all that happy with two more mouths to feed. But I knew my place in the pecking order. These two hairballs were too scrawny for me to raise an eyebrow, let alone exert any energy. Pfft. The midget, the little white guy, made me look like I had got color, so I kinda thought he was okay. But his tail looked like roadkill. The other one made my eyes water. The glare coming off her backside reminded me of greased lightning.

PUFFED UP LIKE HE'D BEEN STRAPPED to an air pump, Bailey exploded:

Just who do you think you blokes are, invading our space?

No reply.

Get out now before I give you a proper boot!

No reply.

Are you daft? One last chance!

JOEY STOOD NEARBY, SILENT. *I was having such fun watching these sad sacks scoot into corners that neither Bailey nor I could reach. Who would've thought Mr. FluffnBuff had the makings of a wild buffalo!*

His take on a cat-and-mouse game continued until it wasn't fun for him anymore. Had nothing to do with how often Mama scolded him into acting more like a doting big brother than a wild animal. In time, he got bored when they wouldn't leave. But I wondered if there might be more to their story.

When Bailey was napping, I checked out Casper for some details. I even found myself feeling sorry for him. The rest of us were blessed with expansive, eye-catching backsides that even a peacock would admire. But this munchkin must have been MIA when the powers-that-be applied the finishing touches.

Joey: *So, what's the scoop with you and your sister anyway? And what happened to your tail?*

[It took a bit for Casper to emerge from behind the couch pillow; but eventually, ever so sheepishly, he poked his head out, eyes lowered.]

Casper: *We had a rough start. Our home was overrun with humans. Most of the time Sis and I found ourselves under someone's foot. Frankly, the place was a pit and we ended up bunking in the bathtub before we'd both be flattened—especially after I got stuck between the washing machine and the dryer. I barely made it out with my life, but my tail never looked the same.*

Joey: *Note to self: Sometimes it pays not to rush to judgment. Now I feel compelled to let him in on a little secret. I'm boss cat. I rule and have the last meow.*

Hey, lil buddy, I wanna apologize for what Bailey put you and Chloe through. It was uncalled for and quite out of character. Like he got clocked by some evil spirit and needed to put you and your sister through some kind of initiation to prove you're worthy of acceptance into this family. Total hogwash. If I'd known he'd be that overbearing, I would've given him a good thumping when I had him under my own paws when he walked into my life.

Casper: *So you'll keep an eye on him? Chloe and I won't have to worry?*

Joey: *You got that right. Just a heads up, our mama packs a bag every once in a while. You'll soon learn she has no luck with men, but for some reason she won't quit trying to find the right one. I'm on a mission to convince her, no matter how long it takes, that her fur family are all she needs. And now we've just doubled our forces. Still, it may take some time.*

WATCHING BAILEY TURN into a one-cat goon squad against these two rugrats was equal parts hilarious and frustrating. How could I trust him alone with them? Joey had been kind to him in comparison, with a mere hiss or two. No posturing. No intimidation. Bailey has had a mind of his own ever since that hygienic setback during my hiking trip. I could only hope that my two new furballs could withstand this short-term aberration without any trauma.

I needn't have worried. Mars and Venus in the animal kingdom seem to find ways to intersect without going off the rails.

Casper: *GEE, SIS. I was some worried about our transfer when we got pounced upon by this overstuffed polar bear. But just had a word with the one who calls himself "King Joey," and he told me he's the leader of this pack, and he'll take care of things. Apparently he runs the place.*

Chloe: *I wasn't worried in the first place. I just looked scared to make him feel good. We'll be just fine with or without King Joey. We aren't always going to be such midgets. I figure sooner or later I'll be able to face Dough Boy and show him that true power comes from within. We won't be afraid of his bluster. He won't be pushing us around much longer. You'll see. We girls have our own way of taking care of business.*

AT LEAST ALL SEEMED GOOD in my relationship with Big Ben. It felt good to be once again socializing with other couples, and I couldn't do that without a mate. Although I had a host of compatible female friends to keep me company on my single weekends, I still felt outside the mainstream without a man. The sizzle factor was too strong to ignore, and Ben was fun. Once I'd secured a reliable pet sitter, thanks to her referral from my friend Brenda, I could enjoy a getaway with Ben without worry.

We went to Scottsdale, Arizona, home of frequent dual rainbows against the iconic Camelback Mountain. The range offered unique opportunities for a panoramic view quite unlike what's here in woodsy New Hampshire. So when Big Ben suggested a sunrise ride in a hot-air balloon, well, why not? But stuffed in a bucket with strangers, counting on Mother Nature to hold fast to her wind predictions, was no place for this insurance lady. Although we didn't end up in a thicket of saguaros, the landing gave me the willies.

Our next adventure, in the spring of 1997, brought us to the island of St. Martin, which boasts a split personality: one for the its-five-o'clock-somewhere crowd (St. Maarten, Dutch) and the other for the strip-and-go-naked-who-cares crowd (French). At Orient Beach (clothing optional), a visitor can enjoy a "yippee-ki-yah" moment strutting about in his or her birthday suit.

Maybe it was just a bad day, but why would anyone want to waste a minute of vacation for the sake of curiosity—especially if the day's beachgoers are in the over-80 crowd? My behavior may not always have been the most prudish, but at my core I was reserved. Big Ben seemed bent on changing things up, perhaps hoping there'd be some coquette itching to get out.

"Come on. Lighten up. Take off your top. Let me take a picture."

"No, I don't want to. It's embarrassing. Really, I can't."

He persisted and promised the picture was for his eyes only. I reluctantly relented.

We poked our heads on the Dutch side for some window shopping, but it was the evenings spent strolling along the marina in Marigot, on the French side, that meant the most to me. Hand in hand, we lingered by yachts too magnificent for words and basked in the glow of a setting sun. But one night, Big Ben decided to take a quick dip following our seaside dinner. We'd no idea the images on his swim shorts glowed in the dark. We laughed ourselves silly.

Light of heart, enjoying day after day, I was unprepared for a sudden downshift. I didn't have any idea that I was about to slide headfirst into a giant palm. Whatever Big Ben's intentions were must remain a mystery, but can we all agree that a closed bathroom door doesn't require a DO NOT ENTER sign? One evening, as I was pulling aside the shower curtain, in walked Big Ben, camera in hand. SNAP!

"Hey! What are you doing?" I shouted.

"Oh, relax. I'm just finishing up the roll. No big deal. It's just for me."

He later told me the roll of film was developed while we were on the island and the negatives destroyed. I didn't give them much thought, but when we got back to New Hampshire, the relationship began to lose its sizzle. We'd been together for more than a year, feted each other with surprise birthday parties, and enjoyed a couple of vacations, but now we seemed to be treading water.

AS WE APPROACHED Motorcycle Week, in mid-June, a client friend asked if I'd like to join him on his Harley to check out the Weirs, the center of excitement for us locals. Cars are banned during this week; only access is by foot or bike. If there's one thing I'd acquired over the years, it was a spirit of independence. When I pay the bills, no one tells me what to do. We stopped for dinner. I had nothing to hide, but the outing didn't sit well with Big Ben. He asked to come to my house for a talk. This particular evening is still painful.

He seated himself in the chair just inside the archway of the living room; I sat on the left side of the couch facing him, placing us about four feet apart. Joey leapt onto the couch, then stayed alert, snug against me. Big men take up space regardless of their frame of mind, but when they're on the warpath, it's best to stay out of their way. Big Ben started screaming at me, furious that I'd gone on that bike ride. And then he let loose.

"And you tell me this because . . . why? So, I can say 'Good for you. I'm glad you got a chance to hop onto Michael's Harley'? I'm not stupid. I know it's Bike Week. Like that makes any difference? Look at me. Do I look like a doormat—a 250-pound doormat? Like it's okay to wrap your arms around him while you cruise the boulevard? Behind my back?"

He stood up, towering, menacing. "You fancy yourself some kind of big shot now, don't you? Got your own house. Got your own business. Miss Independent. Like you think you can compete in a man's world. Well, I'll show you who rules. You remember those pictures I took of you on the beach in St. Martin? And what about the one of you coming out of the shower? See this envelope? See this address? Yeah, your ex. That's who's gonna get these pics. He'll see you haven't changed a damn bit! What's the matter? Cat got your tongue?"

Joey

I DIDN'T GET WHAT THIS LUG WAS SAYING TO MAMA, but I knew one thing: I'd never seen her tremble. Not like this. The whole darn couch was on the move. He had to pay for screaming at her. He was gonna wish he'd never been born. I was feeling my jungle roots, and I was gonna roar right down his throat. If he made one move toward her, just one step away from that chair, I was gonna throw my whole body right onto his big fat face and drag my paws down his eyes and his elephant ears and leave him bleeding and begging for mercy. How dare he talk to my mama like that!

WHEN THIS BIG MAN was blowing a gasket, my mind and my body were paralyzed—I could neither fight nor flee. I was shaking like I'd been dumped in Lake Winni at ice-out. The thought of the father of my children seeing such pictures pulverized me. Made no difference that they were unposed other than the damn beach shot of my topless self, looking more like a dunce than a coquette. The shower shot was hardly a pole dance. But I was too frightened to think logically or utter a word.

The *what ifs* later crossed my mind. What if I'd hit back with my own fury at his outrageous reaction? What if I'd stood up myself and told him I didn't realize I was dating a guy with such low self-esteem? Neither Joey nor I adjusted our position on the couch. How many minutes ticked by is anybody's guess, but the emotional toll on me lasted a lifetime. Big Ben sat there and glared at me, with the pictures tucked inside his manila envelope. Thanks to Joey snuggled in so close to me, though, I didn't feel quite so alone.

Joey

I SHUT MY EYES and wished myself back in the jungle as a grown-up version of my baby self to take down this creep limb by limb. I bet he sensed what I was prepared to do to protect Mama. He stood up, took one last look at this now shell of a woman, turned, and walked out. I bet he was scared. Mama almost fell off the couch, then locked the kitchen door, ran upstairs to her bathroom, and slammed the door.

Meanwhile, I had some unfinished business of my own. My siblings, those chickens, one by one emerged from their hiding nooks. They approached me one paw at a time. They knew I was hissing mad. And they knew why. Where were they when we needed them? Four of us on the couch would've kept that beast at bay from the get-go.

He'd have known right up front that his goose was cooked if he kept drumming down on Mama. But what did I hear but a bunch of cockamamie excuses.

Bailey: *Oh, bloody hell. I had to use the loo and got sidetracked.*
 Casper: *I-I-I had to hide. His voice was so loud, I couldn't stop . . . I . . . I . . .*
 Chloe: *As Casper's big sister, where he goes, I follow. That's it. No excuses.*

Joey

Argh! If I hadn't been so worried about Mama, I'd have given each of them a good swat across the whiskers. But I figured the past was behind us. No sense beating myself up for not having the premonition that this guy from his size alone would be a problem for Mama if he got out of hand. What we needed to do now was get our butts upstairs and show our support for her.

It seemed like forever, but finally the door to the bathroom opened and there she stood, her face drenched in tears and still bawling. But we could sense that she was relieved to have us there. We all stood at attention for her. She sat down at the top of the staircase and just cried. I knew she needed a hug. I wish Griffin had been here to help. All we could do was stay by her side for as long as it took for that last tear to dry. We'd make sure she was never alone again. Saving Mama became our mission.

As I emerged from the bathroom, a shocking sight awaited me: All four of my kitties stood at the top of the stairs looking at me—not sitting, not lying down, almost like they too were frozen. I'd never seen anything like it. At least these were *my* babies and mine alone. No one would take them away from me. But what threatened to unravel me once and for all wasn't a court hearing but rather an ex-boyfriend who could hurt me in ways I'd never imagined.

His threats are beyond the scope of this memoir. He didn't get what he wanted. But what else could he do to me? The trouble with a broken relationship is that you're left vulnerable from all the secrets shared in moments of intimacy. Big Ben knew, after my children, my pets and my house meant everything to me.

My imagination started spinning out of control. *What if? What if he hurt my kitties? What if he set my house on fire?* Not outside the realm of possibility, as a woman in the neighboring town of Meredith had suffered that same consequence following a breakup. Her house burned to the ground.

Why did a breakup with me require that I be crushed? Why was being with a man so complicated? Did I need to look up, under, and around each dating partner and divine his potential Mr. Hyde? Is there such a thing as a margin of error? And where does that begin and end? My 14 years of reinventing myself seemed capable of being eradicated by a jealous, egocentric maniac. Just when I was back on my feet after a protracted fight for my parental rights, I took this kind of wallop. So much for being around a big guy. But at least I had my fur babies.

Joey

IN TIME WE EACH HUNKERED DOWN for the night on Mama's bed. She wasn't alone. She wouldn't be alone. It was all we could do. For now.

I WOKE UP the next morning with my eyes the color of a December sunset, my cheeks bloated, and my mood deep into my slippers.

I had no clue which way to turn, but I knew I'd have to cancel the day's appointments. As it turned out, I had a birthday lunch date with one of my clients. I sounded so unlike myself; he told me later that he felt the need to drive by my house to assess whether I was okay based on the outside, as if the clapboards could tell him anything.

One of the ramifications from last night's drama was visible when I walked down the stairs and saw Big Ben's truck in the yard. I know I opened the inside door and kept a locked screen door between us as he stepped onto the porch.

"I'm sorry, Claire. I know I went too far. I don't know what came over me."

The evidence of his rage was front and center on my face. When I said nothing, he knew forgiveness wasn't part of the picture. He left.

I'd like to say I never saw him again, never spoke to him again, but that wouldn't be true. Sometime later I met a girlfriend for lunch at a sidewalk café, and being outside meant I could wear sunglasses. She and I had met in group counseling during the early months of my separation from my ex-husband, and now she knew something quite serious had happened.

"Claire, you don't have to tell me what's gotten you so rattled, but you're not yourself. Whatever it is, you've got to unload it."

I thought about it and realized I'd remain powerless to rally on my own. It had already been several weeks and still I was smacked with anxiety and shame. I couldn't bring myself to speak to any of my friends, in fear of retaliation should the news travel. My daily performance in front of clients was worthy of an Oscar, but in my personal life, I was yesterday's crumbs.

Only once or twice did I catch sight of his truck at an intersection, and it sent my sympathetic nervous system into overdrive, like I'd been struck by an intergalactic force. Just the sight of the

WELCOME sign at either end of his town line made me shake. I knew I couldn't remain trapped inside my emotions forever.

I made an appointment with his town's chief of police. There I sat across the desk from the father of one of Ryan's high school friends, the same friend who had accompanied us to the Red Sox game. It was the most difficult, most embarrassing conversation I've ever had. I felt like a tattletale from elementary school. But his reaction was swift and clear:

"Claire, this is your decision, but I know I can bring a case for two Class A felonies."

I hadn't thought about what telling the police would accomplish. I was so stunned that only one of the two do I remember: extortion, criminal intent. There was no way I could press charges. No way I could put myself once again in Superior Court, caught in another link to my ex. If I didn't explain about the threats of the pictures, Big Ben might . . .

But the chief's support put me on the road to healing. My reaction was no overreaction after all. I was victimized and had every reason to be traumatized.

When I got home, I shredded every picture from St. Martin.

Joey

ONCE WE GOT PASSED Bailey's initiation rites and Big Ben's temper tantrum, our newbies caught on to the pecking order of this family tree. At least in my professional opinion— until Chloe started showing some moxie. She was just a girl, for crying out loud.

There were plenty of nooks and crannies in this house to accommodate the most discriminating ego, so it wasn't that complicated: just follow my lead. If I was unavailable, Bailey would step in. But let's face it, it comes down to food. It always does—in or out of the jungle. Fortunately, Casper couldn't care less about tuna, but Chloe made up for it. We called her Queenie. You didn't want to cross her! She was all muscle and would likely take a swipe at you and ask questions later if you didn't watch yourself.

Bailey and I would always outweigh her if we had a battle on our hands. But most of the time these two rosebuds stuck to themselves and snuggled butt to butt in the den. Since the room wasn't by any window where the sun's rays streaked, that was fine with me and my brother. We'd hog every inch of space by the back slider—he, stretched out, full length, belly up, and me catching some zzzz with one eye open.

Pépère was our regular babysitter. I always got along with him because he loved passing out treats and I loved eating them. It was obvious he was a cat man, going all cutesy on us with a squeaky voice. Tia having been such a shy kitty, I usually got a double dose. But when Bailey came on board, it was a different story.

Bailey seemed mesmerized by Pépère, and vice versa. As soon as Pépère walked into the kitchen, there was Bailey ahead of me with his tail wagging (like a dog!) and even flopping onto his back! I'll admit I was a bit jealous, but I still got my usual fill of treats. Things changed drastically for me, though, when Casper and Chloe entered the picture.

Now it was Chloe's turn to outgun us. I don't know what it was about Pépère when she saw him for the first time, but you'd swear he was the Grand Pooh-Bah of feline paradise. It's like she experienced some kind of déjà vu and had eyes only for him and the heck with the rest of us.

She went so far as to turn the volume up on her motor and lead him to the couch in the den in some kind of seduction dance. And here's the embarrassing part: She'd jump onto him with her version of a lap wiggle and then peck away at his baseball cap!

I could say that Pépère, um, lapped it up, but that would be unfair. I may have been a lot of things, but I still had class. I tried not to let it bother me, and then it happened: Pépère called her Sweet Petunia. Puh. Puh. You'd think Bailey would've been put out by being set aside by this little hussy. But Mr. I'm-Fine-Just-the-Way-I-Am wasn't a bit ruffled.

Don't tell anybody, but sometimes I found myself wishing I had a bit more of Bailey in me. Nothing bothered him. And when it did, he handled it and moved on, like owning his decision to scooch on the side of the litter box. When Chloe caused a *scene, as she now did every time Pépère came over, Casper and I were left out in the cold. Just because Casper wasn't the sharpest tool in our litter box didn't mean he didn't care. Pépère even called him Knucklehead.*

One day I was just so frustrated that I reached out and took a good swipe at Pépère—quite unlike myself with humans. It didn't help that I was in a yoga moment and stretched out on my side. No one, *and I mean* no one, *touches my belly. It was off limits. I'll admit, there was no warning sign on my forehead. I was sensitive, that's all. There was enough belly showtime around this house with Bailey. No need to compete with Mr. FluffnBuff.*

But wouldn't you know, the poor old gent sprung a leak and was bleeding. Boy, was he mad at me! It was never the same between me and Pépère. But he was a sucker for a kitty, any kitty, and continued to pass out treats to all of us. It's not like any of us could look the other way because of the new pecking order, all thanks to "Sweet Petunia." Our pride had to make room for our common sense.

MAYBE I DON'T GIVE MYSELF ENOUGH CREDIT. Maybe I should just kick the can of failed relationships down the road and hope to catch a rainbow. Or maybe I'll call this stage of my life just what it is: a ding-dong of broken promises and broken hearts headed away from the goal line.

The year was 1999 and I'd hit the half-century mark. As much as I wished for a home in tony South Down, in the city's north end, a gated community well stocked with trees, walking trails, and a private beach attached to a dock ravenous for attention, the universe pushed back. While the area was safe and pristine and would lend a touch of class to my address, Admin wanted nothing to do with the self-employed, forcing me to open an office in Gilford's Village West, a hodgepodge of units designed for entrepreneurs not yet ready for prime time.

I then considered renting a cottage in South Berwick, Maine, only a half hour away from my ultimate destination, Ogunquit. My four munchkins were easy enough to transport and would keep me company for such getaways. But the French in me tugged at my savings account. I was no risk taker, and another mortgage was akin to crossing the Delaware in a canoe. I was doing just fine with my one remaining anchor, having fulfilled my responsibility on my second mortgage to Andy. With interest rates trending lower while maintaining my initial payment at 9 percent, I was pecking away at the principal. How could I now take this leap and assume my business would support a new burden?

My gift to myself ended up being closer to home. I transformed an early addition of a mud room into a mini–great room. If I couldn't move to South Down, at least I could walk into my humble abode and appreciate an 11-foot ceiling highlighted by a spectacular Palladian window with west-facing casements open to Mother Nature's whims. My new contractor, Ray (Andy had moved onto more expansive villas with a touch of Milan), who preferred home remodeling over scratch creations, offered insightful suggestions for aesthetic balance. Considering the height advantage to this entry, two rectangle windows were installed along with an oval one looking out onto the back deck. Custom window treatments, corner gas fireplace, lighted closet, and commercial-grade Pergo flooring wrapped up one of my best decisions.

Managing the opposite sex, on the other hand, never seemed to be within my skillset. It didn't help that I was experiencing a seismic shift in my biological makeup. Menopause. I didn't get flashed by an aberrant heat lamp and glow, but I did suffer from a malfunction in my eye ducts. All Sarah would have to do is show up in the driveway and just like that, my tear ducts let loose. Like I'd lost control of my bodily functions. I found there to be but one solution: golf. It may look simple enough, but it requires 100 percent concentration, which provided a reprieve from thoughts of my daughter's approaching departure for college.

Unbeknownst to me, my ex and his wife were preparing for a substantive move of their own: An offer presented itself to recalibrate his career and move to a warmer climate. Although our connection in familial terms had long since been severed, there was still a knee-jerk reaction when a piece of my jigsaw puzzle dropped off the table.

And just by coincidence, in walked a McDreamy, a dreamboat—what my mother would've referred to as tall, dark, and handsome. It's one thing to ogle eye candy in the comfort of your living room; it's quite another when it looks back at you.

That was my experience as I sat in the audience in a conference room at the local hospital to listen to a Blue Cross representative bring us brokers up to speed on changes to our sales portfolio. McDee, as I thought of him, commanded attention not only for his artful delivery of bland material but also for his impeccable *GQ* appearance. Had my early fantasy of working in New York or San Francisco materialized, a spit-polished look in men's attire would've been dismissed as ordinaire. But in Laconia, New Hampshire, men like McDee were like rainbows. In fact, clothing seemed to run parallel to home construction: humdrum or stunning; a roof over your head or designed for curb appeal.

McDee had exposure to opulence long before he understood its impact. Not every child has grand ballrooms and elegant soirees in a grandparents' home. Early connections to the General Electric plant in Upstate New York gave his family a leg up in finances, providing ample resources for McDee to indulge his whims. It didn't hurt that his high cheekbones captured a youthful vitality that enhanced his sex appeal. If John Wayne was known for how tall he sat in the saddle, this stunning cowboy could be remembered for his impish grin wrapped in threads befitting a prince.

Although he'd manage to break my heart, McDee still qualifies to be included in this memoir beyond a postscript. It's natural to question the *why* of our decisions when we know the ending, but I'm mature enough to appreciate the patchwork of my history. His block was a far cry from the thunderbolts that characterized my time with Big Ben and more like a scene from Margaritaville.

I learned that McDee had more than a family fortune awaiting him after his tour in Vietnam. The Red Sox were interested in his pitching arm, but injuries to his hand were permanent. His athleticism, though, didn't miss a beat. Be it on a black diamond ski trail or a five-star golf course, McDee could still outshine the competition.

What he failed to inform me as we traveled to resorts across New England and upstate New York was that he was still married. As a single, my eyes were laser focused on a man's ring finger. I was used to insurance men with a gold band on their left hand. How else can you sell insurance for all those late-night appointments and early-morning agency meetings without your better half handling the kids, laundry, meals, and after-school sports?

Instead of a wedding band, McDee's left finger held an intriguing diamond ring that suited his polished look. He told me his wife had a serious illness, and even though they continued to inhabit the same home, they were no longer legally bound and led separate lives. I had no reason not to believe him.

Menopause mixed with empty-nest syndrome created the backdrop for this relationship. In providing occasional weekend getaways to resorts normally off limits to me, he forced me to concentrate on hitting a little white ball or remain balanced on a ski trail I wouldn't otherwise consider. He taught me the nuances of red wine and even introduced me to the Cosmopolitan, the cocktail made popular by Carrie Bradshaw and friends.

Call it woman's intuition or, maybe more accurately, my angel sister, but I wanted to settle the issue of: "Are you married?" After a year of weekend jaunts, with pickups and drop-offs from a Park-and-Ride, I was feeling like some kind of helicopter kid whose parents fly in for a weekend. No one in our business circle knew about "us," as we were rarely seen in the area. One afternoon midweek we met for a drink at a Mexican restaurant in Concord when I point-blanked asked. "No, I'm not," he replied. Surely, he wouldn't lie to me in broad daylight. I never pushed him to move the needle on our relationship, but I was beginning to feel as if the same song was playing on repeat.

Friend Brenda and I planned to meet McDee and his best friend at an upscale bar in Nashua. When we got to the table, only his buddy was there.

"Where's McDee?"

"Ellie found out about you and left the house. McDee has gone after her."

What?

Brenda and I left.

His friend told me later how upset McDee was upon hearing that I knew. "Why did you have to tell her?" McDee left me a voicemail to say that he and his wife had indeed been divorced but had remarried to provide her with better health insurance.

What was the problem with the truth? With someone in a position of leadership, as he was, in one of America's most recognized health companies, his respectability had been part of our personal connection. I wasn't inclined to look under a rug for his authenticity. I seemed to be proving time after time that women can't take anything for granted and need to develop a sixth sense to penetrate a string of lies. I felt like I had no judgment . . .

Was I *in love* with him? Hard to know. We were older and free of the emotional burden of child rearing. We played, and he chose the playground. As to why he kept me in the dark, I don't know. In time, I recovered. Of course I did.

Joey

MOST OF THE TIME Mama spent the day in her office glued to her phone. We were used to the sound of the doorbell. Mama would come running up, but we minions never broke a wink. My siblings had elected me official greeter. They were smart: I was Joey, dripping with attitude and ready to face the big, bad world. Besides, who could resist my topaz gemstones and adorable button nose. I even developed quite a good relationship with Mama's first contractor, Andy. I called him "Boots" because he was always in work boots. Even I could tell he was stuck on himself—but then again, so was I. We developed a bond: I never failed to pay him a visit because he never failed to reach down and pat me. He understood I wasn't just another pretty puss.

But one day a hulking giant walked in, and we could all sense this was no ordinary heavyweight. It didn't help that he ignored me.

Bailey rushed up to me.

Bailey: Well, I'm gobsmacked! Have you ever seen anyone this ginormous?

Joey: Not even close. His head about touches the ceiling and his feet are about as long as the kitchen rug.

Bailey: If he wanted to hurt Mum, she wouldn't stand a chance. This is utter rot. We need to make sure he never comes back.

Joey: I get it. But how are we gonna do that?

Bailey: Just you wait and see, mate. Leave it to me.

Joey

AFTER WHAT SEEMED A MUCH LONGER appointment than usual, we could hear them leave her office and walk up the stairs. Mama was first and about jumped out of her skin when she saw what lay ahead. But there was nothing she could do. Bailey had dropped a big poo, a stinky one, smack dab in the middle of the kitchen floor—his version of a sucker punch. Ever since Mama's last trip, he could poop whenever he needed to make a statement.

Mama was embarrassed, but she understood. The giant would never return. Mama didn't scold Bailey; she also didn't see the paw-bumps we all exchanged. Mission accomplished. Saving Mama.

CATS CAN SNOOZE much of the day because their instincts keep them safe. Such a gift. It isn't like I had a conversation with them before this 300-pounder walked in. Seeing the size of this man took my breath away. Had he applied for health insurance before our state had "guaranteed issue," his weight alone would've disqualified him. Made no difference he was shaving just under seven feet. First Joey and now Bailey proved he was more than a pretty face.

Admitting strangers into my home was the inevitable consequence of being in business. My career was now angling more toward employee benefits, which gave me access to risk takers with a penchant for analysis. As my name again rose to the top of the company leader board, my pride was tempered by the consistent failures in my personal life.

THE ONSET OF A NEW MILLENNIUM struck terror in some of my friends, fretting that when the clock struck 12 on January 1, 2000, computers would crash, air travel would be restricted, and life as we knew would come to a screeching halt. Although a trickle of their unrest couldn't escape me, I still believed the worst was behind me.

Surely any clump of time could never come close to the turbulence of this last run. The separation from a child trumped any hazard from Mother Nature, Uncle Google, or another *Homo sapiens* no matter what year or in which millennium.

Ryan was set to graduate from college in May, and I knew there'd be no invite. I didn't even know what degree he earned or what plans lay ahead. With the needle on the mom meter stuck at zero, my pride had no place to go. At four years apart, Sarah too was graduating. She'd been accepted at the University of Maryland. I'd had a chance to enjoy several trips with her over the years—New York City, San Francisco, Sanibel Island, Nassau, even Bar Harbor, Maine. I lost count of the number of afternoons we spent in Boston, where the Purple Panache at Faneuil Hall groomed her for grander boutiques.

But on some level, I had a score to settle before she headed to college: that damnable spring break. Now it was my turn to treat her to something special. A cruise to Bermuda from Boston Harbor was best for accessibility and affordability. It soon became obvious, though, that I wasn't the only parent with the same idea.

Shortly after we had boarded, when we gathered for the mandatory fire drill, Sarah found herself in the company of classmates. I, on the other hand, stood next to a woman bursting with personality. No idea how many Chardonnays we each had, but I was near catatonic when it came time for our first dinner.

One day my daughter would earn the nickname "Mama Sarah" for managing roommates overcome with liquid refreshments, but she got her start with me. That evening I was giggling so much I couldn't even dress myself. I spent the rest of the week staying out of trouble with morning yoga and sunbathing by the pool. The night before departure, Sarah and her friends poured out of the ship for one last fling on the island. I figured: Why not join them?

Every time I left Little L.A., adventures met me more than half-way, but experience, I thought, would give me some veneer, some protection. My naivete was wearing thin. As a single, I was vulnerable whenever I set foot outside my backyard. I was minding my own business, sipping on a cocktail, when some dark-haired hunk of manhood anchored himself on the stool next to me. I never saw a wedding ring on his finger, so I decided to enjoy his attention. Although he failed to charm me into a beach walk, I didn't see anything wrong with stopping by the next day to say goodbye. I entered the establishment expecting to see him at the bar because I recalled he had some connection to ownership/management. Instead, it was his wife standing there, with a look that said *Here we go again.* I didn't stick around for the fireworks—too busy wiping the egg off my face.

What I had to think about was Sarah's special day, which was followed by the shortest summer on record, given her mid-August departure for college. I was grateful for our many shared experiences. I was the one she turned to when she was invited not once but three times to the red carpet of prom nights in eye-catching ensembles only we clothes horses could assemble. Then there were the annual dance recitals, for which I could count on Sarah being front and center with multiple costume changes. I only had eyes for her as I crept down the middle aisle of the Gilford High School auditorium, balancing on my back leg for one picture after another. The professional video provided more detail, but I didn't want to leave anything to chance. In my objective opinion, no one could rock a dance outfit like my little girl—not with those legs.

Sarah's graduation would've been a golden moment in this parent's life had it not been for the sadness I felt at Ryan sitting with his father and stepmother. I believe I may have seen my son just once over the past four years, at an Italian restaurant. He had agreed to join me for dinner, but its awkward conversation gaps proved a gut-wrenching example of a mother and son disconnected for too long.

At graduation, my boss, Con, and his wife, Kathy, didn't suffer from past grievances and greeted Ryan warmly. They chatted about how quickly time had flown since the days when the Omaha gang organized a family softball game. Con made sure each of his agents' kids played, and Ryan had been assigned to second base. I was grateful for my Omaha family to be able to infuse a spirt of camaraderie I couldn't seem to manage on my own.

My inability to approach my son weighed heavily on me. I probably looked frozen, for all the emotions crushed inside my chest. What would've happened had I walked up to Ryan, his father, and his stepmother like we were a blended family and greeted Ryan with a big squeeze? What was I most afraid of? Ryan not hugging me back?

It didn't help that all around me were those gray-Volvo ladies with their successful husbands and bunches of children by their side. Made no difference how kind they'd always been to me. Made no difference that I too now drove a Volvo. A black sedan is no match for a station wagon loaded with a boisterous family headed to the airport for a week in the tropics, as I'd come to expect from Sarah's friends every April vacation. It was my annual poke to the solar plexus for being just a part-time mother.

Despite the revolving door of her personal life, Sarah managed to excel in her studies. She was named "Best Dressed" in her high school yearbook—the one chuckle I allowed myself, remembering her comments on my wardrobe while she was still in a stroller. I beamed with pride on the night of the sports awards. She was no one-hit wonder: she had the makings to set her own world on fire. And I was her mother. But graduations bring together families and warrant multiple photo sessions. I could only hope no one noticed the crumbs of my motherhood laid at my feet. No one had walked in my shoes.

Joey

AS THE YEARS ROLLED BY, we four got used to Mama dashing into and out of the house as well as packing her bags and leaving us in the hands of our new sitter, Auntie Shelley. We knew we could count on extra treats from her, and we remained gentlemen and a little lady in her presence just to be sure. When we were alone, however, it was quite a different story . . .

Bailey, for example, could spring onto the counter, walk along the edge of the sink, climb onto the top of the refrigerator, and leap to the top of the cabinets. There he maintained his lookout, or so it might seem. I knew better—he was zonked. Other days, he was on the windowsill of the downstairs bathroom soaking up the morning sun before the rest of us even had our breakfast.

Casper was our Olympic high jumper. In one swoop he could bound from the floor to Mama's office-window ledge with nary a misstep—always a thrill to watch. Chloe and I were more content with ground-level cubbies and left the gymnastics to our brothers.

My only quirk was that pillows were for my exclusive use. Perhaps I was a human in a previous era, but for the life of me, I couldn't understand how kitties could be content curling up in a ball or, as in Bailey's case, lying atop a pair of sneakers. To me, a neck was designed to be supported, and any couch or bed pillow would do just fine, thank you.

Life on the home front was nice and quiet since the fallout with Big Ben. I didn't ask questions when Mama packed a suitcase but couldn't resist giving her the cold shoulder when she came home—just to keep her on her toes. I had just passed my 13th birthday, though with little fanfare, I must say. Mama was too busy to realize where I was in life. The books said I had a lifespan of 10 to 17 years. Well, golly, I was well on my way to my next dirt nap, er, adventure. But if there was one thing I'd learned being around humans was that they took life way too seriously, like they had only one shot at getting things right.

Never in a million years would I have wanted to be in Mama's shoes. She couldn't see through the mist of her tears. She was always searching for something or someone to fill the hole in her heart. It wasn't gonna happen. No one could do it for her. She had to be whole herself—or at least, in front of the world, pretend to be. Pretend she was a queen bee and ruled with a deadly stinger. Maybe because I was on a path to be king of the jungle but got reassigned to Team Mama, I still felt the call of the wild stirring in my loins, and no one could take that away from me. No matter that I was a mere pussycat. Too bad my cattitude couldn't replace her "Attitude determines altitude"—as if that ever did her any good.

SOME WOMEN GET MARRIAGE right the first time and live happily ever after. Some women find lasting love with marriage number two. And if some women are brave enough to go for number three, good for them. But what if a woman strikes out all three times? Does she hide in a cave designed for wasted talent? Would she be . . . any number of adjectives could work here (*brazen, stupid, numb*) . . . enough to try again? What was wrong with finding a steady guy yet not co-habitating? Why didn't that idea make sense to me? Why didn't I even *think* of that possibility? After three failed marriages, why would I hold on to my childhood notion of marriage as the only *right* way? Because I'm brain dead when it comes to men.

Eight years had elapsed since the termination of my 18-month marriage. That's a reasonable amount of time for a woman to get her bearings and appreciate the freedom of being a single woman. But not me: I was still stuck on tradition. Marriage was the be-all and end-all to live in Little L.A., and sooner or later I would get it right.

With that in mind, I was comfortable enough with one of my female clients to ask if she knew of any eligible "good" men. She did, she said, but he was already taken. A friend of his, however, was free to meet me. So began a journey unlike anything I'd undertaken before, and it had lasting repercussions.

John, the architect in a design-build company, was nine years older than I. We met over dinner, during which I learned he'd been the first in his family to graduate from college. His company had built an impressive array of high-end homes along shorelines and mountain ranges. He appreciated the fruits of his labor but was never one to boast.

Born into a poor Midwest family, he was the only son within a trio of sisters, which meant he was comfortable in the company of women. He skied, biked, played tennis, and was a remarkable dancer. A dry martini guy, he could pop two in a matter of minutes and then be done for the evening. Efficient and predictable.

As summer wound down, it was time for the long drive to Maryland. My friend Brenda offered to drive Sarah and me in her Chevy Suburban. Packed tight with not an inch of space to spare, we set forth for the ten-hour ride, during which I learned a new word: *rubbernecking*. Brenda had once traveled across the country, so she was familiar with folks craning their necks to look at a crash site while on an expressway. It doesn't take long to create a pileup, especially if you're crossing the Tappan Zee Bridge into New York.

Leaving Sarah was bittersweet, but our goodbyes were nothing new. Fifteen years of a truncated relationship had a way of softening some of the sadness. I was happy for her. She'd get the experience I never had. A four-year education away from home would extend her knowledge of life far beyond her snow-white community and provide a better chance to develop the intuition women need regarding men.

Brenda and I weren't about to make it a one-day round-trip, so on the way back, we decided on an overnight in Danbury, Connecticut. A comfortable bed was a requirement, and I got that. The next morning, as I was watching *Good Morning America*, I remarked on one of its guests.

"Bren, look at that guy. He barely opens his mouth when he talks and he speaks in a monotone. John is the same way. Sometimes I have to force myself to pay attention because there's never any animation in his delivery."

"You think this could be a problem for you?"

"Maybe. I enjoy his company, but I need some fireworks and get almost frustrated. I'm a dreamer. Pure Aquarian. I see life in a kaleidoscope of colors. Nothing ever changes with John. Steady Eddie. I haven't figured out if I wish I was more like him or that he was more like me."

We may not have matched in temperament, but otherwise we were quite compatible. There was so much that was right about "us," but even a merry-go-round comes to a full stop. The question is: Do you hop back on for another spin or do you head for the Ferris wheel? Or maybe the Tilt-A-Whirl?

AS THE HOLIDAYS APPROACHED, peering ahead for the *what ifs* of a relationship took a backseat to a four-week blowout of mixing tradition with an ever-expanding client base. Still a kid at heart, I embraced the intensity of Christmas, as did the cats. It seemed these rascals, especially Bailey, were attuned to the first sound of my opening the closet door in the den. It didn't matter if they were chin deep into their afternoon nap when I thought I might get the chance to wrap, um, unassisted. Mayhem always ensued, driven by Bailey.

Joey

GOTTA HAND IT TO MY BROTHER. Such a natural showman. Dang him! He usually carried an air of poise and sophistication, but something happened to him at Christmas. Who'd have thought he could transform himself into a wild boar at the first hint of rustling tissues and bows? The mere sound of the sliding door exposing all those holiday wrappings had him up like a rocket and headfirst into whatever lay in his path. Given his recent transgression to the wild side when we first met the sibs, I was getting the impression that there was way more to my brother's backstory than he had told me.

Anyway, when that door opened, we all had to see what Bailey was up to—such a commotion! Lord knows that between the sound of crinkling paper and Mama's stern "No, Bailey. Stop it," sleep was out of the question. For all the nonsense he doled out to me because of my so-called carnival roots, this snowball could suck in a ribbon spool faster than any sword-swallower on the circuit.

Poor sister Chloe. She was no match for this magician. She tried her best to show her moxie, only to end up swallowing a plastic-bag tie that walloped her intestines and sent her to the vet with Mama in tears. An overnight stay and she was good as new, although a wee bit humbled.

Still, barring this one-time setback, we were in a free-for-all if Mama turned her back. Soon she figured out that wrapping presents on the floor was a bad idea: Bailey was faster than a speeding bullet and leapt onto each bit of tissue with ribbon coming out of his mouth before she could stop him. Mama had to start over but, like on Saturday mornings, she gave in to these shenanigans. Even presents upside down under the tree didn't keep us from enjoying a spell of mischief in the dark of night.

Casper, on the other hand, discovered his weakness: plastic, anything plastic. He took credit for carrying the holiday season through the upcoming year with bits of chewed-up plastic deposited in every corner. And there were lots of corners.

ON DECEMBER 23, I was like a kid again anticipating Santa, only now it wasn't the tapping of hooves but instead that Sarah smile as I waited outside the jetway. Not since she'd been two had we been together without a switch from one house to another. Now I'd have her all to myself. (Let's not talk about fall weekends when I flew her home to watch her quarterback boyfriend run a few plays.) We'd set a precedent for having a late dinner at the Hanover Street Chop House, on the menu surely some of the finest steak, seafood, cocktails, and ambience in New Hampshire.

Our house was fully decorated when we came home, thanks to a team of merry elves coming to my aid. Here's when it takes a village. Stringing lights, especially up a ladder for porch enhancements, requires the agility of a chimpanzee and the arms of an octopus. The next day, Sarah and I were working on a floury counter for our annual bake-off of cranberry bread and sugar cookies outlined with the same red cutters I'd used all her life. I know how far I'm capable of drifting from tradition, but my love for Christmas was strong enough that we were the only ones in the neighborhood with luminaries—paper bags filled with sand, each with a lit candle inside, along our side of the split driveway on Christmas Eve. *Why not?*

The following morning, Sarah gained an Etch-a-Sketch of memories just as special as those my own mother had made for me on Christmas Day.

Mom and Dad were expected by early afternoon for our gift exchange. Guaranteed that Mom would bring Sarah's favorite desserts, date squares and magic bars. Joey and Bailey rounded out the holiday entertainment with leaps in and out of boxes and rolling in tissue paper. Sarah and I spent quiet evenings together following dinners of steak tips and crab legs, settled in on the couch for our three favorite movies—*One Magic Christmas*, *All I Want for Christmas*, *Love Actually*—while I ran my fingers through her hair for tangles, as I'd done for years.

Away from the madding crowd during these few remaining days of the year, I often pondered the issue of child rearing. Bringing a little being into the world is the easy part, maybe even the fun part, but the clock starts ticking from the moment that hospital door swings shut. Having had but a fraction of the normal interactions with my children, I felt great relief that they had both emerged from high school relatively unscathed. Of course, it was impossible to assess just how my son would navigate his emotional ambiguity toward me. I could only hope maturity would soften his stance. Surely, his intellect fronted by a warm smile and his grandfather's piercing blue eyes would serve him well.

Sarah struck much closer to home. Only now did I realize I didn't want her to be a mini-me. I wanted her to use her voice, to stand up for herself when she felt misjudged or misguided, to trust her gut—the seat of power capable of stirring the pot of doubt. I knew I was as close to her in spirit as I had hoped to be. It now fell upon her to make the right choices as she gained her footing as an adult.

On the other hand, my generation took it upon itself to distance itself from the female members of the Greatest Generation. Although my love for my mom held fast, we never saw life through the same lens. She couldn't relate to my life choices. But how could she? Between her brothers and my dad, she'd always been sheltered. I give her credit, though. Not once did she chastise me for my obvious transgressions from the Ten Commandments. The only frustration she expressed had to do with my not calling her every day, as she had done with her own mother. She couldn't appreciate my love/hate relationship with the phone, based on its being the link to my financial freedom.

In addition to spending much of each day with the handle tucked into my right shoulder, the last thing I wanted to do off hours was to chitchat. Now I realize that she wanted to hear my voice, not necessarily what I had to say. She needed some "us" time. I had sought a much different relationship with Sarah, even if it meant rubbing a magic lamp. But even without a genie, my wish for us to talk about anything without embarrassment was fulfilled. At least at this point, we were reading from the same script.

Still, my relationship with my mom weighed heavily. She showed much love and affection toward me and my brother, but it didn't extend to animals, not even cats. My brother, Dan, and I were enamored of kitties and between us had as many as seven at one time. They made our lives richer. But for my mother, it was her children who brought her joy.

With time and maturity, I was able to process the gulf between us. I found a way to navigate our differences through trips that would bring her outside her hometown and into a camaraderie with her daughter that had been missing. We had visited New York City, but it was only when we ventured away from the familiar and touched down on new territory that our relationship caught a breeze.

I decided to bring Mom as my guest on my next Omaha reward trip, to San Diego—a four-star getaway for members of the President's Club, its second-tier honor club agents. I accepted that the years of being part of the gilded Chairman's Council were over, but the company didn't scrimp on us second fiddlers. We were treated to a visit to the city's well-known zoo, no coincidence a microcosm of the company's brand: Wild Kingdom at our fingertips.

The company also managed to secure a hangar at the Marine Corps Air Station Miramar, where *Top Gun* was filmed. A picture of Mom and me in a mock-up model still sits on my bookshelf—the two of us with a salute. Robert and Lyman, my two now forever friends from the trip to Egypt, lived nearby and invited us for a sumptuous lunch at their hilltop home. They treated Mom like they'd known her all her life.

As was the case with these award trips, some time was allocated to business. When agents were at meetings, their guests could wander at will. My mother, though, was most unsettled whenever I left her alone. She wouldn't leave the room. I couldn't fully appreciate what happened to a woman who was protected all her life from the vicissitudes of what I'd consider independence.

Mom would probably say the highlight of her travels with me was our trip to Branson, Missouri, on a bus tour for seniors—a one-stop, winner-take-all *American Idol* convention. Paul Anka, Frankie Avalon, and their partners in song, dance, comedy, and magic transported us from one venue to another. All details were handled for us, and I never left Mom's side. A perfect week for this mother/daughter duo in the heartland.

MOST OF US RING in the New Year with optimism and maybe renewed goodwill toward man, but who can forget the drama that rocked our world in the year 2001. Long before the 11th of September (by coincidence my son's 24th birthday), I was being forced to reconcile the difference in affection between John and me. For a woman who'd yearned to complete her own Cinderella story, the subject of marriage with John never set my heart aflutter. It was obvious to our social set that he'd do anything for me. After a year of play, though, I couldn't pretend what I didn't feel. Our merry-go-round had run out of tickets.

I was no longer the desperate woman of yesterday and could walk away from a man who offered me companionship, security, diversity, and love because I wanted that *whoosh* feeling. No matter that I had felt the *whoosh* with the father of my children; look how that ended. I don't have an answer for why I couldn't fall for this gentle soul. Gentleman that he was, he walked away.

One afternoon some weeks later, with the sun high and the clouds AWOL, I decided to play hooky and drove to Lakeview, a nine-hole golf course and a neophyte's favorite getaway for privacy. As I opened the trunk to retrieve my bag and cart, a dark blue Toyota with Massachusetts plates parked next to me. *Grumble, grunt.* The chances of being either in front of or behind anyone at 1:30 were slim. I was still a beginning golfer and sensitive about how long it took for me to trek from one hole to another. I could do without an audience.

Not to be rude, I gave him a curt hello as I jogged behind my pull cart, rounded the corner to the clubhouse, paid the fee, and headed over to the ladies tee at a brisk pace. It was a par-5 with a right dogleg uphill. A look back toward the tee box—all clear. Everything was fine until I nailed a nice chip onto the No. 4 green, and wouldn't you know it, Mr. In-My-Face yelled out "Nice hit!" *Ugh. Caught.*

"Thanks," I replied, and off I went toward the next hole, which would again separate us from each other's view. I had completed six holes in so little time, having maintained my pace between holes, that I found myself annoyed and frustrated to have to wait at No. 7: As a par 3, no one tees off until all other golfers complete the hole. Just my luck there were four golfers still on the course. I couldn't go forward and I couldn't go back. Didn't they realize I was desperate to get off the tee? But I was sure this stranger was still far enough behind me that he wouldn't see me play out my game after all.

It wasn't the sound of footsteps or even a chip onto the No. 6 green or perhaps an aberrant hit in its sand trap, but I sensed someone. I turned to my left and was surprised (and not happy) to see the gentleman who'd parked beside me yet remained well behind me suddenly approach.

He came up to me like a long-lost friend and extended his hand. "Hi, I'm Tom."

Yikes! What was that?

"I'm Claire," I told him, wondering if I'd stepped on a live wire. The electricity from that contact was startling.

Tom wore a white golf shirt and tan pants and was as affable and relaxed in chatting me up as I was fried at the thought of striking a golf ball in front of him. Fuzzy faced with a full head of white hair, a bit shorter than average height, he looked like he'd just risen from a long afternoon nap.

"Want to buddy up?" he asked.

Sigh. What was I supposed to say? No, I've spent the last 90 minutes staying away from you, and now I'll be stuck for these last three holes?

"Okay," I replied, barely audible. *Like what choice did I have without looking like an idiot?*

Thank goodness, when it was our time to tee off, I hit the damn ball straight down the fairway.

"Good shot," he said.

His shot wasn't too much better, and later I realized it was by design. The eighth hole once again separated the men's tee from the ladies', but just ahead lay another par-5: the longest on the course, especially if you're a hack. But Mr. Personality managed to stay back with me as if he were also navigating a new sport. In fact, he'd been playing since he was a kid.

As we maneuvered away from the brambles on the left and the ruts on the right, he directed the conversation on a familiar enough basis but without divulging much personal information. He joked he'd been living out of a suitcase for several days (*it showed*) and was bunking at his family's home on Lake Winni for a brief respite. He mentioned a tour of duty in Vietnam, which made me aware that we were of similar age, but left out the details. When we completed our round and approached our cars, Fate decided to have some fun.

"The next time you and your daughter are in Boston, give me a call," he said. "I'll take you both to lunch." He handed me his business card.

"I'm not sure if we'll get back before her return to college, but thank you."

We said our goodbyes. I didn't expect to see him again, although he was quite warm and chatty, considering he came out of nowhere. When I got home, I glanced at his card and promptly experienced another jolt. VICE PRESIDENT, CONSULTING DIVISION, PRICE WATER-HOUSE COOPERS. *What?* The accounting firm attached to the Academy Awards? He sure hadn't been dressed the part.

Less than a week later, I got an envelope in the mail with PwC as the return address. In it was a "nice-to-meet-you" letter, dictated to his secretary to type up for his signature. He repeated the luncheon invitation, but as Sarah was going back to UMd by mid-August, there was no opportunity for a shopping day in Boston. It might've remained just a weird memory, an invite relegated to a drawer; instead, Tom called me for dinner when he returned to Boston from a business meeting on the West Coast. We were to meet at the New Hampshire border at Exit 1, the Sheraton Tara, about an hour-and-a-half drive for me.

I got there first and wandered around the lobby amid the usual scrum of day-trippers, conventioneers, tourists, and businesspeople, given its central location for large-scale gatherings. He was wearing business attire, and I was dressed to the nines (well, the eights), as if I could even the playing field with this white shirt. I recognized that full head of white hair walking toward me at a good clip, but when he reached me, he commented on a pressing need:

"Be right back. Gotta hit the men's room."

We found a table at the hotel's casual off-lobby café, which doubled as its bar.

When couples are at a restaurant, it's easy to tell if they're married. Singles are into each other; couples are into the menu. When our waitress arrived to take our order, both Tom and I seemed to step up our game and tapped into our respective second languages. Before she knew it, she was being assaulted by a few words in French (from me) and in Spanish (from him, with his South American busi-ness counterparts). Given we'd had little previous communication, we found ourselves chuckling through this one-upmanship banter.

Our chatter was lively and we never lacked for conversation, but there was one bombshell:

"I'll probably always be married," he said.

Not a sucker punch, and at least he was honest. Playing a game of catch-me-if-you-can at golf, I hadn't bothered to check out his ring finger. His consistent contact with me made me assume he was available. He was and he wasn't.

He was separated, he said, his wife's idea. Their 20-year marriage included two children from her first marriage, whom he not only raised but also legally adopted. He too had been married before but had no children. He was obviously committed to these now-grown kids. Separated from their mother or not, they were his. Maybe he wasn't confident about it, but I got the message early on: This sepa-ration wasn't going anywhere.

As the oldest of seven children, he knew how to change a diaper and corral his tribe of siblings when they got out of hand. Family was second nature to him. But his stint in the military drove a stake into his commitment. *Leave no comrade behind.* Specifics were necessar-ily vague, but he told me he was recruited by the Army as a student at the University of Alaska. The look in his eyes told them he might be a good fit for their elite division, Special Operations. After several tours, he left the service as a lieutenant colonel, a rank undisclosed to me for quite some time.

When we left the Tara, he walked me to my car, which I'd parked under a set of lights. Once I was in the driver's seat, he asked, "Is it okay if I kiss you?"

Really?

"Um." *One second, two seconds.* "Sure." *Jolt! Zing! Pop!* Sparks flew.

I know he kissed me a second time. We were staring at each other, all aglow under domed lights. Nerve-wracking. I was at a loss to say something memorable, and what came out was, "This is what I look like with my glasses on." I mean, what else could I say? *Wow! You're an amazing kisser!*

He planned to visit me in Laconia in a few weeks. His work with PwC had him in constant motion and across time zones, but he usually knew when he'd be free. The plan was he'd bed down on my couch. That was the plan . . .

On the morning of September 11, I left home shortly after 8:30 for a 10:00 hair appointment in Nashua. PwC had several clients in Manhattan, some with offices in the Twin Towers. Because Tom was based in Boston, it was typical for him to fly out of Logan to any number of destinations. Listening to the radio, I was beside myself.

In late afternoon I got a call from him assuring me he was safe, although working some blocks away from the crashes. Five of his coworkers perished on those Boston flights, in addition to an entire merchandise group under Tom's wing. With 10,000 partners throughout locations worldwide, it took some time for PwC to determine which staff were lost and which ones had taken a day off. I breathed a sigh of relief that he was alive.

Like most of us that fall, I went numb, unable to make a single phone call. I mourned the loss of so many people and the tragedy of the families they left behind.

I talked with Mom and Dad, after making sure Sarah was safe in Maryland, then wrote a long letter to my cousin Ray, in Valdosta, Georgia. His dad was second in my mother's family of seven siblings and several years older than I. We'd developed a special bond during my first marriage, in the early 10970s, when Ray, as an Air Force pilot, had been stationed in Okinawa.

We'd been exchanging detailed letters for some 30 years. He was more than a pen pal, more than a cousin. He was more like my brother and knew me better than I knew myself. I wrote about Tom and that he had been in New York City on 9/11 but was okay.

"Let me get this straight," he wrote back. "You get led down a primrose path with McDee, who never owns up to being married. Then you turn down John, although he's available. And now you're contemplating a relationship with a man who says he's going to stay married? Are you nuts?"

Ray liked to call me Calamity. Whether I'd already been so anointed or this triumvirate sealed the deal, the name stuck. I embraced it in part because I knew how much he loved me. He didn't want to see me get hurt but seemed helpless to save me from myself. I *was* a calamity. I seem to gravitate toward chaos. But why?

SHAKEN BY THE EVENTS of September 11, Tom may well have reassessed his priorities as well as his appointments. He had long ago left a war zone, but even a seasoned warrior like Tom might've needed a warm embrace. He arranged his schedule for us to meet in Portsmouth in early October.

I chose Strawbery Banke, where residents had re-created a historic colonial village. There was something comforting about being in such tranquil surroundings. I still struggled to concentrate, so to meet my sizzle partner, I decided to leave home early and make a stop at Victoria's Secret at the Steeplegate Mall in Concord. I was too distracted to imagine what impression I was making on my kitties, especially the two seniors.

Bailey: *HEY, MATE, what's Mum all buzzed up about? She's flitting around like a butterfly.*

Joey: *Yep, gotta be a guy. Wonder what this one will be like.*

Bailey: *She's keeping us in the dark. We haven't seen anyone in a dog's age.*

Joey: *That's okay by me. Men are nothing but trouble for her. I wish she realized that we four are enough. Sure, she's sad over Ryan, but a man isn't going to bring him back. We're already a family, and we're here to stay. Why can't she see that?*

Bailey: *Humans seem daft. It's always something—love, money, kids. So glad I'm a domestic.*

Joey: *Agreed. Easy-peasy in the jungle. You either kill or be killed. All you need is a few morsels to chew on, water, and maybe your best girl if you're lucky.*

Bailey: *I'm knackered just thinking about life as a human. Let's grab us a few zzzz.*

Joey: *Good idea. When she fills our water bowls to the brim, adds another one, tops off our food bowls, there's only one reason . . . She ain't sleeping here tonight.*

TOM WAS DIFFERENT from anyone I'd ever dated, but I couldn't put my finger on how. It was unsettling to be hot under the armpits—like I was smoking from the inside out—even as I drove in my air-conditioned car emboldened with my new undies. Bringing my A game when I was already weak in the knees was going to take some work.

But what if he didn't show? What if his plane got delayed? What if he got into an accident? I was a wreck by the time I arrived at the B&B. The hostess told me my friend had already arrived, and I breathed a sigh of relief as I recalibrated in nervous energy. Our last goodbye carried considerable weight in light of the tragedy he had narrowly avoided

One of my clients had recommended an Italian restaurant known for its homemade cuisine and its romantic setting. Side by side but not hand in hand, we made our way to our destination chatting comfortably. Tucked into an alcove, we could peer out without being near other diners. When our waiter came for drink orders, I asked for my usual glass of red wine. Tom ordered a bourbon rocks.

Whoosh! "That's a pretty strong drink," I said without thinking. I couldn't help myself. The few times I'd been with him I'd felt at ease, but he'd been sober. And now, faced with an overnight, I wanted him to remain sober.

When our waiter returned with our drinks, Tom said, no hesitation, "Never mind, thank you. I don't want it." No explanation. *Gulp.*

It took more than three holes of golf and one dinner for me to grasp the full monty of this man. Here he was just off a flight from California and looking for a relaxing meal with a woman who intrigued him, and she throws down the gauntlet about what he can and can't drink. I can't say why exactly, but vestiges of Big Ben must have come into play, like somehow he'd have control over me. I didn't know that no amount of alcohol could match what Tom had been trained to do in seconds. His hands were lethal weapons. Woe to anyone who hinted at an assault to someone connected to Tom.

Our time at the inn was straight out of a romance novel, but I must relay one story about it. I couldn't sleep, and Tom wasn't the only reason. Although it had all the modern conveniences, the inn had been built in the 18th century. Doors lacked locks and wide pine floors creaked, and someone was pacing outside our door. I was sure of it. I could feel it. Was it possible someone had lived or died in this house and was restless for some kind of closure?

What made the experience really eerie was its one-way communication—like the, well, ghost decided to troll the halls because of some unfinished business but left me to fret about whether it would rattle the doorknob. Boo, as I named the spirit, kept walking back and forth in front of our door, with an occasional pause as if considering whether to enter. The feeling that its hand hovered over the doorknob gave me the willies. My heart was beating out of my chest, my body primed for imminent attack, like my whole being was a tuning fork. I kept looking at the doorknob. Boo seemed confused. Maybe we were in Boo's old room.

Meanwhile, Tom slept like a baby, but like a cat he could've sprung into action in a flash. But I'm no cat, and I wasn't dreaming. The murmuring sounds, the shuffling, were as palpable to me as a haunted house on an empty stomach, yet Tom heard nothing. This was an issue for the sisterhood. I was convinced it was our hostess, whose spirit somehow manifested when someone or something tapped into her sensitivities. Maybe we reminded her of a lost love. But she had to know she was trapped in her own world. The soldier next to me was no match for her.

In the morning, at breakfast, I was excited to hear what our hostess would say. Instead, on the table was a note telling us she wasn't feeling well and wouldn't be able to attend to us. No one showed up, leaving us to question the coincidence. This budding relationship appeared resistant to conformity. It was in uncharted waters from the beginning. Expect the unexpected, Calamity, prepare for takeoff.

TOM SPENT MOST OF HIS TIME out of his London office deep in negotiations with a team of international professionals. Working through the holidays was normal. His consulting had become his raison d'être. Shifting from one hotel room to another with wind sprints as his fitness routine kept the malaise of his marital state at bay.

Our time together was relegated to the occasional get-together over dinner and the goodbye the next morning. Flying into New York, connecting to Boston, then driving to Laconia was no big deal for this suited-up vagabond. Only once did he grumble, when he'd flown in from London only to be forced to head back on the next flight because a nor'easter was slamming Little L.A.

Tom placed no expectations for us, partly because of his low expectations for his own success in a relationship. Over the course of his two failed marriages, he'd come to view personal relationships as waiting for the other shoe to drop, which struck me as an oxymoron for someone so accomplished. One email from him tamped down any wishful thinking for a happy ending. Comparing us to a military operation, he called us "two planes refueling in midair." Whether my heart would heed this cautionary flag was another matter.

Regardless of not being together during the Christmas season, I knew how much I wanted to give him something meaningful without backing him into a corner. Never straying too far from a jewelry counter, I found a 14k gold golf shoe charm. In other words, I wasn't going anywhere.

He presented me with a brooch, a replica of one worn by former first lady Barbara Bush, one enhanced by both black and white freshwater pearls against a backdrop of silver leaves. It gave an air of elegance to my calf-length black wool coat and catered to my love of jewelry without making any promises.

After the holidays, a return to normal in 2002 required further processing, especially as it related to airline travel. My trip with friend Brenda to Taormina had me in a bit of a dilemma. Her husband had her as a no-go. Do I lose the money, fly solo, or buy her out and bring Sarah in her place? With no one holding me back, shouldn't I go? Life is short.

Meanwhile, Sarah had already convinced me a semester abroad in Italy for the upcoming fall term would be no more expensive than one spent in Maryland: "And, Mom, isn't this the chance of a lifetime?" I was concerned, because Florence might tempt her beyond what a 20-year-old could resist. I decided to invite Sarah to come with me to Sicily. Her first transatlantic trip would whet her appetite for her term abroad. Italian men were fascinated by young American women, whom they deemed ripe for the picking. She'd get a preview of what a semester in Italy would be like.

WE SETTLED INTO A COMFY BUNGALOW on the beach. It was fabulous to be able to roll out of bed and dig our toes into the sand, and we soon got used to the maidens who forgot their bikini bras. Taormina was full of picturesque views across a landscape of tangerine blossoms and open-air theaters, as in ancient Rome and Greece. But from this mountainous island, the best memories came topside, from the funicular, an aerial tram.

Soon we'd meet "the boys." No matter what we did, my daughter was a magnet for the attention of the Italian male—young or old. Weddings in this part of the world are boisterous, public events: Streets are impassable as the bride and her father and their expansive party make their way to the church. Midweek, no less.

Sarah and I stood among the spectators, a mix of locals and tourists. Among the wedding party was an older gentleman. His Superman eyes homed in on Sarah, and as he made his way past us, walking backwards so he could keep looking at her, my daughter and I had to muffle our laughter and maintain some level of decorum.

That same evening, we made the classic freshman mistake of going to dinner at 7:00. Once seated, the table is yours for however long you want to stay, and tipping is optional: dining is about conviviality. Now, Italians—most Europeans—wouldn't dream of going to a restaurant before 8:30, so we were the sole patrons at this outdoor café. After we ordered, we were chatting up a storm when we got distracted by our waiter. We didn't speak the language, so we weren't able to tell him to get lost. If we were in France, I'd have had the words: *Vas-t'en, garçon. C'est tout, merci.*

"Mom, he keeps staring at me. What do I do?"

I didn't know. What if this young man was the grandson of a Don of the Cosa Nostra? How insulting is it for a local to be told to scram if all he wants to do is wait on you? And has nothing else to do? What if we were kicked out, trailed by a bunch of enraged chefs brandishing copper pans? How could I handle this and find a way to get beyond my rather insular Laconia life? All these questions ran through my mind. Then I thought, *Why not put him to work?*

"*Scusi. Per favore, vino rossa.*" Then I tapped into my French roots and used my hands to demonstrate that we wanted a bottle—maybe *due*. Okay, he was happy, and so were we.

Taormina will likely remain a one-shot wonder. A mother and daughter, unmoored from family and friends, exploring a country blessed with mountains linked to the sea, restored the delicate balance of the need to make a living with the desire to play. With Mother Nature showing off, that night we spent languid hours with the scent of lemon wafting through the air, and I got to give Sarah all the attention she deserved from her mother.

Perhaps my daughter will return one day with her own little girl for a chance to escape the hamster wheel. But if she does, I know she'll come armed with a working knowledge of Italian (*Ciao, mi chiamo Sarah*) and the confidence to withstand any unwanted attention from the opposite sex.

TIME SPENT WITH TOM was like being on an exotic vacation: I never knew what to expect. I just couldn't figure him out. In time, I thought of him as a Stealth bomber: made of steel with the instincts of a fox.

Other than our both being born under the sign of Aquarius (one year and 18 days apart), we were opposites. I lived my life on a banana peel, taking way too much for granted and leaning on others for support. He, on the other hand, could assess a situation and make the right decisions. Whether deep in the bush in camouflage or standing at a podium in front of an audience of hundreds, the man could guide the narrative to his own satisfaction.

Some people know a little about a lot; Tom knew a lot about a lot. With his intellect, he could hold court in any country, any culture, yet his demeanor belied nothing of his power, and if he wanted to, he could come across as your next-door neighbor. And as a date, he made me laugh—the most lethal weapon in a man's arsenal.

He also made me feel like a woman, and I could embrace my femininity without fear of retribution. I knew he'd never hurt me; and I knew that on some level I'd always love him. Such freedom allowed me to be vulnerable in a novel way—like greeting him at the door in a long black raincoat and red high heels. You can't pull that lever if there's a scintilla of doubt you'll come to regret it. Instead, I look back on that particular evening with my best Cheshire grin.

But the general on the home front came calling. His wife had had a change of heart: She told him she didn't want to grow old alone. I had cats, but I wanted to say, "Tell her to get a dog!" What a waste of a good man to force him into servitude because you're in a wheelchair, not because you're in love with him and realize you were an idiot to let him go in the first place.

On a late-spring morning, when the temperature pushed the start button to summer, we left the Sheraton Wayfarer in Bedford, another romantic interlude in the books. Before we got into our cars, we kissed goodbye. Tom, in his white Miata convertible, his matching head of hair ruffling in the breeze, took a right onto the 93S ramp off 101; I, in my black Volvo, sunroof open, wearing a white lace top, took a left onto 93N.

I didn't know it, but that was our last goodbye for quite some time.

NO SURPRISE THAT HE CONTEMPLATED his situation during a cross-country flight. He told me he ordered a couple of bourbons to help with his analysis. On the one hand, there were the familiarity and assets of a 20-year marriage, and, more important, the two children he'd adopted and raised. On the other hand, there was me: fun, smart, engaging, ambitious—ready to snuggle every part of him at a moment's notice. I didn't stand a chance. He broke the news to me just before I was leaving for my niece's high school graduation. Only then did I say for the first time, like I wanted him to know, "I love you."

"In my own way, I love you too."

And there you have it. Once again, my heart broken—this time in a million pieces.

I spent a lot more time home with my kitties.

Joey: *LISTEN UP. I dunno why, but I always have a hankering to give Mama a tissue when she's sad. I can predict a storm, I can sense an uprising among the buffalo, and I can tell when she needs me—us.*

Bailey: *Well, isn't that divine. Thank goodness you're in charge. What's the plan?*

Joey: *I think it's an assignment for the Chlo and Caspie. Can you guys take it from here? Can you save Mama from moping around and feeling sorry for herself? Put a smile on her face?*

Chloe: *Sure thing, chief. Caspie, looks like Mama is making popcorn. You know what that means.*

Casper: *Yup. She's setting up for a movie night. Beat you to the couch.*

VHS VIDEO RENTALS were standard-issue home entertainment. With the couch along the front window and the TV cabinet at a 90-degree angle to the stairs, there was only one position for watching the tube: horizontal. Time with Sarah was now relegated to Christmas, but I had lots of company the rest of the year. I learned early on that once I stretched out on the couch, I'd better have everything I wanted for the next two hours within arm's reach. Both Casper and Chloe liked popcorn. I was always sure to break off the hard ends of the kernels and give them each their stash. They'd then leap onto my legs and settle in for the duration of a movie.

Although Casper and Chloe remained bonded, it was touching to see the connection Casper had made with Bailey, like he looked up to him as a big brother. Except for their points—that is, the color variation at their nose, ear tips, and tail (Bailey was whiter with blue-gray accents; Casper was cream with brown-gray accents)—they were amazingly similar. When they snuggled together on the couch, Casper looked like Bailey's mini-me.

Joey and Bailey preferred their respective beds in the dining room. They had no interest in watching a movie with me. These guys considered the back side of the house where the sun baked the floor from noon till dusk perfect for their naps. Bailey's approach to catching a few zzzz finally caught up with Joey.

Joey: *BAILZ, something's been bothering me ever since I met you.*

Bailey: *I say, old chap, what's on your mind?*

Joey: *Well, ya know how touchy my tummy is, like if anyone comes near it, it's a hot poker to the gut. I have to lash out. So why is it you can expose yourself to the world and sleep like a baby?*

Bailey: *You're convinced that in a previous life you were destined to be king of the jungle—the grand pooh-bah, feared by all, right?*

Joey: *Yup, so?*

Bailey: *Well, I'm sure I was a canine, a testosterone-filled wolf-hybrid primed for the toughest race in the world—the Iditarod. All we did was run. See these size 15s that Mum keeps admiring? Well, they ran in the dark, in arctic temps, in snowstorms, windstorms, even navigated through water and ice. I'm knackered just thinking about it. I mean, what's the point? You want to show the world you can run a team of hounds faster and longer than anyone else? Such poppycock.*

Joey: *Wow. That sounds awful.*

Bailey: *It should be bloody unlawful to push man's best friend beyond his limit. Look at me now. Other than my feet, I'm a mere shadow of my former self.*

Joey: *That explains why you swish your tail from side to side. I mean, what cat does that? Er . . . never mind, I just answered my own question. But one more thing: What's the deal with the tummy-rub nonsense? You go all gooey on Pépère when he does that.*

Bailey: *Listen, mate, if you'd just run your legs off for hours and then fallen in a heap, beat to pot from one end to the other, and big daddy came over and told you what a good boy you were, you'd lie with your backside flat out and take that belly rub like it's the bee's knees of biscuits. You ought to try it sometime. Just saying.*

Joey: *Not in this life.*

WHEN THEY WERE SACKED OUT, only one thing could rally all the troops: my announcement of fresh food. *Whoosh!* Made no difference from which corner of the house each of these munchkins was napping, they hightailed it to the kitchen. Let's face it, kitties do what they want, when they want. We're here to please them, not the other way around.

I appreciated what my kitties brought to the table. Each had a unique personality, and my brood trained me about what they liked and what they didn't like.

Joey

By now, we'd all developed little eccentricities: Bailey had his pooping issue; I couldn't stand having my belly rubbed; Casper bit through anything plastic left in the wrong place at the right time. But Chloe's idiosyncrasies were a marvel.

We all tolerated our annual physicals, but only Chloe mastered the art of hide and seek with Mama. I figured she was either a mind reader in a previous life or she could read Mama's calendar. Without fail, she knew the day she was headed to the doctor. When it was time to leave, it seemed like she'd vanish into thin air. Mama would be at a loss to find her and search the house from top to bottom, knowing full well she left herself just enough time to be on time—always a 4:30 appointment.

Chloe often parked herself at the farthest corner under Mama Sarah's bed. Meanwhile, Bailey and I tried to wipe the grins off our faces as we watched our mama scoot from one place to another, yardstick in hand to reach for our little Houdini. This frustrating practice was the routine year after year, until Mama realized she had to close off all doors first thing in the morning. That way Queenie couldn't hide upstairs or, worse, in the cellar, where all kinds of nooks and crannies awaited.

Our goofball Casper never seemed to know what hit him until he was in the backseat of the car, while Mama was searching high and low for his sister. But once they were under way, I'm told he howled all the way to the doctor's office.

Bailey and I, however, were perfect gentlemen—that is, until we got older. Our nails started getting thicker and longer and required more frequent doctor visits.

Chloe's nails were actually the worst, because she was so hard to round up. They would start to grow inward, and she was lucky she never had to be put under anesthesia for clipping. Although she resisted being brought to the doctor, she was too much of a lady to take a swat or bite the doctor, like Bailz and I occasionally did.

I'll admit I tapped into my jungle roots when it came to this now quarterly ritual. I'm proud to say it took an assistant to subdue me enough to get my nails clipped. Pulling me up by the scruff only wound me up tighter, in spite of being paralyzed to fight back.

Clipping was painful enough but combing the knots on my belly was another story. I couldn't help myself—my eyes would bulge out of my head. Mama had to decide whether she was willing to accept my not-so-beautiful mane with its clumps or watch me as I screamed from the depth of my soul from this agonizing routine. She came to see it my way. She loved me too much to put me through such pain for the sake of vanity.

But I don't think Mama ever understood that I had just turned 15. She had no experience with senior kitties. I was headed in the wrong direction. And so was Mama.

I DECIDED TO RETURN to Ogunquit for another session with the fortune teller. I couldn't help myself. I needed to know what the tea leaves would say about Tom.

Joey: *BAILZ, you gotta see this. Mama has gone wacko.*
   Bailey: *What now, mate?*
   Joey: *She's soaking in the tub.*
   Bailey: *Eh? What's wacko about that?*
   Joey: *Well, it sure as heck is wacko, with the tub stuffed with some kind of pollen.*
   Bailey: *Huh?*

I SHOULD'VE KNOWN that fortune tellers, psychics, palm readers, and others of their ilk make their money by studying clients through a combination of observation and psychology. In my case, this wizard had already seen me twice, albeit a few years back.

She excelled because she had the benefit of layering what she already knew about me, one financial "donation" after another. By now my twice-broken heart was coming through loud and clear. She told me the situation with Tom would require far more than analyzing my hand. She'd need a week by the sea fasting and in prayer to allow the spirits to visit and guide her answer. She convinced me she endured much pain to assist a client with such a complex problem. In purging herself of toxins, she said, she'd become better able to divine the future.

Funny, not funny, how some women handle heartbreak. Sometimes it comes in the form of rage, other times a malfunctioning of the brain. I was vulnerable . . . but still it's humiliating all these years later to admit I shelled out $900 without a single attempt to bargain. Besides the cash outlay, she told me I'd need to purchase one dozen long-stemmed white roses—imperative they be white to ensure the purity of this transaction. I was then to strip each pedal one by one and place them in the bathtub. I remember there was a liquid to be poured; whether it was champagne or something more fit for a soaking bath, I can't recall.

As you can imagine, when I called her when I was supposed to, her response might as well have been in tongues through a mist of vapor. At least when she answered me about my relationship with Ryan—"It will never be what you want it to be, but it will be better than it is now"—it seemed concrete. Now, I'd have settled for a "Wait and see." Anything but gobbledygook. I hung up the phone. I'd been had. Sowing seeds of desperation bears no fruit. Nine Hundred Dollars.

IN MID-2002, I was enjoying Laconia's honey-glazed summer evenings—temps still holding in the high 70s, with mountain peaks profiled in shades of indigo. I remember it well, because my life was about to take a 90-degree spin over an embankment. I survived but required the assistance of search and rescue.

It was on just such a night when a late-model, black two-seater Mercedes convertible came up my driveway, John at the wheel. A year had passed since our breakup. In that time, he sold a parcel of land abutting his home, paid a few bills, and decided to spoil himself. The car suited him well, but the diamond Rolex on his wrist seemed out of character. Not because he couldn't afford it, but as a humble man, he was never one to parlay his success onto the material side of life.

It started off innocently enough. He might've asked if I wanted to have dinner. Knowing then what I know now, would I've have been polite but taken a pass? Tooling around the Lakes Region in the peak of tourist season in a convertible is freeing—like being on the back of a Harley.

John never mentioned anyone he'd dated during our separation, nor did I mention my time with Tom. As we moved into the fall, though, John met a woman. He enjoyed her company, but maintaining a dual relationship was not in his wheelhouse. His upcoming office company Christmas party forced his hand on choosing one of us.

"Claire, for the last couple of months I've also been seeing someone else. I like her. But Claire"—he paused—"I hope you know my heart belongs to you."

I believed (and still do) in angels (and ghosts), and all I can say is that I saw stars, or fireflies (think being clocked by a hard right to the jaw), that swirled around my head in a haphazard pattern to generate some kind of energy for me to answer, an answer that lit the match to the conflagration that would ensue.

"Okay," I said, "we'll be together."

Ding dong . . .

I didn't choke on the words, but why did I reply immediately? Is this what I wanted? Could this companionship evolve into deeper affection? Convinced I'd never again meet anyone like Tom, a super-hero with homespun roots, I questioned whether I'd fallen in love with him because he was larger than life. Would the *snap, crackle, and pop* of our relationship, so evident during the occasional rendezvous at our "refueling stations," last with daily contact? What if these fire-flies were carrying a different message. What if they were trying to say: *Don't do it! Walk away while you can. You enjoy John's company but you're not in love with him. Don't be an idiot!*

I wanted this relationship to work, to be off the merry-go-round and in the arms of a man who was kind and intelligent and had many similar interests. Being with John was delightful. Whether we skied, biked, danced, or traveled, we had fun. He'd have made the best guy friend, but he needed more. I hoped I could deliver.

Back on the home front, I remained oblivious to the number of years Joey and I had spent together and wasn't prepared for what was in store for my precious kitty. It was a typical hot day in late July 2003. I had an appointment with a client who had also become a close friend, Miss Janine.

Joey

MAMA'S FAVORITE COUSIN, *Ray, would tell her that growing old ain't for sissies. Well, I had news for him: It ain't for kitties, either. Was it that long ago when I was nimble as a frog and could leap onto the counter in a second—and at the sound of a tuna can opening in even less time? Not anymore. I couldn't leap to save my tail. Forget the counter, those days were gone, and so were the extra treats before supper. The couch cushions might as well be Mount Everest. Heck, even Mama's office chair was off limits.*

My joints felt like they needed an oil change. My purr sounded like it was running out of gas. Even my roar was barely audible. I looked like an emaciated fur-encrusted skeleton. I couldn't tolerate my comb or brush anymore and don't even talk to me about my nails. I was a far cry from the strong, smart, dependable pussycat everyone admired. I was eating the same food, but I looked malnourished.

I still loved my treats, a sure sign that I was alive and kicking. But I didn't get it: I was young, I was middle aged, and now I was a senior. Just the sound of that makes my whiskers go limp.

I guess I turned a corner: no going back and going forward was scary. That happened to me back in July 2003. It was late morning, already hot and humid, and Mama was meeting a client-friend. Janine left her dog, Fenway, in the car because she respected our feline household.

They had finished their business and were coming up from Mama's office when I began walking toward them to get my usual goodbye pat. Suddenly, my ears started ringing, day became night, plop, all four legs let go, and I did a face plant onto the kitchen floor. Although I was barely conscious, I could hear Mama crying and yelling at the same time for Janine to help. Janine stayed by my side while Mama phoned Dr. Mike, who told her to come right in.

Mama called me Joseph when I was naughty, but also when she was scared, like the time that creep ex-boyfriend brought her so much heartache. Now, she wrapped me in Mémère's afghan because I couldn't walk. She held me on her lap and cried all the way to the doctor's office. When we arrived, we were escorted into an examining room, where Dr. Mike looked at my eyes, ears, and throat and listened to my heart.

He told Mama he would need to draw some blood. Well, I knew what that meant, but I was too weak to protest.

As it turned out, my kidneys were failing, and I was dehydrated. I needed daily injections of fluid and ended up staying in the hospital 28 days. Mama came every lunch hour and carried me outside and lay me on a towel in the grass. She talked to me, but it was tough through all the tears. We both knew I was on my way out of this life. It had been such a good one and for so long. I was 16 years old.

Mama wasn't ready to let me go and brought me back home. I still needed daily injections, but grabbing the top skin of my back and sticking me with a long needle was the last thing she wanted to do. Good that Cheryl, one of Dr. Mike's assistants, came to our house every night until Mama felt comfortable enough to do it herself. Of course, even when she did, all I had to do was move and she would prick herself instead of me.

Meanwhile, Bailey, Casper, and Chloe were pretty much in the dark about what the heck had been going on in my absence. Mama didn't talk to them much, as she probably didn't think they'd understand. When I got back, I clued them in on my prognosis. It would be up to them to keep Mama safe.

That's when I realized just how much my brothers and sister loved me and would miss me. I might be the king of this den, but right now I felt more like a mole searching for a burrow. My gut told me there was no light at the end of this tunnel. Still, I had to save face. After all, this group counted on me to keep the peace and protect Mama for as long as I could.

This year, the annual Hebert family barbecue on Labor Day weekend, which coincided with Pépère's birthday, wasn't the usual funfest. Mama was doing her best to be upbeat, but her sorrow was transparent, at least to me. Uncle Dan and Aunt Donna had to pick me up and hold me while Mama took our picture. I knew I looked awful—my fur was thin and matted and no matter how much I tried to poof myself up, like in the old days, it was useless. I was a bag of bones and just limp.

Even Pépère looked a bit less chipper. He always chuckled when he handed out treats, especially when Mama turned her back and he gave us more than he should. I knew this was the last time I'd see this family. Still, I kept my usual composure, especially since I slept most of the time. zzzzz

In the fall, her busiest season, Mama's work kept her distracted. Not as many clients came to our home anymore, so off she went every day to one appointment after another, usually at business locations. But each night, at around 9:00, she took out the countertop ironing board, made a towel-bed on it, and hung that bag of fluid over the cabinet door. Then she scooped me up and placed me on the towel. As long as I didn't move, we'd both survive the ordeal. But the more the weeks went by, the more I resisted.

My kidneys were failing. I was tired . . . I was weak . . . I couldn't frolic about the house with my siblings, and these nightly infusions were really unpleasant. I was thankful for this life, but I was ready to go.

Joey, October 31, 2003

Mama knew that after three months of managing my failing health, the time had come; but still, she'd need a sign. I knew what I had to do.

In late afternoon, Mama got home from a meeting in Bedford with boss Con and the gang. She looked at me with the saddest eyes I'd ever seen on her—and I'd seen plenty. I was lying on the floor by the TV in the living room, and she offered me two treats. I didn't take them. I knew I couldn't swallow one more, I was that weak. Then she knew. That was the sign. She got her camera and took my picture—pathetic as I looked, but I had no energy for vanity.

Without a word to Bailey, Casper, or Chloe, she once again wrapped me gently in Mémère's afghan and carried me to the car. Once again, and for the last time, I sat on her lap to see Dr. Mike.

On the way she called Mama Sarah and asked if she wanted to say goodbye to me.

I could hear her voice, and I missed her, and I wished for one last hug. I wanted to tell her how sorry I was that I peed in her suitcase, but I didn't have the strength. She probably forgave me a long time ago. Still, I just wanted to get it off my scrawny chest. Mama put the phone near me and Sarah said she loved me.

At Dr. Mike's, I was set, for the last time, on the examining table. I didn't have the energy to give him a hard time. The good news was that I'd never need my nails trimmed again or my belly brushed. The bad news was that I was leaving Mama and my siblings.

The doctor left us alone for a bit. Mama told me over and over how much she loved me and that I was the best kitty anybody could have and that she would never, ever forget me. I feel the same about you, Mama. I hope you know that. Best Mama ever.

I'm glad we kitties don't cry. Human noses ooze fluid like a water-main leak. Mama was caught up in a raging river of tears but stayed right with me. I could feel myself falling into a dream state, like I could hear but couldn't meow. I felt a slight pressure and was suddenly floating among clouds of all shapes and sizes, tumbling head over paws as if I were a newborn puffball.

Then in wafted this one billowy cloud like it had my name on it. It scooped me up and offered me the softest pillow for my head. I must be dreaming. Wait just a minute . . . Is that? Could it be? Wait! Hold up! You, over there, snow white with the blue eyes. Is that you, Marshmallow? Remember me?

Bailey

GOLLY. I DARESAY, I was no wizard, but some beastly scent descended upon this house-hold, and I couldn't get a proper read on it. I'd been discharged from the responsibility of managing family issues—that was Joseph's idea of a good time. He fancied himself the king of the jungle or some such poppycock, but it worked for him—and me as well. When Mum scooped him up from the living room and came back without him and bawling her eyes out, however, I sensed this household was going to be shaken to its core. Then again, he'd been away before. Still . . .

Oh, Mum gave us our usual biscuits. But she didn't look us in the eye and said not a word. Instead, she picked up the phone, plunked her posterior on the sofa, and about emptied a box of tissues. Reserved as usual, I joined my siblings for a spot of water and our evening nibbles.

Wait a minute. What was that family conference Joseph had pulled together a few weeks back? He went all technical on us, forcing us to roll our eyes to the heavens. I viewed my water bowl as half full, so I figured Joseph's issues would be tidied up. After all, we'd managed without him before. But this time felt wonky.

I CAN'T SAY JOEY'S PASSING CAME AS A SHOCK. After all, the past three months made it obvious he wasn't long for this world. None of my previous kitties had lived this long. When mats become more frequent and grooming a chore, was the Grim Reaper knocking on his door? My Joseph, my precious Joey, was gone. Forever. I came home from the vet, grabbed a tissue box, sat on the couch, and called my parents. Mom and Dad had phones by their favorite chairs. The three of us cried together. It was comforting to know they loved him too. When John stopped by, he was sympathetic but otherwise emotionless. I wanted someone bawling his eyes out with me.

I remembered the first time I laid eyes on Joey, a tiny buff fuzzball with an oversized ego strutting over to me like he owned the place—like he was on a mission and had arrived on this planet in this location for one reason. If Griffin hadn't told me about the love Joey beamed my way, would I have even noticed? Was my life so busy, so wracked with anguish, that I considered him "just a cat"? No.

Joey wasn't just a cat. From his early years, like when he stared down Mike Moyer, to his one-time adventure underneath the deck, to the power emanating from his little body when Big Ben exploded at me like a mad man, he was my protector, my King Leo who embraced his position as head cheese.

Now he was gone.

I never took my kitties for granted again, but I always struggled with the reality of their inevitable demise. They might spend their lives sleeping and playing and eating and sleeping some more, but they also found their way deep inside my heart. Memories of their antics came rushing back, and they still do.

Thank God for Team Bailey. I wasn't alone, but Joey left a gaping hole in this family.

One week later

Casper: *Sis, Bailz ain't right. I know he's the quiet one, but now he barely opens his jaw and not once has he come and taken a nap with me. Ya think we did anything to tick him off?*

Chloe: *Oh, come now, Caspie. Bailey is just being his pompous self. We're closing in on the holidays—haven't you noticed Mama piling up the boxes in our room? You know what a wild man he is with wrapping paper and bows. Everything is going to be fine.*

Casper: *Yeah, you're right. He's always minded his own business, so we'll mind ours. But seems like a long time since we've seen Our Leader . . .*

Two weeks later

Bailey: *Blimey. Mum has her suitcase out and that can mean only one thing. Not only is my brother missing again, but now she'll be away too. Good thing we love our auntie Sherry, who watches over us when Mum is out of town. She's kind and sweet and takes good care of us. But I'll be glad when all this nonsense with Joseph is sorted and our family is back together again.*

If only I hadn't been Mr. Laid-Back and agreed to let Joseph be Boss Man . . . if only I had asked more questions . . . if only I'd told him "I love you, bro."

Four weeks later

Bailey: *I was going all to pot. Of course, my constitution didn't allow for any spot of nerve. I demanded my brother return to this house, right now, where he belonged. It was time for our annual holiday mischief and I couldn't manage this task alone. I mean, I could've . . .*

But it was jolly fun having a mate in fantasy frolic—like enjoying a game of hide and seek in a pile of crinkling tissue paper. I felt I had to resist my favorite spools of ribbon until Joseph returned, but it got harder by the day to refrain from sinking my teeth into those curls.

Oh, bloody hell.

AT MY LAST PHYSICAL, the doctor noted my blood calcium levels were off. Okay, not too big a deal, right? Wrong. This was a huge deal, especially when she told me that if I didn't bring them into line, my kidneys would overwork, my bones would crumble, and in time my kidneys would fail. Anything else?

Then, following a repeat blood test, my PCP called. "Good news," she said, "you've got hyperparathyroidism. There are four parathyroid glands, two on each side of the throat. Sometimes one of them becomes overactive, causing the intake of calcium to be rechanneled into the bloodstream. But there's an easy fix: surgery. By extracting the errant gland, your numbers will normalize. No problem with living with three parathyroid glands. I'll refer you to an endocrinologist at Dartmouth-Hitchcock to work out the details."

Wait! So these itty-bitty glands, each the size of a grain of rice, have such a huge responsibility? Getting slit near my sole means of earning a living didn't sit well. There had to be another way. Over the next several months, I consulted three endocrinologists in separate practices who specialized in parathyroid issues. By the time I reached a bigwig at Boston's Mass General Hospital, the answer was definitive: There was no alternative. Two normal childbirths, zero surgeries, and now an excavator with a blade.

Fear holds steady for many reasons; avoidance is often the main one. Ever since childhood, I've been afraid of needles. Getting a blood test always required accommodations: recliner, glass of water, open window, and a shot of orange juice before going out the door. Otherwise, my throat closed, my forehead grew warm, my ears buzzed. I dreaded the needle.

Hyperparathyroidism is guaranteed to get you passed this fear. Blood tests were mandatory and frequent. But the needle of all needles, based on my experience at the time, was the dye-needle, which injected a lukewarm solution for contrast purposes when I was flattened on a steel slab under a massive machine. That was very bad; worse, though, was an impressive instrument used by a skilled specialist to pinpoint the exact location of the little sucker that had refused to play nice and was shimmying way too close to my voice box.

Every year, one of our state magazines profiles "best" doctors and dentists, peer reviewed. I chose a general surgeon who consistently made the list. I tried to find it reassuring when he mentioned he'd performed this surgery for 20 years with only one complication.

"What happened?" I asked.

"I found the gland in his stomach and had to ship him to Boston."

Please God, don't let me be his second.

JOHN TOOK MY MIND OFF the "what ifs" of a surgery gone rogue. When I told him the situation, he whipped out his favorite pencil and got busy. Years of creative effort to appease discriminating clients now benefited me. He had a zillion notes tucked away for some just-in-case home. That home turned out to be ours. I'd never seen an architectural drawing. I'm a visual consumer: Show me.

Weekends we ventured to some of my favorite haunts in and around the Maine coastline and I always pointed to my favorite architectural feature: the eyebrow window. Cut into the roofline, it was a throwback to the good ole days. Even more important was the view—to the western sunset, the one I'd come so close to having once upon a time.

We settled on a plot that offered a view of the Sanbornton hills and the sunsets I'd long admired off Parade Road, smack dab at the top of the hill before descending into Laconia. The thought of sunsets set my heart aflutter. Was this really going to happen? Perhaps because John's company had earned a reputation for outstanding construction, I knew the house would be all that I dreamed of with the throwback window and sunset view. I was dead wrong on both counts.

A small detail John once mentioned shook the rafters on the word *small* and that was his admiration for Frank Lloyd Wright. Had I paid more attention, I would've noticed how much of Wright's style was embedded in John's current home. Still, I was confident my wish for a cottage look with arches, views to the sunset, and especially an eyebrow window would materialize.

Let's talk about the engagement ring. If this artistic guru could fill acres of land, then a teeny tiny band on a finger could be accomplished with his eyes closed. On this, though, John let me be the architect. My first mistake was choosing a shank that resembled the Ponte Vecchio, the medieval bridge in Florence, over the Arno, lined with jewelry stores. Ornate to a fault, it was sure to compete with any stone with which it was forced to coexist. The four c's of diamonds—cut, color, clarity, carat—require balance. Too much of one and not enough of another throws shade on brilliance. But when you're closing in on four carats, what's the problem?

Architects are guided by precision. John's office Christmas party was the perfect opportunity for the boss to make a statement. Having been prompted by the emcee, with everyone's eyes on us, John dropped down on one knee. As I sat at the round table of eight knowing full well what was ahead, I worked my best innocent face.

"Claire, will you marry me?" he said, holding an open ring box to expose a ginormous jewel.

"Yes, I'll marry you." *Kiss. Hug.* And I was happy.

Eight weeks later
Bailey

OH, BLOODY HELL. I couldn't postpone this family meeting any longer. I mean the holidays had come and gone. I did fairly well to nibble my usual portion of ribbon. We felines are tough. We keep our problems to ourselves. When we're terribly put out, we don't get mad; we get even. When we're gutted, we hunker down and hope for the best.

I thought that when Mama Sarah joined us for Christmas, she might confide in me a tad. But no. When Mémère and Pépère were about, I failed to detect any change in them a-tall. Pépère kept the biscuits flowing as usual. But it's utter rot how long we'd been without our leader.

My gut told me my brother crossed some bridge—I learned about that on the telly, animals being old and tired, then becoming young again. I don't comprehend how that can happen. Sounds like poppycock. Er . . . then again . . . hmmmmmm.

But, to the problem at hand: Round up the troops. As usual, I found them butt to butt on the couch in the den.

Bailey: Hey, mates. Straighten up. Time for a chat.

Chloe: Got some news on our Joe?

Bailey: Affirmative. He has departed. He's dead. Gone. Done. Bye-bye.

Casper: Huh? Wait a minute. I don't get it. He's not coming back?

Bailey: Negative. He must have crossed that Rainbow Bridge—something I caught on the telly. When pets get too old to manage, they leave their earth family and get airlifted across this wonky arch to play in a wide-open field with other cats and even dogs. Sounds a bit daft to me.

Chloe: *You mean he lied to us? Didn't he tell us not to worry . . . that everything would be all right?*

Bailey: *You know our Joseph. He wouldn't want to upset us. He rather expected Dr. Mike would make him all better again.*

Casper: *Oi. He was our leader. Who's gonna be our leader now? Not me.*

Chloe: *Not this chick. I hate politics.*

Bailey: *Well, I guess that leaves yours truly. I find I can no longer discuss this sad state of affairs. I must take leave of you and lie down so as to absorb this adjustment.*

JANUARY SAW A STUNNING REVERSAL of our mirth and mayhem. I got the impression that my kitties expected Joey back; after all, they'd managed his earlier stint in the hospital followed by his return. His absence took a while to sink in. And then it was like a curtain dropped and the lights went out. I was witnessing depression in felines. When Tia passed, maybe I could say Joey manned up and maintained his confidence. But this trio was struck dumb. They lost their *joie de vivre*—no interest in food, even treats. I rarely saw them up and about. A tough start to a year that had yet to get off the ground.

My mother always said we never know what lies ahead. Sometimes the simplest of expressions can foretell a tempest of trials.

WITH JOHN BUSY in his studio, I looked for any distraction to mitigate the evil spirits surrounding my upcoming dissection for this pea-sized varmint. But John felt the need for regular sit-downs over these sketches. Incubating inside a stack of undecipherable rectangles juxtaposed one to another was our future home. My eyes glazed over.

John was the professional. He knew which contractors to assign which detail, excavation first in line. Situated on a hill, all trees cut down, it was easy to picture the magnificent view of that elusive sunset. During this year, we spent every weekend on our home-to-be. Days of wine and fun escapes were over. John was immersed in building his (our) dream home. Had he been able to lighten up and let in an occasional sprinkle of relaxation, perhaps we might've had a shot at surviving the ensuing chaos. With a set of workmen on the job five days a week, a patch of dirt was quickly transformed.

I found myself speechless. The house was facing east, toward the neighbors' home, peeking through the trees. Huh? Why would anyone position a home at the top of a quarter-mile driveway away from the view and toward the woods?

"John! Why is this house being built to face away from the view?"

"I had no choice," John said. "It's the topography. Nothing I could do."

"You mean when we chose this lot, and it was all about the view, you knew the house wouldn't face it? And you never told me? Besides, this house looks enormous! We don't need something this big. Please, hon, let's sell it when it's finished and buy a condo."

"This is my retirement home," John replied. "I want my mother and sisters to have their own space when they visit so there's a junior suite. When Sarah visits, she'll have the room over the garage and her own bathroom. Our master suite will command the top floor. I'll build you a deck off the master sliders so you can have your view."

He made it clear there was no going back, no adjustments. What good were all those conversations and the times we spent driving along Maine coast? When my contractor Andy built my current house, he made all major decisions but offered me a few frills. Now, my soon-to-be husband—an architect!—thought it fine to build me a monster house facing the woods. And where was the eyebrow window? This was an eyesore.

John had this house built from scratch; my role was now to turn it into a home. I had done that before, but a five-split-level, 3,800-square-foot building was something altogether different. I had so much else on my plate, so what was my priority—the house, with a move-in date of November 1? Our wedding? The transfer of my agent-broker business? My surgery?

I'D LOVE TO GIVE YOU A VISION of what John created out of a few pages of hen scratches, but that's for another time, another book. I can give you the skinny, though. Considering I haven't laid eyes on it for 18 years, it obviously left an impression. Too bad it swallowed me up.

Despite all this, I relished what I thought would be my final months in my own comfy home with my kitties. All of us, in our own ways, were adjusting to life without our king Joey. Only Bailey, I thought, could pick up the reins.

Bailey: *Hi-ho, listen up, mates. We've got to shake off our misery. Joseph would want us to return to normal. He'd swipe us on the side of the head if he saw us moping around.*

Chloe: *Bailey, you're head cheese now. What should we do?*

Bailey: *Why don't you curl up with Mum when she's lying on the couch to watch a movie? She'll love the company, especially if you lie on her chest and purr your heart out. Love conquers all, young lady.*

Chloe: *That's a good idea. I'll see to it that she stays put for a while.*

Casper: *What about me? Please give me some direction. You know I can't stand bein' alone and I'm afraid . . . I hate change . . . I'm . . .*

Bailey: *Let's wrestle!*

Casper: *Hey, what's up with that? Why you jumpin' all over me? What am I—your new toy?*

Bailey: *No, no. It'll be jolly good fun to topple over each other and pretend wrestle. So what if I'm almost twice your size. But look here, young fellow. You need to up your game. You've been in your sister's shadow all your life. Get a grip—it'll do you a world of good.*

FROM THEN ON, Bailey and Casper scuffled, often right in front of me. Whoever was in the mood would approach his snoozing victim and start batting him until both were up on their hind legs, then tumbling head over paws and chasing each other. Hilarious to watch. Their boxing matches filled my heart with a lightness that was in short supply.

May 2004

SARAH GRADUATED with a bachelor's degree in criminal justice, a field very different from the interests she'd shown in high school. There her cross-country running kept her in shape. She also showed considerable promise in both dance and art, neither of which she pursued. To do anything in law enforcement, she told me, she'd need a master's. I never knew her passion lay in chasing the bad guys, especially if it meant staying in school for another two years. Although I was a bit surprised, I never worried about Sarah finding her niche.

The University of Maryland offered its students two graduations, great for divorced parents. Sarah's high school boyfriend had remained friends with her and joined John and me for dinner in Annapolis. Maybe we looked like a real family.

That was the good news. The bad news was that all of Sarah's sorority sisters had parents who'd been married for 30 years.

I WAS HEADING into the perfect storm. Challenges abounded regarding all sorts of things: For example, the idea of selling my house and moving my home office to the McMansion in the woods left me cold, like I didn't want to go. I had 13 file cabinets, furniture from two offices, the fax and other machines—17 years of business life. John could see I was in some distress, but was quite displeased to learn I was going to hold off selling my home for 18 months to coincide with my 20-year Omaha anniversary and the inevitable transfer of most of my files. The 20-minute commute between houses was manageable in the interim.

"If I'd known you weren't going to have your office in this house, I would've designed it differently," he said.

I defended myself: "If I'd known the house wouldn't face the view, I wouldn't have agreed to this lot."

John was like a bull in the ring—he never took his eye off the red cape. The night before my surgery, he insisted I meet him at Laconia Electric for lighting fixtures. Never mind I'd be under the haze of two prescriptions. Maybe his nonchalance had something to do with the fact that I'd asked my brother to hold my hand through the prep. John had become such a fanatic about this house that I was afraid he'd ask me a question just as the anesthetic was being administered. Dan was good on his feet and would surely have some sarcastic comeback for whatever transpired. He didn't disappoint.

On Wednesday morning, August 4, before being wheeled into the OR, I whispered, "Hey, Dan. Did you get a look at the anesthesiologist? What a hottie."

"Oh, for crying out loud, Claire. Hey, doc, she's ready. Put her out!"

As luck would have it, the surgeon faced his second complication: my gland was MIA. He looked everywhere and made a decision: Remove half my thyroid and hope for the best. It wasn't like he could wake me up and get my permission. There was a 50-50 chance it'd be hiding on one side or the other. Let me be kind: He should stay away from the blackjack table.

What happens sometimes after this type of surgery is a drop in calcium levels—hypocalcemia. Lightheadedness, extreme fatigue, brain fog, tingling sensation, but at least I was flatlined on the world's thinnest mattress. Adjustments were made and two more nights were added to my stay. I was home for the weekend but had no clue that half my thyroid was gone until Monday morning, when the stitches were removed.

"No problem," my doctor told me when I saw him in his office. "Synthroid, a harmless medication, will restore your thyroid function, but you'll have to be on it the rest of your life."

John had accompanied me to this checkup, which, of course, led to another lighting store, this one in Manchester. I couldn't concentrate on what I was supposed to be looking at—which chandelier or set of sconces would look best in which area. In fact, I had to sit down before I fainted.

On our way home, we stopped for dinner at Oliver's, at the junction of Exit 20. When he dropped me off at my house, I said, "John, I'm giving this relationship everything I have, but I'm struggling with our lack of communication."

A few weeks later my friend Judy, who'd stood by my side at my last wedding, came over to catch up on the status of the construction and, more important, to take me out for the day. It was a beautiful late-August afternoon in the heartbeat of the Lakes Region, the town of Meredith. We were two chicks on a toot guided by a native tour guide to the Inns at Mill Falls.

First, we had lunch at the Boat House Grill (now Lago). We both ordered my favorite, open-faced lobster sandwiches, and paired them with Cosmos. We then sauntered along the bay and sat by the water's edge at The Docks, a Margaritaville-themed tiki bar, sipping a chilled concoction of some sort (who pays attention to such details with toes in the sand?). Onward we strolled, toward Church Landing, a beautiful Adirondack inn on the shores of Lake Winnipesaukee. We sat at the patio bar on the upper deck overlooking the back lawn, often the site for a wedding reception. Perhaps by late afternoon, we figured we were ready for dessert—chocolate martinis. From our perch, we watched a business owner marry his sweetheart, photographed by one of my short-term (very short-term) dating partners. I recognized several local luminaries milling about.

When Judy and I found our way to the outside stairs approaching the adjoining foot bridge, I missed the top step and bumpety-bumped my way down, giggling all the way. It was that kind of day—uninhibited fun. I landed unscathed, no need for Judy, a nurse, to administer to me. We thought it was all hilarious.

We crossed the street to the Camp, a convincing replica of a summer sleepaway camp. No one seemed remotely unsettled by the look in our eyes. Judy and I still laugh our backsides off about how we got away with such outrageous behavior. My angel sister was forced to keep her eye on me again.

WHAT'S UP WITH THE YEARS ending in the number four? The fall of 1974 saw the collapse of my first marriage. The fall of 1984 brought the perfect storm to bring about the demise of my second marriage. The fall of 1994 had me knee deep in court chaos and draining money through a sieve. The fall of 2004 could be described by any number of metaphors:

a) peering down the Grand Canyon looking for a conversation with God;

b) climbing Mount Everest with one backpack and a dysfunctional oxygen tank;

c) pedaling for the finish line in the Tour de France with a broken leg.

For the second Sunday in September, John and I had tickets to see *The Lion King*, in Boston. The night before, at dinner, I raised an issue that was bothering me.

"You know this house is way beyond anything I've known. But what's more concerning is that if something happens to you, I'd be unable to manage it on my own. You tell me it has a value of $750,000—I couldn't afford to live in it. Would you consider purchasing a life insurance policy to protect me?"

"No," he replied, rather testily.

I was thinking a simple 10-year term. When you live and breathe insurance, it doesn't sit well when your partner puts you up in a McMansion and lives only in the moment. At the least, a discussion was warranted on a subject of this substance, even one that escalated into an argument, but we never argued. The next morning was the beginning of the end.

Before the 2:00 matinee, we went to a brunch reservation at one of the city's finest hotels. The sight of a bountiful buffet of fat, grease, and sugar stirred a pot within my digestive system that has never returned to normal. I excused myself more than once for a visit to the ladies' room. The subject of life insurance was never again discussed, but our relationship suffered a critical wound. I had too much experience to allow myself, in my senior years, to be placed in an untenable financial position.

With less than eight weeks before our official moving-in date, putting together all the fixings—the lighting, the color scheme, the mirrors, for example—now had a timetable, but we fit in a trip to the Southwest for a visit with his family.

Albuquerque, New Mexico, and Sedona, Arizona, offer some of America's most scenic vistas, and under different circumstances my memories would be more about the views than about the turmoil percolating inside the dressing room of a boutique.

Meanwhile, John and I were both angry, hurt, and frustrated. Our visions of our future had devolved into dread and unhappiness. For six months, the feelings swirling deep within us and the look in our eyes were evidence of our downfall. We just weren't ready to call it.

WHEN WE GOT BACK from the trip, some of John's friends stopped by my house with their dog, a West Highland terrier. Although I had admired this breed from afar, I knew one thing: they didn't like cats, making them a no-go for future consideration. Apparently, it went both ways. Casper and Chloe never failed to disappear at the sound of the doorbell, but Bailey was never the least bit ruffled by friend or foe. He embraced the ready tool at his disposal.

Chloe: *BRO, DID YOU SEE WHAT JUST HAPPENED?*

Casper: *Er, no. But I sure as heck can smell it. Bailey must have his dander up. He pooed outside the litter box again, right?*

Chloe: *Not exactly. You're not gonna believe this. Two strangers showed up and they brought their dog! At least I think it's a dog—it sure wasn't any cat. He was about the same size as Bailey, just not as fluffy. It was instant dislike. Bailey dropped a big load right there in the dining room, in front of everybody.*

Casper: *Oh boy. What did Mama do?*

Chloe: *She kept saying "So sorry." I could tell she was embarrassed.*

Casper: *As soon as they leave, let's have a chat with our leader.*

A few hours later

Casper: *HEY, BRO. What in tarnation?*

Bailey: *Hiiiiisssss. Hisssss. That mangy, good-for-nothing ball of frizzed-up pomposity. Ugh. Pssst. Hiiiiissss. What a poor excuse for a domestic. I bet he thinks he's above a proper belly rub. I mean, he has no clue what it's like to be a real canine— strong enough to pull a team; fierce enough to survive in the wilderness. Now that's what I call man's best friend, not this cheesy lump of fuzz.*

Chloe: *Geez, bro. Tell us how you really feel.*

Casper: *Come on, bro. Put up your dukes. Let's go a round. You'll feel better.*

Later

Chloe: *CASPIE, HAVE YOU NOTICED how cranky Mama's been? This is not the Mama we know. When was the last time we heard her laugh? Or even saw her smile? I mean she still takes care of us and likes our movie time, but she's not the same Mama, like she walks around in some kind of daze and goes potty in the middle of the night.*

Casper: *Yeah. Ya know me and plastic. I had a chance to pounce into some bubble wrap the other day and was biting to my heart's content when she yelled at me to stop instead of just taking it away.*

Chloe: *I wonder what's going on. Whatever it is, I don't like it.*

Casper: *Ya know how I am, sis. Can't handle stress. Promise me. Promise you won't ever leave me.*

Chloe: *I promise, lil bro. We're in this life together—forever.*

FINISHING TOUCHES ON A LONG-TERM PROJECT—the fun part, right? Visual as opposed to conceptual. I was running on empty, though, not just in fuel but also in my heart. I didn't know if I could get to the finish line. My job now was to complete each of the four bathrooms with their linens and accessories. Our country manor was no place for the deals and steals from outlet bath stores. I went to Concord, Manchester, and even Portsmouth for the right combinations.

Paint colors were next, but I couldn't make up my mind. And then there was the array of possible enhancements. I contacted two professionals, an interior designer and a master stencilist. Most memorable was the hand-drawn rose in soft shades of pink and peach with brown shadings perched at the corner of the junior suite stained in milk chocolate. Worth the investment.

John hired his own muralist, to narrow the breadth of the main section. With ladders and staging set up throughout the expanded dining area, the woman used a sponge method whereby subtle shadings off the base color added depth. Lovely. But then, so was the whole package. As we came down the home stretch, handcrafted furniture from Vermont's Pompanoosuc Mills completed the look throughout the main rooms. I continued to concentrate on the lighting, deciding finally on the one piece I'd love to see again—a 20-arm Hubbardton Forge beauty with swirls in every direction. It required a three-man installation, a spectacular gem in a naked space and my favorite: the three-season room.

Bailey: *WHAT ON EARTH is this conundrum? Mum and her girlfriends are moving her clothes into the car and even taking pictures from the walls.*

Chloe: *Bailey, what's happening? Is Mama leaving us?*

Casper: *Who will take care of us?*

Bailey: *Keep your hair on, you two. Leave it to me. I'll put my Sherlock skills to work and find out what's going on.*

Later that day

Bailey: *COME HERE, CHUMS, and pin back your ears. Mum will live in a brand-new house John designed. That might explain why she's been so distracted and grumpy.*

Chloe: *But why does she seem so sad?*

Casper: *Maybe she doesn't wanna leave this house.*

Bailey: *A possibility. But she'll move, then we'll join her after Thanksgiving. The good news is that she'll still work in her office and be among us during the day—she just won't be here at night.*

Chloe: *Well, I don't like it. I love our house. It's cozy and safe. It's the only one I've had since Mama rescued us from that pigpen. No way do I want to leave.*

Casper: *Me neither. You know how I hate change.*

Bailey: *Well, this is certainly a double whammy. Last year I moped through the holidays without our Joseph. Now this year looks bleak too.*

December 2004

I INTRODUCED MY LOVABLE TRIO to their new home, an enormous uptick from our Cape. As embroiled as I was in a mix of emotions, no amount of square footage could hide what the kitties detected. They seemed lost, confused, and frightened. My family—again in turmoil.

With Christmas just weeks away, my attention turned to re-creating "Home for the Holidays." At least for Sarah, I wanted the sparkle of joy I'd been fostering for years to remain intact. A curled-up mother and daughter in jammies sipping champagne was headed for a reboot, but I had a surprise for her that eclipsed our traditions. She'd been dating a coworker, Jason, who'd found her special enough to buy her the kitten she'd been wanting: not "just a cat"—a blue-mitted Ragdoll.

I flew Jason up on Christmas Eve to spend the weekend with us. While Sarah and I prepared our favorite appetizers ahead of what would be a full-course dinner, John drove to Manchester under some ruse. When the garage door opened, I was like a kid again waiting for Santa. I could hardly contain myself as I watched Sarah's eyes grow wide when Jason walked into the room. Priceless.

Photographs of John and me taken over this Christmas weekend showed the pain etched on our faces. We'd stopped trying to hide the disappointment, although I don't think the kids noticed. Sarah was too distracted after she opened Jason's present, a framed picture of Hermès — a precious little boy who'd become her own Joey.

Meanwhile, my kitties were showing their angst, especially Bailey and Chloe. Over the years, Bailey had adopted five "babies"— small stuffies, which one at a time he put in his mouth and carried from one place to another, emitting guttural sounds like a seasoned mouser. He would sally about the house puffed up like a peacock, usually depositing his prize at the top of the stairs. In the new house, he moved one after another onto a different step but never to the top floor. Perhaps he wanted to hold on to something from his old home, something familiar. Or maybe he was showing signs of stress.

Chloe, on the other hand, found a hiding spot too good for me to locate. I knew she was alive because I'd see her scoot to her litter box or the food dish, but she always vamoosed as soon as she finished her business. She wanted nothing to do with me. I'm sure both boys knew where she was, but they weren't talking. Most likely, Casper split his time between snoozing with Bailey and consoling his sister. Casper had always been Mr. Laid-Back Jr.—not one to get his hackles up but rather content to be part of the landscape.

On New Year's we had a different set of visitors: John's couple friends from Massachusetts. I remember making muffins and burning the top of my right hand as I pulled them out of the oven, a scar still visible. Our one fun holiday outing was seeing *Meet the Fockers*. Our last bit of mirth.

JANUARY CAN BE A TOUGH MONTH for New Englanders. Not much daylight or warmth, no birds chirping, no flowers in bud. Instead, Mother Nature shows her most mercurial self, every year in some kind of snit, not able to decide whether she wants to freeze our backsides or thaw our lakes and ponds; skip the white stuff and bring on the rain; or just go with a good old nor'easter. But one thing is for sure: She loves gray.

That was apparently the color of my complexion based on comments. Clients who ran into me at the corner coffee shop later told me they thought I had cancer. I looked that good. I tried to look on the bright side of our new homestead. At least there was one inside view of the Sanbornton hills. All I had to do was grab my glass of wine and come up to the top step on the last landing. There, as I leaned on the railing, I could peer out the rectangle window, designed to allow a ray of light.

One evening, John wanted to tell me how the home his partner was building on Lake Winnipesaukee was shaping up.

"They're just putting the finishing touches on the farmer's porch," he said. "It faces down the lake and out toward the Gunstock Mountain range. You'd like it."

Bailey: *CASPER, HOW'S YOUR SISTER? I have my hands full trying to keep Mum company during my waking hours. I have had no opportunity to investigate her hiding place. She pops out only after John goes to work, and just for a few minutes.*

Casper: *She's a mess. She has constant nightmares. She worries about that giant of a man finding us here in the woods and no one hearing our screams.*

Bailey: *I can imagine. Fortunately, I'm still my marvelous self, but I'll never get accustomed to this monstrosity. This is not a home. It's a museum—ceilings that cause a crick in my neck, sky-high windows so we can't see out, not a single place we can rest and watch the world go by. It's a terrible setup, if you ask me. This place simply doesn't meet our minimum standards.*

Casper: *Ya think we're stuck here forever? How can we let Mama know we want our real home back?*

Bailey: *Let me ponder that—I think I'm having a thought.*

I KNEW I NEEDED HELP. I knew John and I needed help. I found two medical practitioners: one for me and one for us. My primary care, who was a cardiologist, was not one bit happy to see a 250 reading for my cholesterol. That was the good news. The bad news was that John and I embarked on couple's counseling as a last-ditch effort to save the relationship, reminding me of the crew on the *Titanic* lowering the lifeboats as the ship slipped away.

I remember our counselor Dr. William's advice: "Think of your relationship as a canoe. Each of you commands a paddle to move the boat forward. Talk to each other but, more important, listen. Communicate."

John and I took one day to downhill-ski at Gunstock and another for cross-country skiing along Lake Winnisquam. Another set of last times. My birthday came in the middle of February, just ahead of the annual New England Boat Show in Boston. John booked us a hotel room in Beacon Hill and a dinner reservation at an elegant restaurant. I can't recall which entrée seemed the least invasive, given my tendency to spend much of any overnight in the bathroom, but I do remember how insistent John was when it came to some evening special on cocktails. I wanted to take a pass but he pointed to the drinks menu: "She'll take that one," he said to our waiter. John knew I was a Grey Goose–on–the-rocks girl, but I didn't appreciate his ordering for me.

It strikes me that my indecision regarding selling my house, my unwillingness to transfer my office, and my obvious dislike of the layout of this new place contributed to John's frustration; he was losing control of his fiancée. The next day, he used that frustration, as we walked the aisles of the Boat Show, to make a snap decision: a six-figure, 32-foot Formula.

"You can pick the color," he said.

I think we saw Dr. William once a week for a month.

March 24, 2005

Chloe: *I HATE THIS PLACE. I want to go home. Now! Tout fini. Done.*

    Casper: *Me too. Please, Bailz, can we go home?*

    Bailey: *The time has come. Mum is stuck. We have no choice but to take matters into our own paws. It's time to save her. Joseph would expect us to take care of business when she can't take care of it herself. I have a plan, but Chloe, you must be brave.*

We've been in residence in this makeshift palace long enough. Mum requires a push. I don't know if the water over here is spiked or what, but she looks like she's sleepwalking. We want our old Mum back. We want to go home.

You two are aware of how annoying John finds me, what with me going up and down the staircase at full meow after he retires. Chloe, once he and Mum are settled in, I need you to leap on the bed and get right up close to him and let out a howl like your life is at risk. Can you handle it?

Chloe: Geez! I've never done that before, but I'm in. I'm miserable and beat up from squeezing myself at the back of a bookcase, shaking in my paws because I'm afraid a monster will break in.

Bailey: Good girl. Now wait until I've brought up all five of my babies. Then head on up and Casper and I will support you.

BAILEY WAS LOUDER than ever that night, as one by one he brought his babies up the staircase. But it was Chloe who jumped smack in the middle of our bed with a howl like from another world. She seemed to pull off a 360-spin, like she was possessed.

John shouted—the first time he ever raised his voice—"That's it! Your cats are no longer allowed in here!"

He dropped anchor. The cats were off the bed in a flash, and John slammed the double doors shut. I knew there'd be no compromise. I knew what I had to do. Tomorrow we'd be gone.

After John left for work, I began a marathon of gathering my favorite personal belongings and filled my Volvo to its roof. I drove to my house, unloaded, and drove back in record time. I refilled the car, a little less this time, and began scooping up the kitties.

Chloe stood in the middle of the living room, just looking at me, waiting to be picked up. It was surprising: She was ten years old and never eager to go anywhere, and it was like now she knew it was okay for me to pick her up. She was going home.

Meanwhile, what to do about the ring and how to approach John required a third-party perspective. I called my friend Brenda.

"What do I do now?"

"Put the ring on the bureau. Meet him at the bottom of the drive-way and tell him you're leaving."

I took her suggestions. I got out of the car just as he arrived. I kept it simple.

"John, I can't do this anymore. I'm sorry. I tried. I'm leaving."

He looked at me and said in his emotionless voice, "I'm disap-pointed in you."

There was nothing further to say. I got in my car and drove home.

I DON'T REMEMBER what I did that first night, if I called anyone, if had any dinner. I hadn't lived there since November. What I do remember is that there were three fur-bodies wrapped around me that night, for the first time in ages, and that their motors were run-ning. Home sweet home.

MY NEW NORMAL took some adjustment; it was a blessing, though, to wake up each morning away from a pair of sun-drenched, east-facing glass doors.

Within the week, I arranged with John to return for the rest of my belongings, but I was in for quite a surprise. John wasn't there, as planned. Instead, I was greeted by an array of photographic equip-ment set up throughout the main living area. Turns out, John had already sold the house. Cash deal. The market favored sellers, and John got a comfortable profit toward his next dream house.

He was soon dating, someone he had met at his hair salon. He started sketching his next house, proposed to her, got married within 18 months, and moved into their new house. Atop a hill. With a 360-degree view.

It was difficult for me to dust myself off and accept it for what it was—a mismatch. Beyond the money I'd invested, there were pressing medical issues for me to manage. Our breakdown had lit a match to my gut. I was being rocked from the inside out. The doctor referred me for a colonoscopy, and off I went to the hospital.

It wasn't my first. That one was a "no sequelae," a no-trauma, nothing amiss experience. Not this time. Let me be kind: She was a butcher. I was awake and caught sight of the technicolor image of my colon . . . let me stop there.

I went from healthy to not. Welcome to microscopic colitis, a condition defined by its predictability to rear its nasty side whenever I was stressed. Next was red in my bladder output. Great. Now I was referred to a urologist for a cystoscopy to determine the cause: infection? cancer? Once again, I needed my buddy Brenda. I called her.

"You know what a baby I am. There won't be any anesthesia. Will you come with me?"

Of course she would, and she even stayed in the room while the urologist poked and prodded.

A relief to learn it wasn't serious, but I had to have an annual test to assess any changes.

Next was the state of my teeth. The periodontist did his thing and recommended more appointments with the hygienist.

MY MOTHER LED A SIMPLE LIFE, never coloring outside the lines, no knack for sports or hobbies, content as a happy homemaker. She never pined for more than being a mother. The empty-nest adjustment never morphed into a new adventure.

Mom herself had a mix of issues, requiring a boatload of drugs and all with side effects. She dealt with a second bout of breast cancer. She broke her ankle coming down the stairs. It was a bad break in two places and required pins. There were basic strengthening exercises she could do, but she refused. I brought her to physical therapy, but she was indifferent. She needed an inhaler, but she wouldn't use it.

Now, in early June, she fell ill and was taken by ambulance to the hospital. Already 2005 was in the running for Worst Year Ever.

When Mom got to the hospital, she couldn't walk, and cardiac and lung distress necessitated a transfer to St. Francis Rehab and Nursing Center. By early August, we were reaching Medicare's limit, so I made an appointment at the Medicaid office. Dad, Dan, and I visited her regularly, but she was miserable. She wanted to come home.

"I want to go home" became her constant refrain, but she couldn't walk and her house wasn't accessible for a wheelchair. She stayed at St. Francis.

August 5 was one of those spectacular summer days. I asked Mom's attendants to help us out onto the patio for lunch. It took two of them to secure the Hoyer lift, which looks like a hammock, and then transfer her to a wheelchair. I pushed it to a comfortable spot, away from other residents, and made small talk; she didn't respond. Her appetite was near zero, so I had brought along a yogurt. I opened the container and spooned out a small amount. Mom was a card-carrying member of the "clean your plate" squadron, but what I placed in her mouth drooled off to the side. She refused to swallow.

I had recently met with the medical director and we'd discussed life support: Did she want to be resuscitated? Did she want to prolong her life? I had said no.

The attendants helped me get her to her room, and I left utterly demoralized—I wanted my beloved Mom back to her old self. I returned that evening and as I leaned toward her in bed she said, almost inaudibly, "Hospital." She wanted to die there.

There wasn't time.

Her nurse called me that night, around 11 o'clock:

"I happened to walk by your mother's room and checked in on her. I'm sorry, I saw her take her last breath."

I wish I'd have known she wouldn't make it to morning. I wanted to be there, to hold her hand.

I learned that the doctor had stopped her Metformin, which she had been taking for diabetes for some 20 years. *What?* I had said no to heroic measures; we certainly hadn't talked about helping her die. I was miserable. I called Sarah and we cried about Mémère.

This was the first funeral I had to plan. I was thankful for the folks who had made many of the decisions; it was on me, though, to inform distant relatives, who'd be offended if not invited for final goodbyes.

I gave the eulogy. Many of the extended family and our friends went to the cemetery for final prayers and then on to the reception. Some were there because of Dad, some because of Dan, and others for me, most strangers to one another. It was comforting, though, that so many people came to show their respect.

Thanks to Sarah's bereavement leave, she was with me and gave me the hugs I needed, but we were painfully aware of our loss. When it was time for her to go, I drove her back to the airport. Neither of us was prepared to step back into our routine.

On my way home, as I approached Exit 20, I saw beautiful white clouds, stretching and swirling, as if in a lyrical ballet. I knew my mom and my sister were reunited somewhere beyond these wisps of fluff, and that offered me some solace.

Chloe: *I'M SO CONFUSED. Mama Sarah was here, but now she's gone. Why would she just pop in, then pop out? It's not Christmas. What's the deal?*

Casper: *Maybe cuz our mama seems extra sad. Something is wrong, but she won't talk to us. Maybe if we knew, we could give her extra attention.*

Chloe: *Humans haven't figured out that we're more than just a pretty face. We have feelings too. We're no longer roaming the countryside living off the land. Humans have domesticated us. But we must go by their rules. When they talk, we listen. When they don't, we must move on.*

Casper: *You think we ought to check in with Bailz and see what he thinks?*

Chloe: *Nah. We keep Mr. FluffnBuff for the big things. You know how much he needs his beauty sleep. We have each other. Let's go spoon on the couch.*

Casper: *Sounds good to me. What would I do without you?*

Chloe: *Not to worry. We're in this life together—forever.*

MY FRIENDS ENCIRCLED me at my mom's reception and referred to themselves as "Claire's girls." Made me feel warm and fuzzy—until it didn't. The one who coined the term drove a knife through my ego when on my next birthday card she wrote: "I hope someday you find what you're looking for." *Whack!*

The chill in the air across a wide swath of social connections since I'd left John made it obvious that I was the one who was frozen out. To them, girl meets guy; guy falls in love; guy buys ring; guy builds dream house; girl plops ring on bureau; girl says she's leaving; girl drives away.

I felt like I was the one on trial in *Twelve Angry Men*, a movie center-ing on deliberations in a murder case. Was the defendant innocent or guilty? Henry Fonda plays a juror who tries to go beyond what *must have* happened to understand what *really* happened.

Folks thought I was a fool for walking away from a man who would do anything for me. That's what they *saw*; they were clueless about what *really* happened. When I moved on with home renovations and overseas travel, the chatter got louder. They didn't understand the depth of my despair at another failed attempt at finding the white picket fence of my childhood. I wanted to live with a husband, two children, and my kitties. I wanted family.

THE 2005 HOLIDAY SEASON was our first without Mom. No one felt like celebrating, but at Thanksgiving, I felt the urge to hear Dad sing his favorite carol, so I brought the sheet music for "O Holy Night" to my brother's house. I appreciated that he and his wife, Donna, stepped up to host. Well, perhaps for nonprofessionals, a cappella is best in the shower. With Dad standing between Dan and me, we trilled through the first chorus, but my poor sister-in-law had trouble maintaining a poker face. I think we quit while we were behind . . .

I'D ALWAYS ENJOYED SINGING around the house. I remember belting out "Dancing Queen" through an imaginary microphone while baby Ryan admired himself in the mirror on his playmat. In 2006, I had the opportunity to test my chops in a ballroom filled with Mutual of Omaha home office brass, managers, and agents to celebrate boss

Con's retirement. The company had thanked him for more than 50 years of promoting its products with—for starters—a beautiful set of golf clubs.

Con gave me my career, turned my life around, believed in me when no one else did, gave me the opportunity to be financially independent. I had amassed a trunk full of awards that proved his faith in me. I wanted to serenade him with "To Sir with Love"—I was that grateful, and the lyrics were a testament to how special he was to me.

I practiced before the event and on the way, and I thought I sounded okay. The schedule had me perform somewhere amid all the speeches—when we'd all had a drink or two or three. Even though I had the song down pat, it's not like I had a regular gig at some club. When the master of ceremonies introduced me, I made my way to the podium. Confident, and wearing my favorite black slip dress, and once again a cappella, I sang as if my life depended on it.

The curtain fell on this shooting star. My secret ambition to be a chanteuse was nipped and tucked away once and for all. But it was important to me to express my appreciation to this brilliant mentor, this great friend. For 20 years we'd been a mighty team. To Con with love.

Now I was ready to transfer the broker portion of my business and assess my next move. How uncanny to find myself sought after by the new owner of the Moultonboro agency previously owned by one of my ex's best friends—the same gentleman who'd encountered me one evening at the Palace Theatre in Manchester. I didn't know what to expect from a man who hadn't socialized with me since 1984.

"You know, Claire, the real money in insurance is on the broker side." *Nice to see you too.*

The broker component had introduced me to new clients, but with no option for deferred dollars: that is, a retirement component. Most companies offer a savings plan and share in its accumulation. Omaha had Deferred Compensation—a ten-year extension of untaxed dollars following retirement from the company. But my broker business was unaffiliated; I was self-employed, on my own.

My business clients understood the need for some kind of transfer, so years of long hours didn't just end in a puff of smoke. It was serendipitous that I found a connection with a respected colleague. Dick and I had worked together through the state's Association of Health Underwriters. Now we agreed to a four-year payout for the transfer of my health business, the one component missing from his having a full-service agency.

Casper: *HEY, BAILZ. What's going on with Mama? I'm glad to be home and all, but it doesn't seem like home. You know what I mean?*

Bailey: *Oh, bloody hell. If it's not one thing, it's another. Her head has been in a whirl ever since we returned from that dreadful manor. But now nothing is ever enough for her. I'm sick of the pounding nails and the paint cans all over the place. Joey was right: Humans can get their knickers in a twist over nothing. We must get her attention and shake her up.*

Casper: *What do you have in mind?*

Bailey: *I say, she seems to have cast us aside for other pleasures. We must get in her face when she'll be forced to pay attention—dinnertime. Watch what I do and then come up right next to me. And don't you be giving me any stick, young man. I'm pulling rank, so you know your place. If I eat, you eat.*

Casper: *You think we should get Chlo in on it?*

Bailey: *Negative. Sometimes it's a man's job. The Brotherhood and all that. We bring in Queenie when the sting is needed. We can handle Mum.*

I HAD NO IDEA what got into Bailey and Casper. Every time I poured some wine and sat down in the three-season room with a hamburger or a piece of salmon, these two rascals leapt all the way onto the table looking for a taste. And they were in my face, bold as bees to nectar. Like they were here to help themselves to my dinner, no invitation necessary.

Who thinks animals belong on the table? But with no sharp rebuke, kitties rule. So okay, a tiny piece of hamburger for one and then the other. Okay, a few flakes of salmon for one and then the other. Night after night. Surely, this new routine was an aberration. Whatever happened to cat treats? Why was my meal suddenly their treat? There were meals when I felt like I hadn't eaten, but these boys were too cute to resist. Besides, they were good company. They were all I had.

A YEAR LATER, Dad and I traveled to Dan and Donna's for Thanksgiving; Sarah was here for a few days at Christmas, Dad joining us in the afternoon. These traditions were our last with the same cast of characters.

A turning point for Dad was on the horizon. Was I paying attention to the fact that he was 91 and had already surpassed both his parents by 20 years? Did I think he'd live forever? Now that I was vested with Omaha and no longer carrying the full weight of my broker business, didn't I have ample time to go see him?

Mom had always been a bit uncomfortable when I came for a visit and almost immediately headed for the back room, where Dad often sat to watch his TV shows. She wanted to know what we talked about when she wasn't with us, but I just wanted to attach myself to Dad.

Like somehow even for a few minutes I could be his buddy. Now, were there any questions left to be asked?

Dad was a huge Boston sports fan. I know I joined him for Super Bowl Sunday, not so much for the game itself, although I was taking note of the Patriots' handsome new quarterback; I was mostly into the commercials. (So many years later, I still had the sour taste in my mouth about getting an F in physical education in junior high.)

Over the years, there hadn't been a lot of opportunity for solo outings with Dad, who had no interest in movies and theater. He was a man's man, but women loved him because he was cute and kind. In fact, some of them on his mail route met him at the door in bikinis. Really. Music, though, he loved. Two of his favorite singers were Anna Maria Alberghetti and Gisele MacKenzie, whom he'd catch on television every so often. And like his sister, my aunt Marie, he enjoyed opera.

Meadowbrook (now renamed Bank of New Hampshire Pavilion), a local outdoor concert venue, was hosting the Irish Tenors, and Dad agreed to extend his bedtime to attend their evening performance. Dad always enjoyed classical music on PBS, and listening to a live concert of voices straight from heaven was worth the price of a late night. It could have been a disaster, though.

When it was over and time to find the car, there weren't any lights to show us the way. With Dad shuffling along with his cane and me at a loss as to which direction was best, we were like two blind mice searching for their hole in the wall. Maybe my angel sister guided us, but eventually, there was the car.

I joined him for lunch on occasion. Dad had picked up where Mom left off, making his dinner at noon with meat, vegetable, potato, and a slice of white bread—we didn't have a routine. If we had, I'd be feeling a whole better, knowing we had enjoyed every opportunity to be together.

MY MIND WAS ELSEWHERE. I had watched too many couples walking their pooch in the evening or taking strolls by the lake on a summer afternoon. It was time for me to be part of the mainstream and quit working day and night like a madwoman. My work schedule had lightened up, and I was ready for a dog. Finally. The pull of having a pal to accompany me outside of the house—whether for a walk, a hike, a Sunday drive—was so strong, I didn't consider the immediate difficulty in bringing a canine into a feline household.

Even though I can't say I had friends who had both—usually it was one or the other—I knew on some level it was doable. Kitties bring much companionship, but they're housebound. I wanted more than that. I needed more that. It was now or never.

Perhaps on some level I was willing to forgo my picket-fence dream. It had brought me nothing but pain. Instead, I'd find myself a pooch and together we'd figure out a new balance. After all, these kitties were well advanced in maturity. They'd continue to sleep their days away.

Reading the classifieds in the newspaper, I stopped at ads that said FOR SALE PUPS across the tristate area and Massachusetts, the distance I was willing to cast my net. I now had an envelope stuffed with prospects.

What suited me was either a cocker spaniel (à la Griff), a poodle (such intelligent dogs), or a Shih Tzu (cuteness overload). A pooch on my walking route caught my attention. Milly was a springer spaniel and such a sweet girl. I wanted my own Milly.

As it happened, there was an available male springer spaniel puppy in nearby Gilmanton. Why not check him out? Maybe I was hoping for kismet, but the little rascal couldn't bother to look my way—I didn't even warrant a *woof*. So what? I still wanted a dog.

Then I heard about a golden retriever pup that was part of a new reading program at the Gilford Library called Tales for Tails—an opportunity for young children to learn to read with a friendly puppy in the room. I thought the idea was brilliant, but the dog would have to be certified as a Therapy Dog.

Chloe: *HEY, LIL BRO. We need to talk.*

Casper: *I'm all ears for you, sis. What's up?*

Chloe: *I keep hearing Mama use the word* dog *when she's on the phone.*

Casper: *I've caught that sound too, but I like to live in the moment. I don't even worry before my next doctor visit. I just howl when I know it's gonna happen.*

Chloe: *Do you remember when Bailey got his dander up when John's friends visited and brought along a strange beast we'd never seen before? Do you think that was a dog?*

Casper: *By Joe, I think you may be on to something. We can't forget how upset he was over that invader. I think if Mama were to bring in something like that, our trusty leader would take care of business and know he's not welcome here.*

Chloe: *Yeah. You've got a point. That's why we elected him our leader after Joey passed. We'll leave it up to him to pass judgment. I know it won't take long. But why do you think Mama would even want to bring in another animal, especially one who doesn't look at all like us?*

Casper: *Maybe you need to take a hint from your little brother and live in the moment.*

Quit worrying. You know Bailey will protect us—and that's only if this creature got the stamp of approval from him in the first place. We are together forever. Nothing else matters.

Chloe: *I just love you, Caspie. I feel better already. Now let's head for the couch.*

Since age 40, Dad's heart had been cranky, first with a heart attack and then, in his 80s, with a quintuple bypass. He'd also had a pacemaker installed and, without being flip, he'd been able to maintain his normal activities without missing a beat.

I was 10 when he had the heart attack, so I didn't remember what life was like with Dad sidelined. The bypass had taken place after he helped me lay red stone tiles as a walkway to the front steps of my house on a hot summer day. Dad showed signs of being tired and had difficulty breathing. He'd always been a well-oiled machine from dawn till dusk. It had been most unsettling to see him struggling.

Once, I found myself in a terrible snowstorm. My street could be a slippery mess for hours, but making a 90-degree turn into a hill to get to my house was my worst nightmare. I'd been visiting the folks, but even their street was treacherous. Dad decided he'd drive me in his car and shovel/snow-blow me out.

"No, Dad. Please. I don't want you to drive. It's too dangerous. Please, let's just give the storm more time to settle."

I was pleading and then I cried—I was that concerned for his safety. But asking him to wait was like telling Dad the bull just blew through the back fence: Let's wait and see if he comes back on his own. Dad got into his Toyota RAV4 with me in the passenger seat, and off we went to brave treacherous roads and square me away in my driveway. He was not about to be dissuaded. When you've been astride a tractor since the age of three and had driven in the worst of snowstorms during 20 years of delivering mail, navigating my driveway was no big deal for this warrior. He never even fishtailed. And then he cleared my driveway.

Dad had always been a man of few words with me; only with his friends would he talk a blue streak. Today, my friends will describe me as a Chatty Cathy with a penchant for details, but when I was younger, Dad led by example.

He was a master of everything, from pool table to tennis court to gardening, from fishing to hunting, even to inventing whatever was needed around the house—like the time he built his own live-animal trap to entice a family of raccoons getting some vitamin D on my back deck. One by one, Dad caught the mother, the father, the teenagers, the toddlers, and the baby—practically a baseball team—and one by one brought them to the edge of Parade Road to drop them off in another set of woods. There was nothing he couldn't do.

Early in my homeownership, Dad saw to it that I had a lawn mower suitable for the daughter of a mechanic. We called her Nellie, a two-stroke engine requiring a mix of oil and gas in specific proportions. She performed her job well, over and around the ruts and slopes of my property line. A good ole girl, she eschewed the electric start. She often required three pulls to wake up. As she got older, she suffered from seasonal affective disorder and needed to soak in the sun's rays before her workday. One afternoon, I couldn't figure why she wouldn't start. I checked this and that and finally called Dad for help.

"I don't know what's up with Nellie," I told him. "She's in the sun. I turned on the gas. I gave her three pulls, then waited so as not to flood the engine. I don't know what's wrong with her." He came right over—of course he did.

Dad, all serious, went over to Nellie, looked at her from all angles, adjusted a lever, and voilà. I hadn't turned on the gas after all. He didn't utter a word, didn't laugh at my idiocy. Nope. Mission accomplished; he left and went home.

More than one person said I couldn't find happiness because no one measured up to my father.

ALTHOUGH DAD HAD MANAGED quite well with a cane, he now found himself at the same facility as Mom had been at, the St. Francis Rehab and Nursing Center. It was an adjustment to see him bedridden, but he was in 24-hour care. He was in good hands.

Now I could proceed with plans for another trip to Europe, a chance to break free from the tentacles of a broken motherhood that enslaved me on the home front. Made no difference that my children were now past school age. Grief has no expiration date, and it still hurt.

But I had come to grips with one thing—the days of schussing down a mountain at breakneck speed or scaling heights that could cause a nosebleed or lying on a beach in a bathing suit trying to look like cinnamon toast or wandering streets in a foreign city without knowing the language: Done!

Now I was ready for comfort and calm, with no decisions other than what to order at the dinner table. A river cruise was the perfect antidote for a life lived on the run. Think smooth jazz on repeat. With only a few more than 100 passengers across a two-story ship and a single dining room that shut down by eight o'clock, it was like one big happy family at Thanksgiving, sans the drama.

Whether you have a touch of ADHD or are soaked to your eyelids in the condition, you must look elsewhere for your entertainment. In other words, like in the fable of the turtle and the hare, think turtle. Otherwise, moving along at 10 mph will make you crazy. The only jolt occurs at daybreak when the ship enters a lock to pass from one level of water to another. By then, you've had your eight hours and it's time to seize the day!

My week at sea was simplicity from dawn to dusk. A few independent excursions cast a long sunbeam of smiles: shopping in

Strasbourg (France); touring a castle and being treated to a collection of white wines made on the premises (France); indoor dining in Rüdesheim am Rhein (Germany), where canines, not children, accompanied their people to dinner.

Welcome to western Europe, where the women are thin and so are the men; where bicycles rule the road; where food is locally sourced and fish is the main course; where canines are ranked one notch above the kiddos. Imagine a yearlong sabbatical from the frenetic lives of us keeping-up-with-the-Joneses types. Maybe in my next life.

Chloe: *Bailz, where's Pépère? Even when Auntie Shelley is babysitting us, he should be coming for a visit. We haven't seen him—do you know why?*

Bailey: *I know, Chlo-Chlo. It's been yonks since he's been here.*

Chloe: *I really miss him. He makes me feel like I'm the most beautiful kitty in all the world. He chuckles and calls me his Sweet Petunia when I push my head against his cap.*

Bailey: *It was obvious to us boys which of us was his pet. Still, I'm the only one who can wag a tail and expose the old tum-tum for a tickle.*

Chloe: *I don't like that he calls Caspie "Knucklehead." Sounds like he thinks Caspie is stupid but he's not—he's just shy.*

Bailey: *Pépère is just kidding. If our boy Casper made a show of cat-footing his way to him, Pépère would love it.*

Chloe: *Yeah, well, I like it the way it is. I'm Pépère's girl. But where is he? I miss him.*

Bailey feels the love. (1995)

Brothers from another mother: Joey and Bailey anticipate a treat. (1996)

Casper and Chloe, soulmates for life. (1996)

"There are only two ways to live your life.
One is as though nothing is a miracle.
The other is as though everything is a miracle."

—Albert Einstein

PART THREE

ACROSS A BRIDGE, in a faraway land, where the sun shines all day long, lies a place called Rainbow.

Marshmallow: *Snookums, why so quiet?*

Joey: *I've got a lot on my mind, sweets. I've just been given a new assignment.*

Marshmallow: *Oh no. You're gonna leave me again? Don't tell me your mama is in trouble.*

Joey: *Not exactly—she wants a damn dog. I thought she'd switch me out for that overpriced flame-point Persian she once drooled over at the cat show. Nope. Now she's got it in her head that a dog will make a difference in her life, that she won't be alone anymore.*

Marshmallow: *My goodness, and what about your brothers and sister? And why can't she be happy by herself?*

Joey: *Because she's a mama. She won't forgive herself for letting her children go. She wasn't thinking straight and got very bad advice and now it's a lifetime of feeling sorry for herself. You know, sweets, you and I never had a family of our own. Relationships are complicated.*

Marshmallow: *But what does she think a dog can do?*

Joey: *I not only kept an eye on her, but I also made sure my four siblings saw things my way. I was pack leader. This new assignment isn't for some newbie. Dogs still love to roam in the great outdoors, but their job is to please their owner. This time I'm determined to finish what I started. This mama will learn the secret to companionship, and no damn court document will ever take it away from her.*

Marshmallow: *Sounds like a lot of work. Good to be a cat curled up on a cushion without a care in the world.*

Joey: *I see it more as an adventure—maybe even the life I was supposed to have in the first place. Not exactly king-of-the-jungle stuff, but at least the dog is descended from the wolf. Better than nothing.*

Marshmallow: *How long will you be gone?*
Joey: *Not as long as the last time.*
Marshmallow: *I'll miss you, Snookums.*
Joey: *I'll miss you too, my sweet, but I'll be back.*

Early January 2008

THROUGHOUT MY CAREER, my favorite time was Sunday morning. No phone calls, no paperwork, just breakfast in my three-season room (post-2002). Smooth jazz CDs purring through the new sound system; a scented candle; the corner fireplace glowing warm with its doors open; the winter sun's rays streaming through the white birches; a stack of homemade pancakes glazed with butter and a drizzle of locally sourced maple syrup; and the two-pounder Sunday paper. It was the one day when I cherished my solitude.

Today I began with the classifieds section and was hit with this: FOR SALE. COCKSHEPOO PUPS. THREE MALES LEFT. PARENTS ON PREMISES. And a phone number.

Cockshepoo? as in cocker spaniel, shih tzu, poodle, all rolled into one? and local? Holy cow . . . um . . . cats . . . um, dogs! But was I ready? With a bulging envelope of 2x2" puppy ads tucked into a basket, it wasn't like I was rushing to judgment. For how many years had I wanted to walk a dog, no longer peering through a hazy lens of *Why-can't-it-be-me?* A dog struck me as more like having a baby. It was sure to be a lot of work, especially for a newcomer. But I wanted a dog. I dialed the number.

"Hello. I'm calling about the puppies you advertised for sale."

"Oh," said the gentleman who answered. "You'll have to speak to my wife. She's not here right now."

Turns out the breeder was familiar. In fact, when I started out with Mutual of Omaha, she rejected me when I approached her about disability insurance. No hard feelings. We set up a time to meet. The town of Gilford is Laconia's upscale sibling, what with its Governor's Island inhabitants of elite entrepreneurs and other superstars who want mountaintop homes. Longridge Farm Road brings balance, with its more-affordable housing and expansive farmlands where pups might await their forever homes.

Situated on a corner lot attached to a doggie day care/grooming center, the modest Cape belied the energy pulsing within its walls. The welcoming committee came out from every which way. Mother Daisy, a 14-pound cocker spaniel with a few shih tzu genes from an unknown beau, had such short legs that she could've been mistaken for a dachshund. These were her first puppies. Dad Boomer was a regal 28-pound cream poodle. The quiet one, he let his mate do the talking. Keesha, Daisy's grandmother, and Oreo, Daisy's aunt, and one domestic kitty rounded out the menagerie.

The breeder, Grace, took me into the parlor, where tucked against a wall was a pen with three tiny chocolate brown pups, looking like they'd been rolled in the mud. Only three boys remained from the litter; two girls had already been adopted. As I approached the pen, one pup separated himself from his brothers, who were yapping against the side of the pen. This little guy came forward and looked at me like he knew who I was. *Do I know you?* he seemed to be asking. He was so adorable! It was obvious from his short legs that he took after his mom.

If I was going to raise him to be a Therapy Dog, I'd need one with a calm personality. I picked up this cocoa puff and set him on a table so I could get a better look at him. It was just for a second—he wanted to be near his mother.

"I like him," I told Grace, "but I'm not sure I'm ready yet. I think I'll have to wait another year."

"Just so you know, this is my last litter," Grace said. "Their birth has changed Daisy, and she's become ornery. I don't want to chance passing on that trait to another litter."

So sweet, this pup. *Do I walk away and hope to find one just like him a year from now?* I wondered. I realized it could be a challenge to introduce a canine into a feline household, and without experience. He'd grow up to be between his parents in weight. I could carry him if need be.

I just wrote a bit of, um, doggerel:

> Not sure if I chose to walk away
> Or called back within a day,
> But why not take a giant leap forward
> Perhaps to be scorned or maybe rewarded.

Somehow, I felt compelled to act. I wanted this little guy.

Joey: *HOW MANY TIMES would I need to reinvent myself? First, I was a lion cub destined to rule the jungle. When that fell through, I was reassigned as a smooshed-in-faced domestic. No royalty there, but I had chutzpah and my siblings let me rule the household. At least we were all cats.*

Now I was on a real adventure. But it was all about Mama. For some reason, she had her heart set on a dog. Then doggone it, I'm in. But dang, this time around I wasn't even a purebred—just a mutt with a price tag. And I was a damn midget. My brothers lucked out with Daddy's legs and already towered over me.

Of course, this transition could've failed miserably if Mama hadn't made that call to Grace. I hoped she'd want a boy dog. Good that both my sisters were adopted.

I knew Mama didn't recognize me. How could she? She didn't possess the instinct to steer herself away from trouble or recognize a gift when it was staring her in the face.

That's where we besties come into play, and that's why I'm back. She's still feeling sorry for herself because she's not like the other mothers in town.

Besides, it wouldn't be an adventure if I came in with a bullhorn. I had my marching orders: Make eye contact; ignore the jostling of my brothers; and keep my mouth shut, so I could seem to be the quiet one. I had eyes only for her. Again. Maybe I'm not quite as adorable as my former self, but as everyone knows, puppies are irresistible.

I HAD TWO WEEKS before he was old enough to leave his mom. I needed a name; I needed *stuff*. Facebook friends helped with the name. It came down to Toby or Brady. Tom Brady, the Patriots quarterback, had just come off a 16-0 season. I tried it out: *Brady, Bailey, Casper,* and *Chloe.* Yep, that was it. Thanks for the suggestion, Diane.

My friend Helen, a seasoned canine mom, advised me on the minutiae of doggie life. She even set me up with a run from the deck to the shed—very handy for midwinter midnight potty calls for the young and untrained. I took a deep breath. I was as ready as I could be.

Joey: *FOUR YEARS, THREE MONTHS, 15 DAYS. That's how long I'd been away. Embarrassing to be carried in like a baby, but I hadn't exactly mastered the art of staying upright. Mama set me up with a playpen next to the desk where she spent her day working. At least she was no longer in her office. Good thing I hadn't been told about this level of confinement, though, like I was incapable of being trusted. Pfft. Not for long—I was gonna be outta here sooner rather than later. Hopscotching seven years in the space of one, I figured I'd be pushing my weight around in no time.*

Some things didn't change. Casper and Chloe beat an exit to their favorite couch in the den—butt to butt, of course. Like Mama, they had no clue who they were dealing with. Bailey barely lifted his head, but I knew what he was thinking: What took you so long? It's a bit weird not to use a litter box cuz it's always staring me in the face, but I must remember who I am and where I come from (this time).

We jungle dwellers don't need our mothers to lead us by the nose to do potty. But I was stuck with Mama's schedule. The good news was that this stage of my life would be short; the bad news was that I was reduced to using pee pads for an emergency. But Mama was no dummy and took me out every couple of hours. Friends told her I'd never be able to hold my bladder if she kept this up. She ignored them. Good for her.

My first night was the worst night of all my lives. I was alone and caged. I wanted O U T and was plenty vocal about it. I guess Mama could hear me even though she was nowhere to be found. I missed my siblings (again), and Bailey was no help. Mr. Fluff-nBuff hadn't changed a bit. Nothing interfered with his beauty rest.

THAT FIRST NIGHT was a tough one for me. I was ensconced upstairs, far from the entry room where I put his crate. Because he was so tiny, Helen advised me to divide his crate in half to provide him with a little wiggle room to do his business should the need arise. But I swear he never stopped crying. A pitiful wail. I'm sure being away from his mother and siblings for the first time didn't help. As I say, it was tough.

Thank goodness Helen stopped by after work the next day. I hadn't slept much—I felt helpless about getting Brady through this adjustment period.

"I thought I'd check on you and Brady," she said.

"Oh, Helen. I don't know. I may have made a big mistake. He cried all night and I'm exhausted. And I cried too, because that's what I do when I'm tired."

"It'll get better, I promise. Please give it time."

Of course, Helen was right, and I'll always be grateful for her reassurance and kindness.

Brady: *MAMA WASTED NO TIME introducing me to the outdoors, with little walks in the neighborhood. Three times a day. It was exhausting at first, but it gave Mama a break from her work and got us to bond.*

I could tell how nervous she was. She didn't know yet that I could sniff out her moods—that I knew when she was sad and even frightened. She kept talking about taking me hiking, so I had to get my legs in shape. Our walks opened my eyes to what I hadn't been able to see with my nose pressed against a windowpane. In fact, my nose took some getting used to. Seems like I could detect scents well past my neighborhood and deep underground, but I couldn't for the life of me figure out what belonged to whom.

One week later

Chloe: *BAILZ, WHO, WHAT is this stranger living with us?*

Casper: *Yeah, I mean it wakes me up in the middle of the night howling or crying—I can't tell which that noise is.*

Chloe: *It sure doesn't look like us, and it's be getting bigger by the day.*

Casper: *If I wasn't twice his size, I'd be scared stiff.*

Bailey: *As your commander in chief, it's my duty to inform you that I'm fairly certain it's really our brother Joseph back from the beyond.*

Chloe: *No way.*

Casper: *How can that be?*

Bailey: *Really? With all my leadership skills you've admired for years, I can't believe you'd even think of questioning me. Mum calls him Brady.*

Chloe: *That does sound like a boy's name.*

Casper: *Why didn't he come back looking like his old self?*

Bailey: *Listen up! Let's give the little chap more time and see if he can cut it.*

ONE DAY I CAME HOME to find Chloe inside Brady's pen—curiosity had gotten the best of her, I guess. But it didn't take long for her to exit, stage right. Just long enough for me to grab a picture to prove I wasn't hallucinating.

Brady: *HEY, WHAT ARE YOU DOING in my space? This is mine.*

Chloe: *Oops, so sorry, my mistake. I'm outta here.*

Bailey: *Well, I'll be gobsmacked. You could knock me over with a feather. Is this really you, Joe? Pray tell, what took you so long?*

Brady: *Yep, in all my glory, bro. My last mission with Mama got me rave reviews from the brass, so I got promoted to Special Ops and granted a pass to address a brewing crisis. When Mama got it in her head to get a dog, I couldn't very well hang around with my sweetie and watch her bring any old ragtag mutt in here to take charge of my family, now could I?*

Bailey: *So I suppose you've returned to save the day, to quote, well, you.*

Brady: *That's it in a dog bone. But I gotta tell you, bro. Being a canine takes some getting used to.*

Bailey: *Knock yourself out, big boy. Over and out. I'm exhausted from heading up this household. It's all yours.*

Brady

OF COURSE, HAVING BEEN AN INDOOR KITTY, I never got a chance to meet our neighbors. I guess Mama hadn't either, what with her busy schedule. So now, one day after a snowstorm, we tackled a longer route from home and saw a lady shoveling her walk. She came over to check out this fine specimen of puppyhood and introduce herself. Her name was Mary and she and her husband, Herb, had been living in their house for more than 40 years. Although she didn't have a cat or a dog, she loved them both.

She oohed and aahed over me. How appropriate, right? I knew we were going to see a lot more of her.

Weekends were spent with Auntie Helen and her boys—Jack, a beagle-hound mix, and Duffy, an all-black poodle—at Ahern State Park, a large tract of land on Lake Winnisquam. In time I learned there were many trails, but in these early weeks, we kept to the main one. Both Jack and Duffy were off leash, and Auntie Helen encouraged Mama to turn me loose because I would follow Jack. Something about pack mentality. Whatever that is. With some hesitancy, Mama agreed, and I was off and running best I could to keep up with him.

Whee! That was way more fun than I thought it would be. Way more fun than lying around all day sleeping my life away. But uh-oh. Seems I had a real issue with being ten weeks old. All of a sudden, I was neck deep in frigid waters! I'd followed Jack a little too close to the shore and broke through the ice. Mama was practically hysterical, watching me do the dog paddle. She didn't know I could swim—and, by the way, wasn't I fabulous!

Cool cucumber Auntie kept calling "Come, Brady, come" until I got close enough for her to pull me in the rest of the way, soaking wet and shivering, Mama opened her parka, put me inside, and zipped me up while almost running to the car.

It was a good thing my siblings were still at paw's length with me and didn't ask any questions, except, of course, for Mr. FluffnBuff.

Bailey: *What in the blazes . . .*

Brady: *Let me put it this way. Life outside these walls is full of surprises.*

Bailey: *You always did pine for the great outdoors. I remember you once got out and climbed a tree. For observation, you said.*

Brady: *Yeah, I remember. That was great. But now I want to hear what happened in my absence. I see we're all still here, same house. What happened to John?*

Bailey: *Good grief! What a pig's ear that was. You're not gonna believe this, but it was Chlo-Chlo who saved the day.*

Brady: *Our Chloe? No way!*

Bailey: *Abso-bloody-lutely, old chap. She owned it! We were in the new house—I thought it was like a mausoleum—and John was being a stuffed shirt about everything. Mum was pasty-white and kept drinking some kind of liquid, like she needed extra hydration, but I don't think it was tuna water. In any event, we had to do something. So I worked my magic and drove John nutty singing "God Save the Queen" as I went back and forth to bring each of my fave stuffies up the giant staircase.*

Brady: *Cool! Then what happened?*

Bailey: *It was do or die time for us, mate. I needed the Chlo-Chlo to jump onto their bed when Mum and John were ready for sleep and scare them. Casper was riding shotgun in case she needed help. The little minx really got into it—she bounced around, screeching out some mumbo-jumbo. The language, mate! She played an absolute blinder.*

Brady: *Can't believe this! She barely left the couch cushion with Casper unless Pépère was visiting.*

Bailey: *Well, Pépère was nowhere to be seen. Maybe that's it—when I told her the plan, she gave it all she had just so she could see him again.*

Brady: *What did John do?*

Bailey: *Blimey! He shot off the bed and yelled, "That's it! No more cats!" Chloe with Casper in tow leapt off the bed and the three of us blew down the stairs in the blink of an eye. John slammed the doors. I don't know what happened after that.*

Brady: *Wow! I'm so proud of you sibs. Don't think I could've done better myself.*

Bailey: *So the good news is that next day, after John left for work, Mum loaded a whole bunch of stuff into her car. She left for a while, came back, and loaded more, but left enough room for us. She then scooped me up, and Casper, and Chloe was last. All the time we'd been living there, Chloe was nowhere to be seen. But that day, she knew. We were going home, and she stood smack dab in the middle of the living room and let Mum pick her up.*

Brady: *You never know about girls. Maybe that's their ace up their paw. Unpredictable. One of these days I'll have to thank her for her service.*

Bailey: *Good luck with that. She's pretty skittish around you. Never seen a canine before except when John and his friends brought in some scuzzbucket. I quite knew how to get him to leave and not come back. As for our Chloe, it'll take some work.*

Brady: *Well, I'm not head cheese of this family for nothing. Soon she won't be able to resist my adorable self. Now let's have ourselves a snooze. I can't take any more surprises. Zzzz*

Brady

IT WASN'T EASY BEING ME—*super pup with an eye on the past and a nose for the future. In our own ways, Mama and I were together to forge ahead, like in damn the torpedoes. Mama and I pushed ourselves to cross that bridge at Ahern so we could walk along the lake without Auntie Helen watching over us. I liked the chill of snow halfway up my legs, almost to my boy parts. I figured I might as well dip my nose in the white stuff too. After all, I was a Sagittarius.*

When we were in the woods, I felt like this was who I was supposed to be. It was amazing to be able to mark my territory everywhere I went. What a rush to know that whoever came behind me would know I'd been here—me, king of the animal kingdom. Goodbye, litter box. Hello, tree.

Now I could run like the wind. Who cared that these stumps for legs could get me only so far. Still, even on leash, I leapt over logs and brush, and the sensation of my ears flapping in the breeze made me howl with glee. Mama kept right up with me. She wanted to make sure I didn't take another dip. But it was frustrating—actually, embarrassing—that I couldn't manage a simple staircase back home. Hoping none of my siblings caught sight of my flips and tumbles.

Casper: *Whoa, I never thought I'd see the day when hot shot Joey-Brady couldn't get his butt up or down the stairs. Sure wish I had a camera.*

Chloe: *You know, bro, from how fast he's growing, I have the sinking feeling that before we know it, he'll conquer the stairs and start pushing us around.*

Casper: *It's times like this when I wish I wasn't such a wuss. But I can't help myself. Being the runt of the litter has damaged me for life.*

Chloe: *That's okay, little brother. That's why you have me. I'll protect you against big bad Brady.*

By late April, except for that unfortunate dunk in Lake Winnisquam, my new little boy and I had settled into a comfortable routine. It was easier than I thought, or maybe I got lucky. He amused himself or napped in his playpen while I worked. His toilet training was a breeze—like he already knew what to do.

What with the kitties asleep most of the day, it was often just the two of us. For 20 years I'd been alone in my downstairs office, with an occasional visit from Casper when he wanted to nap atop the window or Joey when contractor Andy had an appointment. With a phone glued to my right shoulder, I barely left my desk. I was too busy to pay attention to how much of my day was spent alone being serious. Now I found myself giggling over the least little thing. Brady loved the snow, sticking his nose in it and shaking his head side to side. So cute.

Soon we met a woman who changed our lives forever. Stacy ran a canine day care named after her chocolate lab, Kovio. She too went to Ahern. Helen was with us the day we were introduced as she and Kovio were approaching the parking lot. A few minutes one way or the other, and we'd have missed her. But here was an angel. Not that she looked like one—none of them does.

She was the Pied Piper of canines. Made no difference regarding breed, dogs who were accepted into her day care knew better than to cross her. She commanded respect and expected obedience, and dogs loved her for her consistency. She was the Alpha. Stacy was Mama 2.

Meanwhile, I was noticing a change in Dad. Now when I visited him, he often spoke of a particular nursing assistant. She was of color, and she was large, very large. Something triggered Dad's attraction to this woman. He probably recognized not only that he needed her, but also that she was caring for him, and he was grateful.

He would tell me he loved her. I wish I'd asked a few questions—all I know is that somehow their conversation turned to the Second Amendment, and Dad gave her one of his prized rifles. I don't remember which one, but it must have had special meaning for him to have kept it well passed his hunting days. But he held on to the .38 Special he kept under his pillow at night as he lay in wait for any possible marauder.

WITH DAD STABILIZED, I felt it was time for Sarah and me to begin a new adventure: mother-and-daughter Mother's Day trips. Brady was under Auntie Stacy's care and the kitties were now tended to by Auntie Taia, a granddaughter of Mom and Dad's best friends. My goodness, the woman had a menagerie of ten Maine Coon cats.

For two years I had flown to Maryland to experience any number of epicurean delights, boutiques, and rooftop cocktails with my mini-me. Savannah was our first official after-college weekend getaway. I even prepared myself with *Midnight in the Garden of Good and Evil*, by John Berendt, a fascinating tale about the murder of a local celebrity of sorts, with an array of colorful characters. Anyway, the weekend was a huge success. From a hotel bordering the historic district, we were in walking distance of just about everything.

Sarah was working for TEK Systems, the nation's largest privately owned IT HR firm, following stints in banking and insurance. During our weekend, she occasionally had to be on the phone managing a prospect, and I found myself sipping a glass of wine as I waited for her.

I took her picture beneath a tree dripping with Spanish moss. She was no longer the shy teenager of our Boston days and was happy to pose. Another one, taken on this inaugural trip just after a wine-tasting, is one of my favorites: the two of us side by side on a bench.

We had a full schedule of shops, a spa, restaurants, a ride in a horse-drawn carriage, a ghost tour, even a Sara Evans concert. It couldn't have been any better—until it couldn't have ended any worse. My brother texted me on Saturday morning to say that Dad had been transferred to the hospital because of a combination of respiratory and cardiac issues.

My cousin JP, who was an EMT on that service call, told me he thought he was going to lose Dad in the ambulance. Dad was stabilized, and Sarah and I would finish our stay. But on Sunday morning Dan called: "I think he's waiting for you."

SUNDAY EVENING, when I got home, I went straight to the hospital. Dad was lucid, and I couldn't take in that he was going to die. The next day I got a call from hospice's Dr. Carrie. She told me she'd approved morphine for him, and that bothered me a little. I contacted the hospital to ask if I could bring Bailey for a visit. I'd brought him a few times to the nursing home and Dad enjoyed seeing the kitty. (I would've brought Chloe too, but she was a wiggle worm and skittish away from Casper.) Bailey—Mr. Nonchalant—could travel anywhere. That lump of fluff, huge as he was, and with his size 15 feet, was portable. The hospital said okay.

Dad was always so happy to see Bailey. When I set the kitty on Dad's belly, Bailey stayed—for a minute or so. Still, I felt like I was doing the right thing. I told Dad I'd be back later. Brady needed his afternoon walk, and I wanted to get dinner started to make it easier for me when I got back from our evening visit. For the walk, I remember I decided on Garfield Street, which extends the length of South Main and pretty much guaranteed we'd be gone for a half hour. I wasn't there when Dad's friends and neighbors came to see him. I planned to be with Dad after his dinner.

When I arrived, Dad was sleeping. I remember leaning down and whispering, "I'm here, Daddy." I thought he was dozing. I had brought the *Citizen*, the local paper, to read until he woke up. I sat in a chair near his bed. I could hear his steady breaths, in and out, and then—nothing. I stood up and walked over to him. He was too quiet. I ran out of the room to find his nurse. She looked at Dad, frowned, and left hurriedly to get her stethoscope. She put it to his chest: "He's gone."

Wait a minute! I didn't get to say goodbye. The nurse said Dad knew I was coming back—that I'd be with him when Yvette came to get him. But I didn't hold his hand. I didn't tell him how much I loved him. This was it.

THERE'S SOMETHING ABOUT THE DEATH of the second parent. When I lost Joey, both my parents were there to comfort me. When I lost Mom, there was Dad. For the first time in my life, I was the real grownup, the oldest Hebert. I was the matriarch, but in my case, the matriarch of what?

I called Sarah. Most of the funeral arrangements were already in place. Dad's best friends were pallbearers. Dan gave the eulogy. I remember the ending: "Dad, I guess I'll see you on the other side."

Brady

I MAY HAVE BEEN A YOUNG PUP, *but I wasn't stupid. I was quite capable of grabbing a crumb here and there and putting two and two together. We lost my siblings' Pépère. Mama brought me over to meet him after she picked me for my cuteness. She plopped me onto his bed, but frankly, our meeting wasn't a where-have-you-been-I-missed-you-so-much visit.*

He just wasn't into me, and I'll be honest, I wasn't into him either. We weren't a good fit. He was in a bed, unable to offer me a single treat. I was far too rambunctious to sit quietly. Heck no, I just wanted off that bed.

Mama Sarah showed up. Of course, she cooed over my adorable face, but she didn't recognize the real me. For that matter, neither did Mama. I figured I'd mind my p's and q's and bide my time like a good boy.

Brady

WHEN I WAS JOEY, it was my decision to forgo a life of leisure and keep an eye on her. But there was just so much I could do before I crossed the Rainbow Bridge.

Now, Mama decided I should be a therapy dog. She enrolled me in a Beginner class to learn the basic commands—sit . . . down . . . stay . . . come . . . heel— that is, to boss me around. These lessons were as much for her as for me, though, and I got it. Left to our own devices, I'd be dragging Mama around, I'd investigate every smell, my leash would get tangled and one of us would trip over it, she'd either laugh or cry. Hey, maybe someday I could train her.

No surprise that everyone was bigger than I was. Story of my lives.

I was at Mama's mercy when we practiced the commands on our walks. The one I was weakest on was "heel." Ugh. I hated it. If Mama could've thought like a dog, she'd realize that a first-time pup wants nothing to do with walking side by side. How could I protect her if I wasn't out front keeping an eye out for an enemy?

I wasn't the star pupil, and maybe that's why she decided I needed another trainer, for private lessons. Really? I wasn't pleased with this interruption in my otherwise wonderful life. We met the woman at her barn in Belmont, a few miles from home. I didn't like her from the start, and it was probably mutual. She gave me the heebie-jeebies. Like don't ever cross her. She didn't compare with Miss Jeannine, my group trainer.

She already acted like she was mad at me. She grabbed my leash and deposited me at one end of the barn. Now I was facing her and Mama, who stood some distance away. I couldn't understand what she wanted me to do. This was no way to talk to my pint-sized but always adorable self. I stood, frozen. Then she started yelling at me and scared me and, oops, I peed myself. Mama scooped me up, called me her precious boy, told me it was okay, that it was "stress pee" and that she wouldn't let anyone scare me again. We never went back. Mama regrouped and thought of a better way to complete my education.

Bailey: *I'M EXHAUSTED WATCHING YOU arse over elbow these days.*

Brady: *How quickly you forget.*

Bailey: *Not true. Here you are, a pint-sized version of my former sled-dog self, and I still see you tripping over yourself. Don't go silly-billy on me.*

Brady: *Hold on. You told me you dreamed you were a famous sled dog suffering temperatures unfit for canine. That's not the same. Look at me. I'm the real deal.*

Bailey: *Oh, so now we're in a reality competition? Who's the one all stuck up about being king of the jungle? Real or not real?*

Brady: *Why do we always have to get into it? Can't you accept the fact that now I have it all? I'm back in my cozy home but also get a chance to poke around the neighborhood. I even have a big-boy seat in Mama's car so I can see out the window. But the woods—now that's the dog's bark.*

Bailey: *Well, good for you, not-so-big boy. Enjoy it while you can. Life moves at a much faster pace when you're a dog.*

Brady: *I'll take that under advisement, but right now I could use a snooze. Zzzzz*

Brady

I WAS ONLY SIX MONTHS OLD, but already I'd taken another giant step in my development: I passed inspection for Auntie Stacy's day care. She didn't accept any old (or young) mongrel. She was fussy about who could come into her home—any shenanigans from either the human or her pooch and it was bye-bye. Call us the pick of the litter.

Kovio was the pack leader and showed us the way along a path in the woods. Auntie wasn't taking us to Ahern, so it was a new adventure. It was important to stay on the trail, or Auntie leashed you up. Then you wouldn't be able to investigate the bushes or grab a quick drink downstream. I'd never been part of a pack, but it was cool being surrounded by wagging tails. Of course, doggies always look for a lost tail or two and can't resist a quick sniff up the backside. Auntie was okay with that but drew the line at—how can I be delicate; I guess I can't—humping. It was kind of scary not being in control of my impulses, but sometimes I felt the urge . . . Anyway, if I wanted a treat, I had to be a good boy. No humping. Hmmm. So much to remember.

It dawned on me that housebound felines couldn't miss what they never had: family. But they did have friends—each other, and then me. I was grateful for Bailey, Casper, and even Chloe. So what if the feeling wasn't mutual with her? But at day care, I got to choose pals, who became like an extended family. I picked Benjamin and Bella, both black peekapoos. Because I was a bit bigger, they followed my lead, and I could wow them with my unbelievable cuteness. Auntie Stacy took us young'uns for just one walk a day, but big boys and girls got two. I was having so much fun that I didn't even wanna nap. But at home, back in my crate, after all the fresh air and exercise, my eyes closed before my head even hit the cushion.

Meanwhile, back on the home front, the more my leash walking improved, the farther Mama and I ventured from home. One day, on our late-afternoon walk, we headed up Pine Hill. I was tired but too proud to show it. As we turned around for home, Mama saw one of her clients. I was cool with strangers so of course I headed over to him for a pet. Well, no sooner did I get close to the man than his own dog blew out the kitchen door and started to pummel me. He was a flipping boxer, for crying out loud! What chance did I have against this towering machine of lean muscle mass with a face only a mother (or father) could love?

Mama was again beside herself, scared to death her beloved pup was about to be eviscerated. Thank goodness, the man grabbed the mongrel and hauled him back into the house. "He's just excited," he tried to explain. That was my first important outdoor lesson: Beware the consequences of encroaching on another canine's property. I got it, but I knew that having stumps for legs would be my downfall if I didn't develop a strategy to protect myself.

Brady

I WAS STILL SOMEWHAT CONFUSED about the differences between dogs and kitty cats. For example, one cat's day is much the same as another. Another example: Owners are at their beck and call. What I was learning was that canine adventures were a mixed blessing. A dog can handle most of life's ups and downs, his and his owner's. Of course, some challenges might require the right attitude.

Let's take my grooming day. As a pup in training, I was trusting when Mama dropped me off at Barking Bubbles. Frankly, a better name would have been Chamber of Torture. What happened to my tongue as my washcloth? Why can't I regain the luster of my beautiful mane with a few sweeps of this trusted organ? As if being dunked in a tub of sudsy water attached to a humongous nozzle wasn't humiliating enough, getting a haircut with a blow-dry was the ultimate indignity. I guessed I could forget about a third round as a Bouvier des Flandres or a Grand Basset Griffon Vendeen with benefits of height, weight, and distinctive breeding. Those hot shots probably required weekly maintenance. Maybe I needed to rethink the darn boxer—no haircuts needed, just a spray from the outdoor spigot and he would be good to go.

Bailey: Goodness gracious me. Where have you been? Auditioning for a movie? And what's that odor?

Brady: I'll keep it simple. It seems dogs aren't capable of managing their own hygiene—we need a groomer for a bath and a clip.

Bailey: *Fancy that. I'll hold my tongue. On second thought, I could use a little sprucing up myself. Excuse me while I clean up a bit. My face needs a good lick.*

Brady: *You really know how to hurt a guy.*

Bailey: *Before I laugh my tail off, it's high time you reacquaint yourself with your two other siblings.*

Brady: *But bro, you know me—love being boss man. Now I just walk in and they scatter. What a rush!*

Bailey: *Slow down, big fella. We're still a family. They've never seen a dog, and you're bigger than we are. We're all fine with your being our leader again, but help them understand that you're still the old Joey.*

Brady: *Okay. I get your point. I'll go find them.*

A minute later

Chloe: *YIKES. HERE COMES THE WILD ONE. Let's hightail it out of here.*

Casper: *Beat ya.*

Chloe: *The countertop! Now!*

A minute later

Brady: *NO LUCK. THIS ISN'T MY DAY. First, I'm clipped almost naked by a stranger. Then my own siblings taunt me with leaps onto my favorite counter. I refuse to have a conversation while they tower over me. How do you think that makes me feel?*

Bailey: *Snap out of it. Think positive. Look at all your exciting adventures. No day is ever the same for you. Give us cats our due. We sleep . . . we eat . . . we purr . . . we use our litter box (usually). And yes, we leap onto counters, desks, chairs, and tables. We even climb curtains. But that's the total of our existence.*

Brady: *You're right. You've always been the brains to my brawn. In fact, you've worn me out with your logic. Zzzzzz*

Brady

BAILEY WARNED ME MY LIFE would proceed at a much different pace. I had graduated to Miss Jeannine's Intermediate class. "Wait!" and "Leave it!" were tough, considering my innate stubbornness. Although I was a delightful blend of both my parents, it was Mom Daisy's obstinate nature that kept me from being anybody's pushover. But love for Mama meant I tamped down that aspect of who I was, and I settled in once again as the obedient student.

Mama recognized a woman at the class and off we went for introductions. Gil's pup, Emma, was an authentic cockapoo (unlike me, with the "oops"). She was full of spirit and loved to stand on her long back legs. She towered over me. (Okay, everybody towers over me.) Mama suggested that Gil bring Emma to Auntie Stacy's day care for an outlet for some of the pup's excess energy.

In a few days, Emma joined Ben, Bella, and me, and the four of us romped through the woods together. At naptime, though, Emma wouldn't settle down—only after Auntie Stacy set her in my crate would she be quiet. I was cool with her company—fed my ego.

My home crate was another matter. I waited a lifetime for the freedom to express my true self in the great outdoors, and I did appreciate most of my new adventures. But being stuck in this crate was getting on my nerves. It didn't help that I had a direct view of the countertop, where Casper and Chloe kept tabs on me from their aerial perch. It was all crushing my spirit.

Being a dog among feline siblings took some adjustment. I felt like I had a paw in each world. For example, just relieving my bladder was confusing. Sometimes I squatted and sometimes I lifted my leg. Was this the difference between being in touch with my feminine side and showing off my manhood? But does it matter? Not in the animal kingdom. Good to be us.

Although I missed leaping onto my favorite hangouts to oversee my territory, I did love the rip-roaring freedom of scouring the woods. At home, I understood that Mama had to secure my whereabouts. I mean, I did chew on one of her new gray suede shoes. And then there was the time I gnawed off the bottom edge of her rolltop desk and nibbled the fringe on her dining room rug. As a feline, I never would have eaten *something for the sheer fun of chewing, but these choppers had a mind of their own. It wasn't my fault.*

I'VE NEVER BEEN GOOD AT GUESSING—need to know my material cold. So, what would happen if I let Brady on my bed, a haven for three cats? Would there be high-pitched screeching like I remember as a kid? What happens in the woods when a lone wolf invades another's den?

A friend warned me that there'd be no turning back—no U-turn if I gave Brady access to my bed. I debated. Brady had learned quickly to wait for his walk instead of using our home as his litter box. He showed amazing bladder control. But could he share me with the cats? Would the cats accept him?

Chloe: *I REFUSE TO SLEEP with that mutt. I don't care who he was . . . who he is . . . who he will be. I have my pride. If Mama was one of us, she wouldn't sleep with her opposite.*

Casper: *Um, did you forget the whole John mess?*

Chloe: *Of course not. We all remember how that turned out. She doesn't learn her lesson. She ignores her little voice and ends up upset and frustrated. Follow in my paw prints, little brother, because I've been watching her for a long time. We can learn from her mistakes. I'm sticking to my guns.*

Casper: *Maybe it's a guy thing, but I don't think he's all that bad.*

Bailey: *You twits woke me from a good dream. What's all the ruckus?*

Casper: *Chloe is all riled up that Mama is letting Brady out of his crate. Now he leaps onto the bed and sleeps with her and Chloe refuses to accept this new situation.*

Bailey: *You know, Chloe, you're shooting yourself in the paw. Brady is a lot younger than we are and will likely outlive us. Do you really want to give up snuggle time with Mum just because your nose is out of joint?*

Chloe: *Look, I know I'm stubborn. I know I'm giving up a routine I love. Still, I'll walk away rather than compromise my values.*

Bailey: *What a piece of work you are! I've seen you in action, and you can be a formidable adversary. Have you looked at your nails lately? You have any idea how quickly you could rearrange Brady's face if he invaded your space? Mum's bed is plenty big enough for all of us.*

Chloe: *Bailey, you've always been wise and sensible. And maybe part of me agrees with you. I'll admit it—I've got a heaping dose of cattitude. But that's my choice . . . my prerogative as a female. So let me go sulk on my couch and feel sorry for myself. You coming, Casper?*

Casper: *Count on it.*

ONCE BRADY GRADUATED from both his playpen and the crate, I bought him a dog bed with his name stitched across the top and a couple of others that were fleece-lined—just because. I put them between the dining room and kitchen, and of course the cats gravitated away from their own furry mats to these new beds. After all, they used any piece of furniture to snooze on—maybe they thought these too were part of their domain. What struck me as strange, though, was that Brady liked an old oval cat bed and would cradle his head against the side for support. It was too small for him, even from the beginning. But day after day, that's where I'd find him, spilling over the sides. Why?

Wait just a minute!

That was Joey's bed! I thought about Brady's soulful eyes. Why did he seem older than his years? Was I seeing things? Was it simply a coincidence that he chose Joey's old bed? It was like he was right back at home. I thought back to our introduction. He had picked me before I picked him, just like it had been with Joey.

Brady

THERE WERE MORE ADVENTURES at Ahern for Mama and me before we moved on to less hazardous duty. I'd just graduated from Intermediate class, and Mama knew she had to trust that I'd follow her command once she unclipped me from my leash. She was so nervous. I could almost hear her prayers that I wouldn't bolt and run. No, Mama. I'm a good boy. I'll stay.

I roared whenever Mama's car came onto the dirt road leading to the woods and I recognized where we were headed. Most of the time we had the whole place to ourselves, like it was my personal playground, and it brought out the beast in me. I couldn't help myself. I was at full bark. King Brady had arrived.

I was having the time of my life—until.

I didn't see them coming. We were heading home, just about at the top of the hill before the downhill to the parking lot and who caught sight of me: two hooligans who at full sprint were barreling toward me. Holy dogs! What could I do? Where could I go? Where was the trusty picnic table under which I could crawl away from hound dogs with long legs? Darn, that was only at the beach, where loose dogs were common.

Two English bulldogs with their wide-body frames and short stocky legs absolutely pummeled me. The nerve of them! Didn't they know who I was? I was squealing like a pig. I had no clue I could even emit such sounds. Well, that's what duress caused, a sound of submission: Take me. Mama was frantic. The dogs' owners took their sweet time grabbing ahold of their animals. "Oh, they were just excited," they said. I sure could use less excitement.

I wish I could say it was all smooth sailing after that brawl, but a few days later another setback awaited us. It was a typical morning outing with Auntie Helen, Jack, and his new brother, Sparky (a perfect name for this Jack Russell). By instinct, his nose took him to all the hidden treasures deep underground; rapid digging was his modus operandi. We were on a side trail with Sparky in the lead, my adorable self close behind. Jack rarely joined us, as his interests lay in discovering some decayed yet delectable carcass. (Auntie Helen was never thrilled to see a leg bone off a poor deer protruding from his bloody mouth.)

Anyway, Sparky got into a nest of sleeping yellow jackets—and were they hopping mad. Sparky and I, low to the ground, were covered with stingers. Mama took the hits on her legs and started screaming. We all bolted for the main trail to get us to the beach. Unscathed, Auntie Helen grabbed me and carried me to the water to cool me off. Mama's cell phone was in the same pocket as her insect repellent. Both were trashed.

WALKING IN THE WOODS, especially on side trails, required strict attention to be alert for half-buried roots, rocks, even critters capable of assaulting a lumberjack. The yellow jackets came out of nowhere. I'd never been stung before, let alone 15 times by a squadron of furious pests. Mothers must think first of their babes, but I was just screaming in pain and fright. Thank goodness Helen escaped harm and knew enough to scoop Brady up and get him in the lake. Somehow, I managed to drive us home.

I called Dr. Mike and got a late-in-the-day appointment. Helen appeared at my door with Benadryl. She knew a lot about first aid, so I gladly accepted the bottle. As I discovered much later, I'm hypersensitive to pretty much anything the FDA approves. And also simple, over-the-counter Benadryl.

It was like I'd walked into a dark cloud with no air. I couldn't concentrate or get out of my own way. Nausea set in. It was a day spent sacked out on the couch. By late afternoon, I was fit enough to get Brady to Dr. Mike, but I'll always remember Brady vomiting up little white worms on his evening walk. And it cost me $200 to replace my cell phone. Brady and I recovered, but that was it for side trails, and we never again went to Ahern by ourselves. We stuck pretty much to the neighborhood; we'd landed on our feet/paws through a few challenges, so why tempt fate?

BRADY AND I WERE MADE FOR EACH OTHER. Wherever I went, he followed. Whatever I asked of him, he complied (most of the time). The only drawback was losing my kitties at bedtime, especially Chloe. She couldn't get used to him, no matter that he never growled at her. Had she thrown him a hiss or two, or a swat across the whiskers, Brady would've given her a wide berth. The boys, on the other hand, were unruffled by his presence, and I often saw them side by side with Brady in their version of musical beds. My dining room now had the look of a dorm room. The look of a family.

How intimidated I'd been by this pint-size pooch, but he hadn't been that tough. Maybe all puppies are easy once you know how to manage their needs. Already our first year was almost behind us. I didn't have a man in my life, but I had a dog. Whether running errands, visiting friends, having breakfast on the porch, or taking long walks on Sunday morning, we were a pair.

IN NEGOTIATING MY BROKER BUYOUT, I'd agreed to work a four-day week. When I went to Moultonborough, I knew Brady would have five hours, including my commute, to stay in his cage. That left four hours for paperwork. As soon as I got home, I clipped him to his leash and outside we'd go for his business. I was still struggling with his identity, though. He was still just a dog, right?

Perhaps a lifetime of kitties led me to see little fur bodies as self-indulgent couch potatoes, here to please when and if it suited them. And someday it'd be time to say goodbye. Never had I considered the possibility of a rerun, but the little voice in my head was doing too many back flips. Brady seemed, somehow, *familiar*. Would anybody believe me? *Did it matter?*

But, goodness, there was another "little boy" waiting in the wings, except he was no longer a little boy but instead a grown man, age 31. Fourteen years had separated Ryan and me. Almost a generation. He and Sarah were now roommates as well as workmates, just outside Washington, D.C.

A client was going to North Carolina to spend time with his siblings on a motorcycle tour of the Blue Ridge Mountains and offered me a ride on his Harley; I could fly back. I'd never been on the back of a bike for more than a few hours. This trip was two days plus an overnight in New York.

He was a long-term client and a friend (without benefits). He was kind to stop for breaks every couple of hours. All was well until we met rain in Maryland on our final leg and hit a toll on the turnpike. I was wet and cold. He looked to me to drop in a few coins. I could barely function and was this close to crying. By the time we arrived for our rendezvous with Sarah at a hotel, I was wobbly, pale as a ghost. I made quick use of the ladies' room and then went straight for the lobby bar. Vodka rocks helped me regain my sense of humor. Riding on the back of a Harley in the rain on the highway is not for a rookie.

I had booked a room at a hotel near where the kids were living. When I got to their apartment, Ryan was out on the deck. He came in and our reunion began with a hug. The three of us went out to dinner, and we chatted about Laconia and reminisced about some of the good times. I stayed another day, but Ryan had made other plans.

Where was I on the Mom meter? Is there such a thing as simultaneously numb and joyful? Could I let myself believe my son and I were back together? On how many Mother's Days had I cried? On how many September 11 birthdays had I cried? On how many Christmases? On how many "just-because" days? And how many grocery store run-ins with mothers of Ryan's classmates asking, "How's Ryan?" had I endured? And now, how tentative was this connection? Would he stay in touch? How did he feel about me?

That was the future; for now, I was grateful. I had seen him. I had hugged him. We chuckled. There was hope.

Brady

I WAS STILL A PUPPY, but my first couple of years as a canine took their toll. What with catapulting into frigid waters, facing the wrath of an angry boxer, being assaulted by a pair of drooling bulldogs, then being stung by a swarm of yellow jackets, I can't say this life was quite what I expected. I'd envisioned myself as a Chow Chow, the closest I could come to my roots. But no. Mama wanted a half-pint. So here I was, with daddy's face, mummy's body, and some ostracized relative's tail. Not exactly show quality, but I made do.

Brady, for goodness' sake!

Look, Mama, I'm all of six inches off the ground. How do you expect me to defend myself as a midget? You can't stop me. I'm going to stand upright on my back paws and display my boyhood for all to see. That ought to keep us safe from attack. Genius.

I couldn't believe my eyes. Here was my adorable pooch exposing himself every time a dog (or a human!) had the nerve to cross our path! What happened to my well-trained boy who could conduct a meet-and-greet with tail a-wagging? What command is there when your dog raises himself on his back paws and can walk like a circus animal?

I thought my idea to flaunt myself would elicit awe and respect from Mama. She missed the point, though. I knew I wasn't guarding my jungle home, but doggone it, we lived in an asphalt jungle among potential enemies who outweighed me and cast a long shadow over my munchkin self. Brazen ruffians who have the audacity to encroach on my turf posed a threat: to me, because I'm a shrimp; to her, because she'd get bruised and battered protecting me. (Okay, maybe I'd get the worst of it.) Whether I was a lion cub or a mere pussycat, at least I had claws—no such weapon as a pooch. I had a bark but no real bite. In fact, my bite was worthless. I didn't even know how to do it. Anyone could tell you that I gummed treats. Gentle as a lamb. I was a mess.

Brady

*Y*UP*, I* WAS BACK IN SCHOOL *for advanced training. Good Citizenship class was the last stop before the testing for Therapy Dog. Miss Kelly was hands-down my favorite teacher. She had a bubbly spirit and made it fun to follow her lead. Called us "Best in Show." This class taught me to focus and not be distracted by dogs or their owners, yet still accept a pat from a stranger. After six weeks of steady repetition of all the basics plus expanded separation time from our owners, we were ready for our final test. We all passed. Of course we did.*

I was full of pride, and why not? When you've got the call of the wild in your loins and the lion king in your family history, how can you be anything else but a Top Dog? Only two of us were looking for titles and heading to the big city of Concord, where we'd be tested against not only unknown competitors, but instructors as well.

This formal evaluation blew the doors off my puppyhood. Mama and I had rolled paw in hand through three levels of training—today I was alone, adrift in a sea of scowling strangers. My adorable brown eyes and cute upturned tail couldn't sway these judges. It was time for me to call on my inner beast. I pictured this frosty group as my lowly subjects, and potential targets for my next meal. Hear me roar!

I admit it took all my concentration. I knew Mama was hooked on this designation. Besides, I didn't believe in coincidences. There's a reason I was born in a day care center. It was my destiny to work with children, and the only way was through Therapy Dog certification. I needed to manage a series of exhausting exercises designed to weed out the undesirables. Only a perfect score would do. Any portion of the test where despite distractions from wheelchairs and crutches I failed to sit, stay, heel, leave it, come, or perform a down for as long as the evaluator held my paws to the fire was an automatic decline. So much pressure.

My biggest hurdle was the darn three-minute drill. Of course, I'd already been tested on this portion in Good Citizenship class, and Mama and I practiced this drill over and over in an empty church parking lot near our home. It was one thing to remain still with my mama and quite another to focus when surrounded by sourpusses. It took discipline and determination; and yes, I had plenty of both.

My heart about burst out of my chest when I saw the look on Mama's face. Her eyes filled with tears of joy, and isn't that why I came back? She scooped me up and told me over and over that I was the best. I'd heard these words before—in my last moments as Joey. Now I took it up a notch with a title: Brady Hebert, Therapy Dog.

WHEN I SAW the run-down location for the test, I wondered if this operation was set up to assess another dimension of behavior for prospective Therapy Dogs. It was a hole in the wall up a staircase above a pet store. There lacked an orderly way to register, but there were no tussles, no who's-on-first; after all, these were trained pooches. But I was ill prepared to handle my nerves once I released Brady into the hands of a stranger, to be taken behind closed doors, on the other side of the hallway. Time stood still, like all my senses had taken leave. On one level, I knew few dogs train for Therapy designation. It wouldn't be the end of the world if my doggie missed a command.

When I heard the element for distraction with noisy wheelchairs and shopping carts, I knew his test was nearing the end. When Brady emerged and I was given the nod that he'd passed, I gathered him up and tried to squeeze him with love. He, of course, was feeling too dignified for kisses; he wanted d o w n. On our way home, a special treat was in order: I stopped at Jordan's, in Belmont, for his first ice cream. He licked and slurped the cup clean.

Bailey: *WELL, BLOW ME DOWN. Don't you look like the cat's whiskers. What have you done now? Chased some poor chipmunk into his bunker?*

Brady: *Bro, you're looking at Brady, Therapy Dog Extraordinaire!*

Bailey: *So, you mean now you get to sit, wait, and get down for folks in wheelchairs?*

Brady: *Hey. You think it was easy practicing my moves in front of you guys night after night? Now I can visit folks in hospitals and nursing homes. I'm most excited, though, about being around kids who have trouble reading.*

Bailey: *Hey yourself. Let's bring Casper and Chloe into this conversation.*

Chlo-Chlo and Caspie, yawning, saunter into the room

Bailey: *GUESS WHAT! Our brother just passed his big test.*

Chloe: *Oh, geez, what am I supposed to do now . . . salute when he walks in?*

Casper: *Sis, you're still pouting over giving up Mama's bed. He's really a cool guy.*

Chloe: *I can't believe it—my own brother siding with the enemy. Call me a dinosaur, but I loved Joey just as he was—he was one of us. Now he's decided to cross over to the dark side. I may be stuck sharing space with him, but that doesn't mean I have to like it. Dogs don't impress me.*

Bailey: *Come on, Casper. I gave up trying to figure out the ladies a long time ago. You never know which way the wind blows with them. Let's grab ourselves 40 winks. Zzzzz*

Brady

MUCH TO MY CHAGRIN, *size mattered. I had to find a way to manage the stress, and I finally found a solution to being tiny. Whether with Auntie Stacy and the pack or walking with Mama in the woods, I tapped into my genetic heritage with Mama's favorite quote, "Attitude Determines Altitude." Too big to be carried and too small to go eye to eye with the average mutt, my attitude was my only weapon. I could make my bark sound like a ROAR: Be afraid. Be very afraid.*

On hiking days with Auntie Stacy and the gang, I always jumped out of the car ahead of the pack, circled Auntie's car a few times for an energy boost, and took the early lead up the hill. Usually my taller counterparts sniffed my butt along the way, which annoyed the hell out of me. In the rare instance when I was able to cast a downward glance at a compatriot (love you, Benjamin), I understood the attraction.

Then again, lest I run into trouble, I had to make friends with the giants: Helix, my Doberman guard dog on the trail; Barco, my Portuguese Water Dog in the stream; and Gus, my jumbo golden retriever buddy on the home front, whose water bowl required me to be on tippy-paws to grab a drink.

Brady

FINALLY, IT WAS MY TURN *to shine at the Gilford Public Library, Children's Room. My tail was ramrod straight, and I strutted in like I owned the place. After all, not every library gets the attention of someone of my caliber. I figured that little kids from near and far would see me and wrestle for my attention. Mama's schedule limited us to Thursdays after school, which caused a bit of a hiccup.*

Maybe if I'd been in a classroom all day, I'd have felt that 3:30 in the afternoon could be better spent, well, not reading. But these kids were screwy. They didn't want to come sit quietly in a library. They didn't want to play. They didn't run around blow-ing off steam. Instead, they wanted to plunk themselves in front of a computer screen. Still, I remained positive—they'd get bored and want to pick up a book, I thought. How naïve! I continued to prance in like this Thursday would be different. Trouble was, my crowd kept dwindling. Mothers encouraged their children to pick a book and read it to me, but they weren't interested. What?

Mama and I were mulling this over when a woman with four children—four attentive and respectful children—came over to me and one by one they sat and read me a story. Now I was in my glory. It also gave me a chance to grab a little shut-eye.

Soon Mama got in touch with Gilford Elementary's literary specialist, Dr. Wallin. Mama's work schedule lightened up, and now we could be part of the morning reading program for Grades 1 and 2. Playtime was off the table. Move over, computer screens; I was the center of attention. Mama always sat right next to me and held onto my leash just in case I got a whiff of something delicious, like the day I scoped out Dr. Wallin's lunch bag and found a cookie.

"No, no, Brady, that's *my* lunch."

Every week Mama and I went to school and rang a buzzer to be let in. Once we were in the office, I could count on getting my usual dose of oohs and aahs over my cuteness. I looked for lunch bags, but Mama had warned them I could be a cookie monster. Just my luck. Anyway, a call would go out to Dr. Wallin to have the children ready to read. Two at a time came and sat with me. All their teachers were nice, but one was my favorite: Auntie Rebecca paid me so much attention that I had to cuddle up next to her while the children read with Mama.

I was proud to help the kids learn their words. The girls liked to read—they paid close attention, following each word with a finger. Some of the boys got restless and distracted, but they always sat right next to Mama and me. They even chose books they thought I'd like, usually a story about a dog. It was a lot of fun to hear about some of my brothers and sisters out in the world, but none of them had a title like mine.

LIFE WAS GOOD for me in the year 2009. Another milestone birthday, but I was calm about it. I no longer worried about Mom and Dad; Sarah was doing well at her job; even Ryan was (sort of) back.

Walking Brady was an incredible pleasure. He and I eventually moved away from Ahern, where there were too many assailants lurking in the shadows. With Brady attached to Auntie Stacy and her brood of merrymakers to wander about on private property, his life was full with his neighborhood walks with me. And Brady found a way to bring the woods to him. I got a chuckle when we strolled along and he spied a stick. He'd grab it as if it had his name on it. Sometimes he bit off more than he could manage and needed to tilt his head up for balance. With his tail reaching for the clouds and its feathery tips swishing side to side, he picked up the pace to get home before he dropped his prize. What with the hill to our driveway, though, he usually dropped it before he could show it to Bailey.

His tail took on a life of its own whenever he saw two special friends. Grammie Mary always greeted us with a Milk-Bone or two or four. I learned soon enough that once a dog gets a bone—any bone—his brain is encrypted with the location of this delicacy and he won't be dissuaded from staying at the site.

"Brady, Grammie isn't here. We'll come back later."

No, Mama. We're gonna wait right here. I don't understand a word you're saying.

This happened most mornings, and it was an effort to get him to go in the direction of her mailbox, where she squirreled away extras just in case. He continued to stare at her door, convinced Grammie would open it—treats always tasted better with a pat on the head, an admiring comment ("How handsome he is!"), and her fingerprints. It took awhile, but in time he figured out that when her car was gone, so was she, and he let me lead him right to the mailbox.

Uncle Jim, Brady's second special friend, provided treats in the afternoon as well as the morning. He was a mail carrier, and Brady was obsessed with him. My doggie soon learned to distinguish the sound of his truck, even when it was down the street. In the middle of an afternoon nap, his ears pricked up. *Mama, he's here!*

I'd been pining for an extended family, and Brady's special friends became mine, too. Auntie Stacy, Grammie Mary, and Uncle Jim filled a void.

I WAS CLOSING IN on my four-year broker business buyout, but the universe gave me a poke. My agency's owner had been thinking about retirement and selling his business, something he'd never mentioned. He waited until the night before he inked the transfer to tell his staff that effective January 1, less than a week away, the agency would be in the hands of a much bigger player, a competitor with a sizable platform across New England.

The news was a shock: we were a team—a small but mighty one. Con Grace had been the best, but Dick was excellent. I was reluctant to begin anew, to negotiate schedule and compensation with an unknown.

I called a colleague, a specialist in health insurance, to see if I could join his agency for the remainder of my working years. Bill had launched his career at Melcher & Prescott, where I'd worked part time in high school. Now it was a five-minute walk from my house. Would there be an opportunity for me? I wondered.

First impressions, for better or worse, rarely change. But given my history with men, why would I presume to be a good judge of character? Well, occasionally, I get it right.

Shaun, the CEO, was intelligent and empathic with boy-next-door charm. He approached my potential employment with a surprising twist during the interview.

"So, if you had a chance to do anything, what would it be?" he asked.

"Honestly, I'd love to do what I did before I went into insurance," I told him. "I was activities director at a retirement home, but

I brought the residents into the community with a newsletter as well as art exhibits and crafts that would benefit charities."

He listened carefully, then said, "I think we could use a marketing representative. Let me give it some thought and come up with a job description, then I'll get back to you."

Change can be effortless or seismic, and this one effortlessly retooled my identity in a wonderful way. In a matter of weeks, I was in my own office with the mandate to expand Melcher's footprint in the community. Then it was a postcard dropped on my desk that brought a seismic change.

Adopt-a-Spot was a city initiative to improve its downtown curb appeal during the summer. Whiskey barrels filled with blooms sat at the front of most businesses. This spring happened to coincide with the official opening of a recreational trail, some ten years in the making, that would highlight my stay at Melcher. The WOW Trail, a 1.3-mile paved path representing our three adjoining lakes—Winnipesaukee, Opechee, and Winnisquam—was announced with great fanfare. It made sense to me to bring Adopt-a-Spot onto the trail.

Now I could pick up the phone and ask anyone for money, especially for something tangible. What's $100 in exchange for a pocket of posies for the city's newest nonprofit in return for some advertisement for their support? In a few months, I and Ryan R., from an up-and-coming technology company, were on our hands and knees planting flowers in the woods. It made the front page of one of our newspapers, the *Daily Sun*, and from that I met one of its reporters, Adam.

In the next year, Adam asked for an interview about what motivated me. Already I'd expanded beyond pots of plants to murals: ask questions, learn about local artists, appeal to them to get involved, and convince community-oriented Trustworthy Hardware to provide discounts on paints. With that success, I jumped into big-ticket items, such as granite benches at $1,000 each, while promoting another local craftsman, Kevin. It was one photo op after another.

And this was just the beginning. I got the attention of the WOW Trail Board of Directors. Would I be interested in becoming a member?

"I'd be honored," I said.

Brady

I WAS MARVELING at my wonderful life. I mean, what more could I want? Friends and family surrounded me, and Mama looked happier than I could remember, even as far back as my Joey days. If she had a tail, it would reach for the sky (just like mine!). Then, everything went black. Well, not exactly.

I was spoiled and set in my ways. And darn, suddenly I had competition in the neighborhood. His name was Toby, and he was a cat! And not just any old run-of-the-mill feline.

Tipping the scales at 20 pounds, just like me, this copycat barrel-chested preening tom acted like he ruled my home network—including my beloved Grammie Mary. He was so full of himself that he abandoned his kittyhood home and moved right in with her and her husband, Herb.

Grammie had been taking care of my sweet tooth since I was a pup, handing out yummy Milk-Bones as if there was an unlimited supply in her pocket. I had no intention of losing my treats because of this smug marauder. I no longer had claws of steel; I had my bark and my attitude—that was it. I had a sinking feeling that neither tool would rock that bad boy's world.

TOBY WAS A FORCE to be reckoned with. All muscle and a chest remarkable in its breadth, Toby ambled about his yard like a sergeant-at-arms, ready to brawl at a second's notice. I told Mary he must've been General Patton in another life.

Toby had already taken matters into his own paws one morning and attacked a neighborhood pooch, more than twice his size, who had been on an innocent walk with his mother. Despite this, Brady was hell-bent on invading Toby's space and getting the usual Milk-Bones. No fear, no caution, just in-your-face barking.

Mary and Herb hadn't had a pet for decades, and now they found themselves the adoptive parents and aunt and uncle of a cat and a dog vying for their attention. Raised on a farm, Grammie Mary was good at assuming control over an animal, and hoisted Toby into her arms to make room for Brady. In time, Brady seemed to accept that Toby was here to stay and backed down from testing the dog's patience—blessedly, the barking stopped.

In appreciation of Grammie's and Toby's understanding, I thought it appropriate to tell the neighbors to approach with caution and commissioned a garden stake, with Toby's picture on it, inscribed TOBY'S TURF. I hoped to avoid any more intruders to shake up the truce.

IT STARTED OUT as a typical girlfriend outing: Miss Janine and I went to a spring fundraiser replete with flowers, wine, and a silent auction. Held at the Opechee Inn, on the shores of Lake Opechee, it was a chance to relax with an old friend.

Among the many items in the silent auction, one especially caught my eye: a pet portrait.

A pet portrait? I liked the sound of it, but wondered how it would be to bring the brothers Bailey and Brady together. I started the bidding on the sheet and monitored it, hoping mine would prevail.

When my number was called, I did my best to keep my emotions under wraps. But by the time I returned to our table, I was in tears.

"I can't explain it, Janine. Something is pulling at me. In all the years of having kitties, I never thought of such a thing. Now I'm so emotional about a picture of Bailey and Brady and done by a professional."

I let the hot, humid weather pass and made an appointment for late September with Tim Cameron, of Achber Studio. He'd taken Sarah's senior pictures and done a great job. My boys had never been together in the car. Bailey sat on my lap, Brady in his seat.

Bailey: *WHEE! LOVE GOING FOR A RIDE. Hey, how come you're coming along?*

Brady: *Haven't a clue, bro. But I can tell you one thing: Mama is a jumping jellybean. She'd never make it in the jungle, where nerves will get you killed. She's not even saying a word to us. When was the last time that happened?*

Bailey: *Back to my question. Where am I going and why are you coming too? I'm not big on surprises. I thrive on routine. In fact, I need it for my emotional stability.*

IT WAS A SHORT RIDE to Achber's and I was already sweating, wondering if this was going to work. Tim was probably wondering too—he had admitted he'd never done a side-by-side with a cat and a dog.

I was relieved to find a parking spot close to the studio and brought Brady in first. At least he knew what *Wait* meant. Then I carried in Bailey. Unlike his reasonably patient brother, Bailey was a senior housebound kitty with only one other significant outing besides his medical appointments: attending a dance class of Sarah's. He had sat on my lap and purred throughout the whole hour, content as content could be with all the attention.

Now, Brady sat still while Tim made various adjustments. Bailey got restless.

Bailey: *THIS IS RUBBISH. I quite like when Mama and Aunt Sarah take my picture, but I've never had to pose or sit still. I look quite regal on my own, thank you very much.*

Brady: *Well, embrace your inner pooch, bro. Mama is on a mission.*

Bailey: *Well, how about if you embrace your inner cat? You know we do as we darn please—humans take direction from us. Blimey, since when does this top cat take orders? Be right back: I want to sniff this place and check out all the contraptions.*

Brady: *The photographer dude is annoying, that's for sure. But you gotta admit he's kinda funny-looking, jumping around, making faces at us like we we're paying any attention to him. If I wasn't so concerned about losing my Therapy Dog certification, I'd join you and we'd really give this guy a run for his money.*

It seemed to take forever, but within half an hour and maybe 50 shutter clicks, we were done. A few weeks later, Tim called me to make an appointment to review the pictures. All I needed was one.

ONE DAY, THE FRONT-PAGE PICTURE in the *Citizen* made me do a double-take. There, looking back at me, was a woman walking her itty-bitty dog on the WOW Trail, just ahead of our first floral planting. Reporter Gordon captioned the photo simply enough: "BOW WOW Walk." I recognized Lisa, one of my earliest clients, but her dog, Boo, shook me up. I'd heard the name several times from Stacy. Here was the same eye-popping miniature mix of Lhasa, Yorkie, poodle I'd seen with her nose up against the windowpane at Stacy's front door. That's Boo? And she belongs to Lisa?

If reporter Gordon hadn't happened to come upon Lisa and Boo just as they were leaving the trail, would my next project have ever taken place? I stared at the picture while my brain roiled like on steroids. Could I? Would they? I walked into the next WOW Trail board meeting and asked for a few moments of their time.

"What do you think about our hosting a BOW WOW Fest, a dog parade?" I asked.

The members looked at one another. For years their main fundraising event, the WOW Ball, took place on the third Saturday in May. If we held the WOW Ball for the big money and the smaller WOW Fest in the fall for additional fundraising, why couldn't we add the BOW WOW Fest the first Saturday of May, for marketing and public relations?

I could envision a canine event where proud dog owners could not only enjoy a meet-and-greet with other canine families but also acquaint themselves with the new trail. I saw it as a win-win (along with the eye candy for canine devotees to see multiple breeds side by side, kind of like the Westminster Dog Show).

As it happens, the area police departments for the past decade had recognized the benefit of a K-9 unit. Laconia's dog was set to retire at year's end, and donations were being sought for its successor. I'd just hit the jackpot—not in dollars and cents but instead in filling the vacuum that had existed within me for years. This was an event I could organize using all of my strengths, and the BOW WOW Fest was born.

Laconia's chief was the same Mike Moyer who, as a young officer, had stood flashlight to paw with Joey across a windowpane. I set him up as Grand Marshal to lead this first parade with his cocker spaniel, Sunny. It was almost too easy, but for year two, a platoon of volunteers was needed to run the show.

My connection with artists led me to Holy Trinity's art teacher Katie, who had grown up with my son. She was instrumental in carrying the marketing torch for BOW WOW. The students in all her classes, from kindergarten to eighth grade, drew their versions of a dog parade. Our other elementary schools joined in the fun, and many of the sketches were displayed for the public. The most imaginative was formatted onto cardboard and placed in retail-store windows, all thanks to another dedicated volunteer, Janet, from the superintendent's office.

A T-shirt was next. What identity could we create? Kiwi, a real dog connected to our screen-printing company, Body Covers, was irresistible. Black and white, like a soccer ball, and cute as a hedgehog, his image graced our T-shirts as well as our calendars, which had pictures of four-legged participants and kid drawings. Several local businesses agreed to sponsorships, enabling us to cover the costs of production and provide a free T-shirt for early registration. All of these marketing tools supported the WOW Trail.

BOW WOW did well through the years I managed it, but then I needed more help. Ann Saltmarsh, chief of all things administrative from the Public Works Department, had more connections than the mayor himself and could juggle multiple vendors who offered services relating to canines. One who jumped on board my first year was the son in a new father-and-son bakery, Brendon. He was thrilled to create dog-friendly cookies shaped like a Milk-Bone, at the same time bringing his father's homemade muffins to a new clientele.

While I organized a crew of parking attendants, Ann managed the heavy lifters, those who set up the rigging. Her creative juices flowing, she added novel surprises. How about Dalmatian costumes for high school girls to guide folks to the venue? Yes! How about coworkers building a doghouse in their spare time? Yes! How about a kissing booth, sure to attract lots of money for our front-line K-9s?

Yes! How about securing prizes for our top three winners in the costume parade? Yes! Ann was amazing.

Local celebrities, such as Mayors Mike Seymour and Ed Engler, State Senator Jeannie Forrester, and Governor's Councilor Joseph Kenney, judged the costume parade. This first year, the winner was a breed unknown to me. A senior Italian greyhound called Angel, wearing a wedding veil and weighing less than 10 pounds, was as precious as her name, cradled in her mother's arms to accept her prize.

There were also police K-9 demonstrations, and I—a sucker for a man in uniform—felt my heart pumping as I watched these officers with their canine partners run through some drills. I realized then that few people are even aware of these trained dogs: after all, they're never at the wheel of the cruiser, risking their lives when they pull over an errant driver. No, these dogs are on the front lines when a child or a senior takes a wrong turn in the woods or a feckless burglar thinks he's home free after a heist.

K-9s, especially German shepherds, have a stomach that can twist if a service call comes in shortly after a meal. Stomach stapling was a $1,500 procedure. Not since 1988, when I'd won every award, did I feel such pride in being able to protect these officers, in large part thanks to a local celebrity whose appearance on *Good Morning America* had caught my attention:

Hulk tipped the scales at 175 pounds and lived in harmony with a chihuahua and a three-year-old boy in northern New Hampshire. He was a pit bull, a breed whose reputation suffered thanks to the shenanigans of a few. Hulk was a lovebug who howled when the little boy played his harmonica but remained calm with all the attention, whether walking down Fifth Avenue with *GMA*'s Sara Haines, basking in the glow of a live audience with the women of *The View*, or patiently taking command of a photo booth at BOW WOW. He was a wow, and so was the moment I handed over checks of $1,500 to

K-9 officers Evan (Belmont Police Department) and Adam (Gilford Police Department).

Casper: *Bro, NEED to have a word with you.*

Bailey: *What's on your mind, mate?*

Casper: *Something's up with me. I get this crazy urge to blow out my nose. It's not like I can reach for a tissue, and this junk flies every which way.*

Bailey: *I'm glad you brought this up, mate, because the other day I was grateful to be supine; I thought I was caught up in a meteor shower.*

Casper: *Maybe it'll go away as fast as it came. But don't tell sis. You know how she frets about me.*

Bailey: *Understood. Her nerves are shot about Brady. Any setback with you could be her downfall.*

IT WAS FALL 2011 when I noticed how often Casper was sneezing. When he did, he expelled a glop of white goo that sometimes traveled quite a distance. It could land on the wall or a pillow, but wherever it ended up, it was there for keeps. It took the paint off walls and the color out of the upholstery. Otherwise, he seemed fine: His appetite was good, he enjoyed his treats, he looked the same.

FINALLY, A RAINBOW across the bow of the Hebert family tugboat. The woman who happened to be on eHarmony at the same time as my son had caught more than his eye—she stole his heart. She was a Brit on a five-year visa working through the embassy. She was as lovely and pretty as she was smart, and also sophisticated, a veteran of traveling solo to foreign lands. My guess is that Ryan, now in his 30s and handsome and bright, had to up his game.

This young woman wasn't interested in baubles and bling, two accessories that seemed to rub Ryan sideways since he was in high school. I met her when I visited the kids over Thanksgiving and liked her enormously. Sarah is the one who told me he had fallen in love.

It was somewhat of an emotional roller-coaster for me. I was happy for him, but what about the family waiting for her back home? Do I regain my son only to lose him again?

February 2012

IT SEEMED MY PETS often suffered setbacks on Dr. Mike's off days. With four animals in my household, I thought it wise to add a second medical office. Drs. Chris and Julie had opened an animal hospital in nearby Meredith, and as a partnership were on call six days a week. Casper's nasal discharge was the same, and nine months had passed since I first noticed it. Dr. Julie checked him over and suggested a cytology, a minimally invasive procedure to clean out the affected nostril and provide an analysis of its cell structure without a biopsy. He'd be home the same day. I agreed.

It was rhinitis, an inflammation of the mucous membrane. Although this cleansing might alleviate his sneezing, there was still a real possibility that the underlying cause was a malignancy, which called for significant testing. But a wait-and-see approach seemed the right decision.

Brady: *HEY BRO, why you looking so glum? You keep telling me how much you love riding in the car with Mama, even if it's to the doctor, that it beats pulling a pack of loudmouths.*

Bailey: *Mum got some bad news today. My blood work shows hyperthyroidism. And to add insult to injury, now I have a heart murmur. I need an echocardiogram at some fancy hospital called CAVES. I'm not keen on the sound of that. But if I can survive the coldest temps on earth, I'll emerge from this hideaway in fine fashion.*

Brady: *Good grief. Sounds like something for humans.*

Bailey: *I bet Pépère had one—he had all kinds of heart problems. It's rubbish to be in this position.*

Brady: *That might explain why he got so grumpy when I swiped at him in my previous life and made him bleed. Promise me you'll maintain your good disposition.*

Bailey: *No guarantees, bro. In human years, I'm closing in on 80 myself.*

BAILEY'S ANNUAL CHECKUP showed an uptick in cardiac concerns, and the recommendation was a trip to the veterinary hospital. If I had to transport one kitty 30 miles for an evaluation, I was grateful it was Bailey. All his life he'd been like a jar of honey left on its side in the heat of summer—as unflappable as could be, until he got his dander up. When something disturbed his equanimity, he knew how to set the record straight.

Bailey

GOING FOR RIDES in the car with Mama sure beat pulling a team of ne'er-do-wells through the gloom of night on an empty tum. I knew I'd be a boy of leisure from the day Mum Sarah scooped me up and cuddled me. A roof over my head, a full tum-tum, and a house to myself to wander at will—oh, I was a jolly good fellow even when I was a mere nipper. Only a roll with my brothers nudged me off my backside.

I realized that my luxurious coat covered a host of evils, such as my advanced age. But today struck me as a bit dodgy. Sitting on Mum's lap while she drove was like sitting on a bag of ice. It was taking a lot longer than usual, which meant we were going to that pet hospital to have an echocardiogram.

I'd always been a healthy chap, except for the misalignment of these hips, which never did straighten out. (That's one of the many things that make me extra special.) The only problem was an occasional digestive issue. Lately, though, I was feeling my age. I was stuck in a ground-level existence, as I couldn't leap onto desktops or chairs anymore. I missed being able to keep a look-out for hooligans, and I missed catching the morning rays in the loo window.

Since Joseph saw fit to reenter our lives, I felt blinking blessed to have my choice of plush dog beds. It was jolly good fun to see him glued to his old cat bed, which was way too small for him—it was a mystery why he didn't want to stretch out like a normal pooch. But maybe when you're lucky enough to live not one but two lives, you can pick and choose the best of both worlds and enjoy the perfect life.

Anyway, I was feeling like my life had gone to pot. I did my best to sort out Mum's problems ever since the sibs elected me their leader. But now Casper was falling apart; Chloe wouldn't function without him; and I had trouble dragging myself out of bed. I ached all over. At least I could still manage the distance from my bed to the food mat; I continued to be good with biscuits. Maybe this cardiac test would kick-start my engine.

Mum carried me in as usual—no crate for this handsome chap. The hospital was ginormous—high ceilings, posh furniture, hallways leading who knew where—and we had the place to ourselves. Perhaps they rolled out the red carpet for yours truly. Someone led us to a small room, where Dr. MacGregor introduced himself. He was my first Scotsman.

Mum was nervous, but the test didn't take all that long and my motor ran non-stop. I loved being the center of attention. When it was over, though, I was knackered and wished I were home.

WHEN WE HUMANS have a health problem, we can make adjustments regarding nutrition, exercise, and sleep to improve our well-being. Our felines, on the other hand, are pretty much one-size-fits-all, the-couch-is-my-best-friend, one-day-at-a-time fluffballs.

A heart murmur is rarely a good diagnosis, although an incidental one needn't set off alarms. But it's a precursor, at least it was in Bailey's case. He began a course of treatment involving two cardiac prescriptions.

THE YEAR 2012 had all the ingredients to rock my world—the good, the bad, and the break-my-heart. May saw another BOW WOW as well as a Mother's Day getaway. This year, Sarah and I flew to San Antonio, for a stay on its famous River Walk.

Quite different from on our previous trips, conversation centered on the imminent addition of the new family member. It was heartwarming that Ryan included me when he proposed, and I was thrilled to pass on the engagement ring his father had given me. What made me nervous was that he wanted to show her his hometown. Sixteen years had elapsed since his departure for college. My heart was filled with joy but also anxiety—I didn't want to make a mistake that jolted us back in time. It had to be perfect.

July 11, 2012

RYAN AND LISA were due in Laconia the next day.

Casper had lost his appetite and was lethargic. He was still adorable, although he was down a pound or two from his heyday. I kept close watch on him, and that night he vomited. And there was blood. I called the Winnipesaukee Veterinary Emergency Center, and he was seen almost immediately.

Diagnosis: hypercalcemia, leukocytosis, hypokalemia, serious ocular and nasal discharge. Labs, subcutaneous fluids, antibiotics, prescription. Departure: 1:41 a.m.

I was acting on autopilot. I brought Casper home with instructions to call Dr. Julie in the morning to make an appointment to decide on any treatment. I was told to separate Casper from the rest of the pack to monitor any output in the litter box as well as any further vomiting.

Brady was with Auntie Stacy for the rest of the week; the kitties were nowhere to be found. After all, it was the middle of the night.

On this hot summer night, I tucked him into his favorite dog bed in the three-season room and closed the sliders separating it from the rest of the house. I set up a disposable litter box. In his 16 years and 26 days, Caspie and Chloe had never been separated. It broke my heart to obey the doctor's orders but I couldn't risk infecting Bailey and his sister. As I walked away, I checked on him one last time, and there he was pressed against the windowpane looking at me. I looked back at him and I knew what he was thinking:

"Mama, don't leave me in here. Please, Mama, let me out. Please."

I was torn apart. What if he transmitted whatever caused the vomiting to his siblings? Could I risk it? I went with my gut. I opened the slider. I took out his favorite dog bed. I nestled it in a big chair in the living room and tucked him in again. I couldn't have slept a wink, still seeing that little sad face looking at me. I think he stayed put all night. Did Chloe visit him? I'll never know.

Thursday, July 12, 2012

THE NEXT MORNING, Caspie was curled up in the same position. I called Interlakes Animal Hospital, in Meredith, as soon as it opened and was told to bring him in. Ryan and Lisa were due at Manchester Regional airport at 11:35 and I knew I'd have to leave no later than 10:00 to meet them. Updating the medical records of a sick senior kitty took more time than I'd anticipated, and I was a half hour past my deadline to make it to the airport. Unbeknownst to me, the plane's landing gear had a problem and it had to circle while emergency personnel got to the tarmac. The plane landed a half hour late and I got there just as my son and his fiancée disembarked.

I was grateful for their company and elated that Ryan had returned to his roots with the love of his life. I took them to lunch at a restaurant with a patio and we sat outside and talked about their plans. It was sunny and warm, a perfect day for a comfortable chat.

As we drove north toward Meredith, where I'd booked them a room at an inn, conversation centered on many of the changes in the Lakes Region. That afternoon, we walked the first portion of the WOW Trail, and I told them of my efforts to have murals, garden plots, and benches.

It was obvious that this lovely Brit brought Ryan a sense of peace. There were no awkward moments as we enjoyed a late-afternoon cocktail before returning to my house for a barbecue. Ryan manned the grill.

I didn't ask him any questions—I didn't want to hit any sour notes.

They had use of my car so Ryan could show Lisa around, and she drove. As I waved goodbye, I was overcome with emotion that my son and I, and now with Lisa, had the makings of a complete family. Even with happiness at this long-awaited reunion, I was worried about Casper. He was still in the hospital.

Friday, July 13, 2012

I CALLED THE HOSPITAL first thing. Casper was still undergoing tests, but the doctor set up a late-afternoon appointment. Ryan and Lisa were spending the day with his high school friends, leaving me to fret over Casper's illness. Blame percolated. Should I have taken him to the vet about his sneezing a year ago? Should I have given the go-ahead for the biopsy instead of the cytology? Could he have been cured had he been seen earlier? How could this valiant member of Team Bailey be so sick?

I thought about the first time I saw him, when as a mouse-size cotton ball he was lying, belly-up, in the palm of my hand.

At 4:00 it was time to drive the ten miles to the hospital. Dr. Chris told me Caspie was a very sick kitty. He was still bleeding from the nose and vomiting. His kidneys were failing, he had an intestinal disease, necrosis, hypokalemia, low potassium, hypercalcemia, and ocular discharge. How can so much go wrong so fast?

The doctor's assistant carried Casper into the exam room. A paw was already in a splint. I was unprepared for the sight of my near lifeless little boy.

It was time for the Rainbow Bridge. No hopeful images of perpetual sunny days and flowers blooming and birds chirping eased the wrenching pain of having to send this cherished kitty to his final destination. Dr. Chris, his assistant Sarah, and I were at his side as he lay immobilized on the table. A second later, without a sound or a look back at his mama, Casper was gone.

Brady, 10 months old, checks out the neighborhood. (February 2008)

Brady discovering the great outdoors. (October 2008)

Mama with Bailey and Brady. (September 2010)
Courtesy of Tim Cameron Photography.

"What lies behind us and what lies before us
are tiny matters compared to what lies within us."

—*Ralph Waldo Emerson*

PART FOUR

From 2011 through 2013, I think I believed my fur family would be intact forever.

The ride home from Interlakes Animal Hospital was excruciating. I thought about gathering Bailey and Chloe for a chat, but I decided to play Pretend, give them their treats, and hope they didn't ask any questions.

The next day, I had Lisa all to myself, as Ryan was playing golf with a couple of high school friends and was then staying with them for the rest of his visit. I worried about how Ryan had portrayed me. This one day was an opportunity for her to get to know me on her own.

As soon as we were alone, Lisa asked about Casper, and I stayed calm when I told her he had passed away, as I didn't know if she would empathize. My focus had to be on her, not my pain. Because we'd met only briefly over the previous two Thanksgiving weekends, today was the one day that would set the tone for our future relationship. Tears had to wait.

Brady: *Hey, bro. What's going on? I bunk with Auntie Stacy for a few days and return to a different home. The sun is out, but we might as well have the shades down. Feels like we're under a storm cloud. Too bad we can't place an emergency call. We need my groomer in here with her clippers to cut the tension. And what's up with Mama? Her eyes are rimmed with red and I can't get her to play with me. I want to cheer her up but nothing works. And where in heck is Casper hiding?*

Bailey: *Casper is gone. I overheard Mama say he had cancer. Chloe doesn't know yet. She thinks he's still in the hospital. I don't know how to break the news to her.*

"

Brady: *Say it's not so. I loved the little guy. He was small but he had spunk. His devotion to Chloe was admirable and amazing. They were glued to each other when I was Joey, and it was the same when I came back as, well, me. I wish I'd told him I loved him. Why didn't he confide in us? Maybe we'd have been better prepared to tell Chloe.*

Bailey: *We felines usually hide our problems. You were different when you were Joseph. You spent time in the hospital and then came home for a couple of months. As much as I missed you, Mum and I could see how weak you were. Casper's sneezing didn't cause any alarm. And although we hadn't tussled in a while, he seemed fine last week as we lay stretched out together for our afternoon nap.*

Brady: *I hate myself for taking him for granted. If Chloe could tolerate me, you and I could tell her together. If I was allowed in the den, I'd get in touch with my feminine side and at least give her my best tail wag. I'm afraid this burden falls on you, bro.*

Bailey: *When Casper and Chloe elected me their leader after we lost Joey, it didn't occur to me that I'd have to be the messenger with bad news. What do I know about such a thing? I might be a happy-go-lucky kind of guy, but I'm miserable too about losing my favorite wrestling chum. And I know Chloe won't understand any-thing about the Rainbow Bridge.*

Chloe: *BAILEY, PLEASE, please tell me my Caspie is coming home. He is, right? It's been unbearable over these past few days. We came from the same litter and have been inseparable our whole lives. We're like two sides of the same coin: when I'm down, he makes me laugh; when he's down, I beat him up. Please, please tell me he'll be home soon.*

Bailey: *Chlo-Chlo, do you remember when I told you about Joey and the Rain-bow Bridge?*

Chloe: *No, Bailey. I don't believe it. It's hogwash. Casper wouldn't leave me without saying goodbye. Before he disappeared, I knew he was sick because for the first time we didn't sleep together. I thought he didn't want me to catch whatever he had. You told me Mama was taking him to the doctor to get better.*

Bailey: *She did, but Dr. Chris said there was nothing more he could do. Casper was just too sick.*

Chloe: *You were an only child, so you can't understand what it meant to enter this world with your forever best friend. I feel broken. I can't live without him. I won't live without him.*

Bailey: *I get it, Chlo. But you and Casper elected me leader. Now it's just the two of us, and I promise to watch over you. I'll do anything and everything I can to make you feel safe and loved. Lean on me.*

Chloe: *Thanks, big brother, but no one can mend my broken heart. Not now. Not ever.*

How could this be? We were one month to the day after Casper's passing, and I was back in Dr. Chris's office. Bailey had a lump in the corner of his right eye and the doctor said the mass had to be removed. While my kitty was under anesthesia, Dr. Chris did an oral exam and extracted two teeth. The mass, a cystic hyperplasia, was benign. Some consolation. I took Bailey home, still groggy.

Brady: *Now what? You were gone all day. I had no idea what was going on, and I'm still licking my paw over losing Casper. And what's that thing around your neck? Is it some sort of costume?*

Bailey: *Mumble . . . mumble . . .*

Brady: *What? You're talking funny. And you look like you've been in a fight. Okay, you're too tired to talk about it. I get it. I'm just glad you're home. And, by the way, from now on, you're going to hear these words a lot: I love you, bro.*

The next day

Brady: *BAILEY, SLOW DOWN. You're still talking like you've got cotton in your mouth.*

Bailey: *I'm so done with doctors.*

Brady: *Tell me, bro. I love you.*

Bailey: *You saw the bump around my right eye, right? Okay, I assumed Dr. Chris would get rid of it. I was out for the count and when I came to, two of my teeth were gone! My tongue was finding potholes everywhere. Shouldn't I have signed a release? And there was this cone around my head, so I couldn't take a nip out of the doc when he clipped my nails. Major humiliation.*

Brady: *Oh dear. You've had a day of it. But look at the bright side: your name can be a hyphenate, like all the best people in London. Bailey Hebert Cone Head. Sounds posh.*

Bailey: *You're jealous. You know your claws are worthless. If I were younger, I'd scratch you silly. But I'm afraid those days are over.*

Brady: *You always gave Casper and Chloe sound advice when they were meowing about one thing or another. Now it's my turn. Get your butt to bed. You'll feel like a new man when you wake up. I love you, bro.*

THAT FALL, my stomach was either in a knot or roiling and I couldn't put my finger on why. At least Bailey's lump had been visible, but it had come out of nowhere. And I wasn't aware that he had two rotten teeth. His appetite hadn't changed . . .

November 6, 2012

I HAD A LUNCH appointment with clients who met with me once a year at the 99 Restaurant to review their group health renewal. These entrepreneurs and I also commiserated about the myriad details involved in a long-term business. I couldn't keep our date.

I was walking by the counter on my way to the dining room table for my paperwork and caught a glimpse of Chloe curled up on the telephone cord in the corner near the three-season room. She wasn't moving. And there was a puddle next her.

"Chloe, what's the matter, sweetheart?" No response. No movement.

I called Dr. Mike, at Tilton Veterinary Hospital, and was told to come right in. I started the car, ran back inside to grab a kitty mat and a small afghan, and picked up my Chloe. How many times had she tucked herself into some recess to avoid a checkup? This time she sat on my lap as I drove, like she was numb. I wanted to hold her.

We were ushered into an exam room—the same room I'd been shown with Joey. Dr. Mike took one look and knew: there was nothing he could do. She'd had a stroke. She lay on the table, more quiet and looking more peaceful than she had since we lost Casper. Again, my heart broke and I was back in the bottomless well of grief.

"Chlo-Chlo, I love you so much. Goodbye, my sweet girl."

Just as Dr. Mike inserted the needle, she yelped. *Oh dear, did it hurt her? Did she leave this world in pain?* Neither Joey nor Casper had made a sound. Was she saying "*Caspie, I'm coming*"?

I didn't say anything to Dr. Mike or to the girls at the desk, but I'm sure they understood. I went to the parking lot, got into the car, sat there, and gave in to all the emotions I'd bottled up when Casper died. I hadn't done anything about his sneezing . . . I wept, too, for Chloe. She had been in agony over the loss of her brother. She had howled and she howled, and all I did was tell her to be quiet.

The price I paid has been regret for not being attentive enough to them. I wish I had taken Casper to the vet; I wish I'd comforted Chloe, stroked her, told her how much I—we all —loved her. In the space of four months, I lost half my fur family, maybe partly my fault.

Bailey: *YOU'RE NOT GONNA BELIEVE IT, bro. We've lost our lassie.*

Brady: *You just got back from Auntie Stacy's. How do you know that? No way!*

Bailey: *I know things. She's gone and done it. She told me she wouldn't live without her brother, and she went and gave herself a heart attack or something.*

Brady: *How the heck?*

Bailey: *Listen, I'm no psychiatrist. I have no idea what makes the ladies tick.*

Brady: *Dang it, she never recognized me. Am I in some way responsible for her demise? Maybe if she saw me as the big-brother version of Casper, she'd have found a way to get her purr on.*

Bailey: *Well, matey, it's just the two of us now. Kinda the way it was when we were wee lads in the feline world. At least Chloe and Casper are back together. Maybe over the Rainbow Bridge is a good thing. Let's have ourselves a spot of water and a snooze.*

Brady: *It's not a bad place if you find yourself a sweetie.*

Bailey: *One day at a time, bro. We've got our own sweetie right here who still needs us, though I must say it's been a long time since we've seen a guy hanging around. Maybe she finally sorted herself out. Oops, pardon my yawn.*

Brady: *And who do you think is responsible for that?*

Bailey: *I'm tired and in no mood to think about you as an adorable pooch come here to save the day. Over and out. Zzzz*

eHARMONY WASN'T THAT FAMILIAR to me. I'd never done an online dating platform. While it had been some time since I'd been in a relationship, I had my boys for company. Finally, I didn't need a man. Still, coworkers urged me to at least try a dating site.

"I don't want to meet a stranger. Too scary. What if he's a Jekyll and Hyde kind of character? Maybe I'd consider a fix-up by somebody who knows somebody, maybe." With an emphasis on *maybe*.

"eHarmony is different," they said. "These prospects are serious about a relationship. Otherwise, why would they take the time to answer so many questions? Try it. What do you have to lose?"

Ryan had met Lisa on eHarmony. And I discovered that my precious daughter was also using this same site and already had gone on a few dates. When Christmas and time for our annual mother-and-daughter blowout arrived, it was obvious she was distracted. She told me she was having extended conversations with a guy she'd already met.

"I'm thinking of inviting him to Lauren and Chip's New Year's party," she said.

Uh-oh. A party like that means a premature intimate setting, with a lot of alcohol. She could be giving up the cookie way too soon. During my no-dating period, I'd read a book that adjusted my thinking when it came to men. It was Steve Harvey's *Act Like a Lady, Think Like a Man*—all about the 90-day rule and "the cookie."

Steve said it takes a man 90 days to tap into his feelings for a dating partner who's been hands off. Could he wait? That made a lot of sense. Two of my friends were pushing me to try eHarmony. I could act "like a lady" and find out whether a date had a real interest in me. That was a plan, so okay.

It was a Sunday afternoon in January, and I'd finished the endurance test of assessing every aspect of my character. When it came time to pay online, I got stuck. Either I couldn't figure out how to enter my credit card number or I couldn't bring myself to do it. I called Annie, a techie friend.

"I just finished this damn dating questionnaire and I don't know how to do the payment portion. I think it's not meant to be."

"I'll be right over," she said.

Sigh. She was at my house in 20 minutes.

"Read me your credit card number," she said, and in seconds I was in the universe of singles looking for love.

It might be tough. Laconia was some distance from any significant population. Manchester, an hour away, was as far as I would drive, and all I could offer in the way of a date was time for a cup of coffee. Who'd be interested in so little?

Soon enough, pictures came from men "matched" with my profile. Wait: upstate New York? Northwestern Vermont? A four-hour drive to some guy in northern Maine? A friend looked at the pictures I'd posted and said she knew why there were so few matches and all out of my range.

"Claire, look at yourself. You look like a nun. You've got to show some cleavage—that's what men want."

"Well, that's not what I want. I don't want to set myself up as sexy and then activate the 90-day rule if someone gets pushy."

"The 90-day rule?"

"That's advice from Steve Harvey's book. Keep a man at arm's length for 90 days and see if he sticks around. If he does, you're more likely to begin a real relationship, rather than a wham-bam-thank-you-ma'am situation that makes you feel like yesterday's leftovers."

"Oh."

One prospect seemed promising. He was a retired school counselor with a master's degree. We chatted through the website's email system. I told him how much I'd wanted to pursue a career in counseling. The rub, though, was that he lived an hour and a half from me, in Massachusetts.

Another "match" came my way, with only a picture from a driver's license and no info about interests, travel, education, family. But he lived just 30 minutes from me, in Concord.

I began to enjoy long talks with Mr. Retired Counselor and short exchanges with Mr. Close-By, who wasn't all that forthcoming but pretty insistent about our meeting in person. I never thought to question it. In mid-February, after two weeks of internet chat, I set up back-to-back dates with these two prospects: on Wednesday, for lunch at the Manchester Mall, midway point for Mr. Counselor, and for coffee at Panera in Concord with Mr. Close-By. It was unfortunate but Mr. Counselor realized it was the day before he began a weeklong cruise with friends. Could we meet when he got back? Of course.

THE MEETING WITH MR. CLOSE-BY stayed in place: coffee at three o'clock.

I was a bundle of nerves, but I felt some control: he had a son who worked for a competing insurance agency, and if it went really, really badly (remember Big Ben?), I could call him and tell him about his father's dark side.

I stopped at Talbot's, just up the hill from Panera, to gather myself and remember the two decades of walking into strangers' homes. I got to Panera a few minutes after 3:00 and spied a single guy at a window table.

"Aha," I said. "This must be you." He looked just like his photo ID, and was cool as the proverbial cucumber . . . I didn't know I was date number 54 across six dating sites.

I asked the server for my usual midafternoon snack: a decaf cappuccino and a pumpkin muffin. With such a low-cost order, I didn't offer to pay. Conversation came easily during the time I'd allocated for this meeting: one hour. I'd scheduled an appointment for myself back in Laconia, a good excuse for me to leave.

"When can I see you again?" he said.

"Um, I don't know. I don't get to Concord that often."

I'd just leased a Toyota RAV4, and the company agreed to equip it with winter floor mats, which would be delivered to its dealership in Concord.

"I can let you know when my mats come in and we can arrange to get together."

That wasn't good enough; he wanted to see me sooner. With some reluctance, I agreed to meet him in Concord at a dog park the following Thursday. I'd bring Brady for his afternoon walk.

When I got to the park, I immediately saw his truck. He got out and greeted me with a king-sized grin and something else—he'd called the dealership and convinced someone there to let him pick up the mats for me.

Surprising, but not off-putting. And that was just the beginning. He gave me the mats, then handed me two cards and a gift certificate to Talbot's. He knew from my profile that my birthday had just passed. The first card wished me a happy birthday: from Bailey! The second was signed "Brady"! Only Sarah had ever given me a card from a pet. Holy cats and dogs!

February 26, 2013

IT WAS BRADY'S first dental cleaning. Unlike my sweet Chloe, who had built-in radar for a trip to any kind of doctor, Brady was blase when he didn't get his breakfast, and his tail wagged when I got him into the car. I'd be picking him up at 5:00.

As usual, I went to the office and came home for lunch. Bailey was just to the right of the kitchen counter. I gave him a second look because something seemed off. As I was approaching the dining room table, in my peripheral vision Bailey seemed to spin, then he got still. And stayed still. Something was wrong. I called Interlakes Animal Hospital and was told to come right in. I called the office to speak to my HR director, who herself had a kitty.

"Holly, I don't know what just happened to my Bailey. We have an emergency appointment at Interlakes, so I won't be back this afternoon."

The ten miles up Parade Road to Interlakes provides ample time to worry. Bailey was on my lap, as he always was when we went somewhere, but with a huge difference: not a peep, no humming coming from his outsized motor. I knew in my heart that this might be the end, but I tried to reassure him.

"Bailz, my sweet boy, Dr. Chris will do everything possible to make you feel better. Please stay. I know how much you loved Pépère, and I know he's waiting for you, but I'm not ready. I love you, and so does Brady. We need you. We're family."

In the examining room, I put Bailey on the floor, and he just stayed still. So as to make Bailey as comfortable as possible, Dr. Chris checked him right there. After a while, he stood up.

"Bailey has had a stroke," he said. "If we don't do something soon, this little boy is going to be in a lot of pain."

"You mean in a few hours?"

"Sooner," he said. "I'm so sorry."

I knelt and stroked my beautiful boy. I wanted to hold him, hug him, tell him how much we all loved him, to bring him home for one more night with Brady and me . . . but I couldn't let him suffer.

Dr. Chris prepared the injection and joined me on the floor and we lay there, on our stomachs, looking at my precious boy. Bailey showed no pain, no emotion. In my mind, I told him I'd always remember his purr, his outsized feet, his massive tail . . .

I remembered when he walked away from me at the breeder's and she almost didn't let me take him home; when Joey first laid eyes on him and gave him two quick hisses and that was it; when he met Pépère and swished his tail and rolled on his back for a belly rub; when Casper and Chloe showed up and he looked like he was attached to an air pump; when he lay on my lap through Sarah's dance practice and purred for an hour; when he grabbed his "babies" one by one and deposited them where they "belonged"; when he was forced to take matters into his own paws with that terrible house sitter, with a hulking giant, with anyone or any canine he considered a threat . . .

And then it was over. My third kitty in seven months.

MY CHILDHOOD BEAUTY took himself off for the dirt nap. During my first marriage, Tanya was hit by a car. In my second marriage I lost Mitzy to leukemia. Tia, too, was leukemia.

This brood—Joey, Casper, and Chloe and then with Bailey—had been in a league of their own. Collectively, they gave me the equivalent of 66 years of unconditional love. They slept on my bed, they twined themselves around my legs, they comforted me when I cried. I was so overwhelmed by grief that I had trouble getting up from the floor. But it was time to pick up the only little boy I had left.

Brady

It was supposed to be just an ordinary day in the life of a pampered pooch—it turned out to be the worst so far. I was relieved to know the groomer wasn't on the schedule, but going to a doc never set my heart aflutter, even though I got through his pokes and prods. Today was different: my first dental cleaning as a pup. It was similar to when I was Joey: mouth felt like sandpaper, limbs were a bit stiff from a day in the cage. But then my heart broke.

I knew as soon as I walked into the dining room that he was gone. If I'd been there, would he still have left me? Why couldn't I have been here to stop it . . . or at least to hold his paw and tell him that life on the other side was good. Maybe he couldn't face saying goodbye to me. I hope he comes back for another round with Mama—and with me. Bailey was more than my best bud. He was my brother.

I knew he'd been failing, just like he knew when I-as-Joey was failing. He was on two heart meds. His legs looked like they were made of wood when Mama picked him up. Still, he manned up—more than I did.

Now I had to remember everything he told me to do when someday I was left alone with Mama . . . there was something about making sure she didn't make another mistake. What mistake? Later—now, I was too discombobulated to think straight. Mama, sitting in her chair, had trouble looking at me. I think she was trying to man up.

Boy, I was feeling a whole lot more pressure than I expected. I mean it was so quiet. I already missed Casper and Chloe. Yes, her howling was annoying, but the sounds of silence sent shivers up my spine. And now my Bailey was gone. What with my two incarnations, we'd spent the equivalent of 80 years together, ribbing each other and solving the world's problems.

Our most important goal was—always—to save Mama.

MR. CLOSE-BY was into me in spades—maybe too into me, maybe too many spades. I'd learned to be cautious. Needing a man to complete me had been the worst reason to fall headlong into a relationship. I'd even learned to be content as an independent woman, no longer alone in a world of couples. In addition, what with everyone's children grown and gone, the phrase "single mom" had lost any power.

Now, given our conversational compatibility, Mr. Counselor continued to loom large in my mind. Fate intervened, though, and it was not to be. His ten-day cruise ran into a double whammy of snowstorms in Massachusetts. He held tight to his life up north, but his friends convinced him to remain in Florida. Who could blame him? Maybe if he'd come face-to-face with my baby blues and my wit and wisdom . . . alas.

So Mr. Close-By had me all to himself—but on my terms. Trust had to take time, and I gave him no guarantees. One Saturday in March, on one of those perfect late winter–early spring days that pull a dedicated hibernator away from the heat lamp, Brady and I met him at the Steeplegate Mall, in Concord, for a ride to my favorite haunt, Ogunquit. Walking its beach, during any season, brings me peace and a feeling of tranquility.

When we arrived at the parking lot at the beach, Mr. I-Wanna-Be-in-Your-Life quickly got out of his seat, came around to open the door for me, and then reached in to scoop Brady up in his arms and set him oh so gently on the ground.

"I was concerned he might hurt himself if he jumped down." That single act helped to seal the deal at the end of the 90-day (plus two weeks) probation I'd established.

Anyway, he still didn't know where I lived, but I felt I owed him dinner since we'd gone out on neutral territory or places of my choosing several times. I decided to consult Sarah.

"Sweetpea, you think it's okay for me to have him over for dinner? Then he'd know where I live."

"Oh, Mom, I'm sure it'll be fine. I mean, he could find your address on the internet."

On a Sunday, he came for my usual haddock dinner in my usual 62-degree house. He cleaned his plate, and with nary a shiver. My pooch lay belly-down under the coffee table.

Brady

OH NO, this must be what Bailey meant: Mama never gets it right with men. I pretended he wasn't here. No eye contact, no tail wag. So what if he'd been kind to me. So what if he was all gushy over her. I had my orders, and besides, I didn't want to share Mama. I liked it just the way it was. My former self and my brothers and sisters had gone head over tails to keep her out of harm's way. It was high time for it to be just the two of us.

Mama with Brady: Who needs a man? (2011)

Mama and Brady people-watching on the porch. (November 2010)

*"It is never too late to be
what you might have been."*

—George Eliot

PART FIVE

Mr. Close-By—Dean—on August 24, 2014, became husband no. 4. It happened quickly for this 22-year single girl, especially considering he'd emerged thanks to a website's algorithms. I think he'd begun to capture me when he said "Je pense que je suis tombé amoureux de toi"—"I think I've fallen in love with you" in French, a language he didn't speak—two months after we met. We got engaged after six months.

I was in no rush to marry—until I was. Ryan and his bride were going to live in England. Sarah was engaged and pregnant. I wanted them to be by my side. Dean and I set the date.

Now this Mama Bear speedily organized a gathering of family and friends. Both my children's mothers-in-law were in the wedding party: These two adopted sisters, Ruthie from the UK and Sylvia from Delaware, led the way on the arms of their respective sons. Following them were Dean's son and his girlfriend, stunning in her native Indonesian garb; Dean's daughter, her husband, and their three children, as flower girl and ring bearers; and my own cubs, with their spouses, just ahead of me.

I wore a scarlet satin full-length dress to represent the love I felt. The walk down "the aisle" of the Oval Room overlooking Lake Winnipesaukee at Church Landing with Dean had me glowing like a 1,000-watt bulb. With both my children there, as well as extended family and special friends, I felt whole for the first time in years. All the loneliness and regret had been swallowed up by the joy now filling my heart.

IN TIME, Brady got used to sharing his mama. He and Dean forged their own relationship, and Brady soon learned to love his papa. I retired from my insurance career at the Melcher & Prescott Agency in September 2015, with the intention of finishing off out my truncated education, through the online program offered by Southern New Hampshire University. I graduated in May 2019, the recipient of a master's degree in creative writing, nonfiction, beaming in front of my husband, daughter, son-in-law, and granddaughter.

My Brady bud provided more joy, more emotional tranquility, more companionship than I ever dreamed possible. In other words, the eagle had landed. Sleeping past sunrise suited him just fine, and it was I who was up and about long before he was. The days of *woofing* by the side of my bed were gone; he now slept in. As I busied myself in the kitchen, I kept an ear out for his plop onto the floor. While he waited on the top step, I'd open my arms: "Here he comes to save the day!" I'd trill in my best Mighty Mouse imitation.

TWO EVENTS in late April 2021 threw us into a downward spiral. Over the course of a month, Brady suffered four emergency stays in four hospitals. I never gave up; no one was honest about what was going on. Specialists had said he had pancreatitis. Sure, he needed changes to his food and a few supplements, but that was easy.

Leaping onto my bed and off the bed had always been effortless, until one morning Brady tweaked his lower back and his gait was off. After a day at Interlakes Animal Hospital, Dr. Julie diagnosed a slipped disc. We scheduled an appointment with a chiropractor who had worked on animals. That first session gave us hope, the second one took it away.

On May 1, there was a sudden collapse on the floor of the Northway Bank lobby, and after Brady yelped, he lost control of his bladder. There were two emergency visits, to hospitals in Meredith and Concord, and then we took him to an internist in Scarborough, Maine, who recommended a cardiologist in Portland, the same Scotsman who long ago had administered Bailey's echocardiogram.

Frankly, after hours sitting in a car with the temperature in the high 80s, it didn't feel realistic to schedule a second appointment in another six months. But in Concord and Scarborough, Brady spent time in intensive-care units, receiving the best treatment veterinary medicine could offer. I didn't think beyond the moment. He was the love of my life.

Because he couldn't navigate the stairs, we turned the living room into his bedroom. Two additional canine "couches" gave him places where he could be comfortable as he watched me go about my day. Five medications, with food, at eight-hour intervals, dictated our bedtime. I worried that he'd attempt the stairs to sleep with me, so I removed the cushions on the grownup couch in the living room and slept there. Brady preferred the floor, sandwiched between his doggie beds.

May 2021 was sunny and warm, weather Brady never cared for. Born in December, he was a cold-weather boy. On the hottest days, I still took him to the beach for a quick dip in the water, but we no longer took our morning walks to see Grammie or look for Uncle Jim on his route. Instead, I put him in the car and we drove to Grammie's for a Milk-Bone, then on to South Main Street to find Uncle Jim.

On Thursday, May 20, we went to one of Laconia's smaller beaches rather than the more heavily trafficked Opechee Park, his usual playground. Except for a city employee picking up litter from the shoreline, it was deserted, as I knew it would be, mid-morning, mid-week. I gave Brady time to do his business. The sanitation guy wanted us gone immediately and was obnoxious to boot. I thought of calling his boss Amy, a canine lover, to tell her how rude he was, but when a sign says NO DOGS, I knew I'd lose any argument.

BRADY'S MEDS were administered in hamburger, white rice, chicken—anything to mask the taste. He ignored the food, ignored the pills. But when Uncle Jim showed up mid-afternoon, Brady shook off whatever tummy ache gripped him and loped down the driveway to meet his favorite buddy, his tail up, anticipating as many treats as Uncle Jim would get passed my inspection. I noticed something strange, though. Instead of turning around and walking back to his truck on the curb, Uncle Jim walked backwards and kept looking at Brady.

I found solace at the Opechee Inn grounds, where my BOW WOW Fest used to be held. Brady enjoyed a fishing spot tucked off to the side, where he'd grab a drink. As usual now, I opened the car door and gently placed him on the ground for a short walkabout. That afternoon, though, he just stood there.

"Hey, sweetie. Time for our walk. Let's go this way."

Nothing. I picked him up and returned home. And I didn't connect the dots.

The only signs that his digestive tract was out of sorts were what he ate and the output. His appetite had dropped to zero; his output was tinged with red.

The next morning I discovered that Brady had slept by the side of the couch rather than in the middle of the living room. The first time I'd used a child gate to prevent him from going upstairs, he woofed, looked back at me, and woofed again. What a smart dog: He went from the living room, through the dining room, nosed the door to Dean's man cave, and nudged Dean awake, as if to say *Papa, help! What's up with the gate? How am I supposed to get to bed?* Now, to get to the gate, I had to climb over Brady as he lay motionless. I still didn't connect the dots.

On Friday, Brady didn't get up on his own, and the clock was ticking past 7:30, the time for his morning meds. Dean came in from getting his coffee and the paper, and I told him again that I was seriously worried that Brady wasn't eating. But it was Brady's direct route to the dining room table that alerted me. He immediately lay down, and that was the sign. He was done.

I went through the motions. I called Dr. Chris's office and was told to come right over. Dean got onto his belly to pull Brady as gently as he could from under the table. When I heard Dean say, "Brady, please let me help you," it was too much to bear. I got my pocketbook and went out to start the car to get the air conditioning going. I sat in the front passenger seat, put Brady's dark gray seat mat over my lap, and went numb.

Dean came into Brady's life when the doggie was already five years old, but the two had become great friends. As a matter of fact, Brady had written him a note in a Father's Day card: *I used to wonder why I was the only pup at Auntie Stacy's who didn't have a dad . . . but now I have one.* Dean and Brady and I were a family.

I didn't want Brady to think this was it, the end. Dean was crying quietly, though. When we got to the vet's office, because of the COVID pandemic all of us dog owners waited in our cars for an assistant to come out and take in our pets.

Brady wiggled on this trip up Parade Road, like he was uncomfortable and wanted to get down. I tried to rearrange him but I held him for the 20-minute drive. I couldn't talk. Really, what could I say? I was sorry for every treat, every morsel of human food that contributed to his heart issue. I was glad I'd told him every day of his life how much I loved him or the variation: "Do you know how much your mama loves you?"

Dr. Chris's vet tech Jamie came out for Brady and a quick summary. She brought him in to see the doctor. In just a few minutes, Dr. Chris came to speak with us. I expected him to tell me, as he had about Casper and Bailey, that I had no choice. Instead, what he said was this: "Brady will have more bad days than good days. The left side of his heart fills up with fluid. I can drain it . . . ."

Then I knew. There was only one choice. Perhaps I nodded.

Dean and I were allowed to come in the side door and into the same room where I'd said goodbye to Bailey. Dr. Chris's assistant asked what I wanted to do after Brady was gone. I'm pretty sure I said, "Everything. Please give me the works." She figured out that I wanted his ashes, his paw print, whatever she could give me.

Now, though, we saw a completely different Brady. He was almost hopping around, excited, eating treats like he couldn't get enough. I looked at Dr. Chris:

"What's going on?"

"Sometimes this happens."

How was I supposed to put him down?

I got down on my knees and gave him treats as fast as the vet tech could hand them to me. He was almost delirious with excitement, but out of the corner of my eye, I could see Dr. Chris preparing his injection.

"I'll give him this first injection and he'll calm down."

I lay on my stomach, face to face with Brady, unable to speak. I tried not to think about him trotting in front of me with his tail pointing skyward and swaying side to side, grabbing a stick and balancing it by tipping his head back, leaping off the porch in search of a mischievous chipmunk we named Chippie, doing wind sprints in the backyard, barking happily so loud that Grammie Mary could hear him four houses away, or bounding up from a nap when he heard Uncle Jim's mail truck down the street.

Brady didn't look old, no white scruff around the nose: Folks marveled when I told them he was 13.

I couldn't even utter a final goodbye. I was numb.

After the second injection, I saw a change, and Brady was fading. We were nose to nose. I hope I was petting him . . . did I feel his last heartbeat? I don't know. I prayed.

Our Father who art in heaven, hallowed be thy name; thy kingdom come, thy will be done, on earth as it is in heaven. Give us this day our daily bread; and forgive our trespasses and we forgive those who trespass against us; and lead us not into temptation but deliver us from evil. Amen.

And Brady was gone.

DEAN WAS DRIVING us home. "Look at our boy," I mumbled to him, "up there in the clouds. See? See his face, his two-toned body, his upturned tail? It's like he's running—like he's just seen someone he knows."

AT 9:25 IN THE MORNING a week later, on May 27, as I approached the corner of Pine and Merrimack Streets, I looked up and saw my sweet boy again: shades of tan, upright tail, floating among a few thin clouds. "Brady bud, I miss you sooo much. I love you so much. You're forever in my heart." It looked like he wagged his tail.

AS SUMMER BIT DOWN HARD with its humidity and high heat, not a day went by when I didn't either read one or all of the many sympathy cards friends had sent. He had touched a lot of hearts. I wasn't ready to face the world and return to some new normal. Estivating in the dog days made sense to me.

What was it about this little boy that touched me to the depths of my soul? I'd been a contented kitty mama since I'd been a kid. But it took those early years of my career when Griff and I sat by the town docks in Alton when it was like a lightning bolt for me to see these wigglebutts encapsulating what so many of us driven-to-succeed types couldn't hold.

First, I thought it had everything to do with the freedom of appreciating the joy of every day for what it was. A day to let go and just be.

Then on further consideration, I understood it went beyond the freedom of being detached from the almighty dollar. It was simpler than that. Brady tapped into my motherhood. He needed me every day, no matter how young he was or how old he got. I was his lifeline.

I missed being a mother. A full-time mother. A mother with benefits. Brady in his own way filled my cup, which had been gasping for air and nutrition for so long. It was the state of homeostasis I'd been groomed to have since childhood. Sure, he couldn't talk back to me, break my heart, or grow up. He was a perennial child. And I was his mama.

EPILOGUE

I GAVE MYSELF two years to mourn Brady's loss.

On Thursday, October 28, 2021, Dean was checking out the classifieds in the *Daily Sun* and an ad caught his eye: GOLDENDOODLE PUPS FOR SALE.

"Not ready," I said softly. "Wait! What's the area code?"

"603."

New Hampshire.

"Not ready."

A tide of grief could roll over me at any time: We'd be having dinner and he'd find me sobbing quietly. We could be watching TV and tears would stream. Dean always felt helpless when I cried. What could he do? He had googled doodles because the breed jumped out at us all during the summer and fall. We even saw two of them in the backseat of a convertible, both sitting on their haunches, like they were kids excited to have an adventure. But my excuse remained the same.

"I'm not ready."

Friday passed without any thought about the 603 pups. On Saturday afternoon, I took a break from writing and stretched out on the couch with *Time* magazine. And then: the area code 603 doodle pups. What the heck—I decided to call and find out when they expected the next litter.

The man who answered told me only one male was left. He put the phone on speaker so his wife, the actual breeder, could listen in. I don't know why, but I ended up telling him about all my kitties and then Brady, and then the memoir I'd been working on for six years. And I wept.

All of a sudden, I wanted to check out this puppy. "If it's okay with you," I said, "my husband and I will come by tomorrow morning and have a look. How does ten o'clock sound?"

I got up from the couch, shaking and still crying. Oh my, what had I just done? Dean was in the shower, so I paced back and forth in the kitchen, waiting to tell him what had transpired while he was in the bathroom. What I'd done was compromise on multiple levels. I hadn't vetted the breeder to see if she was reputable; I hadn't ascertained anything about how carefully she took care of the pups; I didn't even know how old this puppy was.

"Well," Dean said, "did you offer them a deposit? Did you ask for the right of first refusal?"

Dean will tell anybody who listens that he's a fixer. If someone has a problem, Dean will try to find a solution. If there's a detour, he knows an alternative route. If we run out of juice, he'll squeeze some oranges. Now he saw a way to "fix" my sadness. He called the breeders to talk about a deposit and first refusal. He was so anxious, though, that when he learned the couple were early risers, he blurted out: "We'll be there at 9:00."

The thing was, someone else had called before Dean did and was queued behind us to look at this one puppy. That evening, a third person called.

This breeder was just ten minutes from us. The house was set back on a country road, and she and her husband greeted us warmly. Then she retrieved the little fella.

Snow-white and small. When I picked him up, he immediately attached himself to the inside of my neck. His mother was going to be bred one more time, in two years. A few issues bothered me: *Why did no one choose him? Was it his temperament?*

I wanted a pup to choose me, as Brady had done. But others were scheduled to meet this pup right after Dean and I did. Then

I wondered: *Is there a reason he was still here? Was it a sign that he was meant for me?*

Dean dropped the hammer. "Why do you want to wait till you're 74?"

I was torn. And then he dropped the sledgehammer: "It'll never be better than it is right now."

No time to think. The next person might want this puppy. Or the one after.

"We'll take him," I said. "I'll call him Toby." That's what I had almost called Brady, and now it just came out—like that's who he was. And that's how Toby came into my life.

IN A MATTER OF WEEKS, Toby had ballooned, like he was being pumped up with air. Milly, his mom, was Brady's size, 22 pounds. His dad, up in Vermont, was 40. The breeder predicted he'd land somewhere in the middle, but I'd thought he'd favor his mother. Ha!

I posted a picture of him in my arms on my Facebook page and got several comments, all with the same theme: He was "huge" for three months. When Uncle Jim met him, the first thing he noticed was Toby's legs: "He's going to be a big dog."

Toby settled down at 32 pounds. He was pure white with a tail in full evidence of his golden retriever lineage. There were two early eccentricities: First, before he learned to sit on command, he sat on his haunches, ramrod straight like a human, thereby launching his nickname: The Tobe. Secondly, he loved—demanded—belly rubs. Lots of them, all the time, from anyone. He likes to sit by me as I write. He leans back, bends his front paws, extends his back paws—size 15, at least—and cocks his head to tell me he's waiting for a long belly rub.

The day of his first snowstorm, we were walking along the side of the house. It was as if he'd been shot out of a cannon; he leapt over mounds like he'd been doing this all his life! I could barely contain his exuberance and was grateful he wasn't at his full weight. I called the breeder to tell her he loved the snow. Then she dropped the mic. "Oh, his mother thinks she's a sled dog."

The following Sunday morning, I was as usual at the 7:00 mass when it registered—pure white, paws the size of a basketball player's, belly rubs, sweeping tail, the genes of a huskie . . . Wait. Just. A. Minute. Hold On!

BAILEY!!!!!

ACKNOWLEDGMENTS

ANY BOOK TAKES A VILLAGE (my circle of friends, or a city (Laconia, New Hampshire, and its neighbors), or an entire region (New England) to produce. Thank you to Mike Herrmann, owner of Concord's only independent bookstore, Gibson's, who led me to Deidre Randall, of Peter E. Randall Publisher, in Portsmouth, New Hampshire. Without knowing me at all, both went out of their way to help. Then my angel guides introduced me to Doris Troy, an editor who loves her kitties the way I did mine. Together, we went through every section of my draft until it was just right. A bottomless bag of treats to the three of you.

Margaret Sanborn, a brilliant linguist and a lifetime friend, introduced me to the need for a "throughline" and a platform. Thanks to her, *Saving Mama* took root. And thank you, too, Margaret, for propping me up in grad school and fine-tuning my thoughts when I got carried away.

Tom Casey, a soldier's best friend in and out of uniform, has a fascinating photographic memory and can chat as easily with the CEO of a Fortune 500 company as he could with a lowly recruit like me. He quickly earned a place in my heart when he stood firm that I coauthor, not just edit, blogs about executive transitions. Thank you, Tom, for taking this private into the elite world of big business.

To Ruth Caple Humphreys, thank you for adding the sizzle to Bailey's voice. His demeanor was so uncatlike that I needed an angle to set him apart from the other kitties, and being Britishly posh served him well. I'm blessed that our children met and joined their lives together (and gave us two wonderful grandchildren).

My special angel classmates in graduate school supported me through my greatest academic challenge. Enormous thanks go to Amy, Jason, Jeanne, Lyna, Megan, Traci, and Dr. Randy. It was a blast and an honor to share the stage with you for our Discussion Posts.

To Helen Becker, who groomed me to be a good doggie mom and was a pal during Brady's earliest months, I'll always remember your kindness.

Stacy Soucy subbed as Brady's mama for day care and overnight stays. From his youngest days, you taught him trust, respect, and friendship on wooded paths. You taught him how to be a leader. Is a thank-you enough? It doesn't begin to convey the love and gratitude I feel about you. You're family.

To Brady's special friends at CVS, especially Renee, Laura, Amy, and Brianna; at Northway Bank, Kyril, Cherie, Lisa, and especially Kara; and to our adopted Grammie Mary and Uncle Jim, many thanks for all the goodies and love you showed Brady.

Shelley Cram and Taia Peters, kitty sitters and adopted aunties for Joey, Bailey, Casper, and Chloe, enabled me to go on worry-free vacations. Brady's groomers, Aunties Becky and Katie, paid kind attention to his needs. Thank you to every one of you.

My connection to Bill Bald, at the Melcher & Prescott Insurance Agency, led me to Shawn Farley, who opened the door for me to expand my marketing skills, which in time led to this memoir. A big thank-you to both of you.

To the WOW Trail board, and Diane Hanley and Alan Beetle in particular, thank you for offering me the opportunity to create a path I wouldn't have found on my own, and thank you for encouraging me to add and add and add to it.

My tech team, in order of appearance—Best Buy's Geek Squad, Southern New Hampshire University's 24-hour tech support, the unflappable Don, of Reboot Computers, and in the final months

Tom, of Lakes Region Computer—helped me through waves of ambiguity without a glitch. Lizy Freudmann, of One More Thing, a strategist on a plan to market my dream beyond the neighborhood, put *Saving Mama* on social media platforms. Heart-felt thank-you to all.

To all the veterinarians, vet techs, and administrative staff affiliated with Dr. Michael Ware and then those working with Drs. Chris and Julie Jackes and Dr. Ann Bruce, I'm grateful for the years of sage advice and guidance about my kitties. During Brady's final months, I was lucky indeed for the connections to Dr. Jeanne Ficociello, of South Shore (Weymouth) Animal Hospital, and team CAVES, with Heidi Miller as liaison and Valerie Lunnon, DC. And to Dr. Jeremy Diroff and his team at Maine Veterinary Medical Center, the compassion you showed to my husband and me during Brady's final days was hugely helpful in stitching up my bleeding heart. Thank you all for your incredible kindnesses to my kitty and dog family.

To Jago and Yogi, of the Laconia Police Department; Ike, from the Gilford Police Department; Max, of the Franklin Police Department; and Vito, from the Belmont Police Department—you led me to my passion for K-9 units. To their respective handlers, Mike Finogle, of the Laconia PD; Adam Van Steensburg, of the Gilford PD; Dennis Rector, of the Franklin PD; and my contact for ancillary information, now, Lt. Evan Boulanger, of the Belmont PD. Thank you.

Gatekeepers Kevin Dunleavy, Tim Cavanaugh, and Steve Smith—thanks to them, I had no concerns about "losing" any patrons. Thank you to Hulk and to the Grennans, for letting us use their photogenic lovebug for publicity. To all our vendors—My Coffee House, Dog-gone-It-Training, Four Paws Inn, Jill Baron, Illustrator, and Happy Tails Dog Park, along with many others (for those I can't name, please forgive my memory lapse)—I appreciated your support. To Nancy Brown for her artistic posters, thank you.

Mike Moyer, former Laconia police chief and county sheriff, Bill Wright, Belknap County sheriff, thank you for believing in my mission and assisting with referrals. To my right hand, Ann Saltmarsh: you were the best copilot!

To Kim, of Winnisquam Printing and Kim-Prints-Everything, who handled everything I gave her—from my personalized Christmas cards to my multiple-choice photo library to my 167,000-word opus to my business card and beyond—you've been a ray of sunshine.

To Tim Cameron, of Achber Studio, who skillfully captured sentimental moments that could never be duplicated, I'm so grateful for your talent.

Lauren, Jeanie, Debbie, Cathy, and Janice Beetle provided limitless support in the various stages of this very long journey. Thank you for your help when I most needed it.

To my friend Marie: Although you're not in this memoir, over the last few years you've earned your place in my next one. You always asked the right questions: How was I was holding up? What progress was I making? Thank you for being the strong shoulder to lean on.

Kimberly Hancock tended to my flagging enthusiasm for almost anything over the past ten years and gave me a peek of angels and spirit animals hovering about me—especially my muse, Brady. Your gift has been priceless.

To my husband, Dean, who was a beacon of emotional support through three challenging years of grad school, words can't express how grateful I am. Your attention to detail was invaluable. And I love you for it.

I also want to give credit to Wendy, for being a good stepmom to my children. Although we were unable to enjoy a comfortable relationship, I always understood that my kids were well cared for under your supervision.

To Con Grace and his wife, Kathy, I can't imagine what my life would have been if the good Lord hadn't set you in my path. There were some thorns to manage, but I'm grateful beyond measure that you welcomed me to be part of your Wild Kingdom. I'll love you forever.

Through *BOW WOW Fest*, I discovered a community's secret weapon. A member of the K-9 unit is a policeman's best friend both on and off the job. At a cost of more than $12,000 for training a working dog or $7,000 for a comfort dog, not all departments are able to have such a partner. I've written this memoir in the hope that at least one will be given the means to add a dog to its roster: proceeds from *Saving Mama* will support a department in need. Please check out the Working Dog Foundation, in Raymond, New Hampshire, and Hero Pups in Stratham, New Hampshire, both 501(c)3 organizations.

Toby hoping for his forever home. (October 2021)

Toby at four months. (January 2022)

ABOUT THE AUTHOR

Claire L. Hebert-Dow is a proud baby boomer, born and raised in Laconia, New Hampshire. Thirteen years at Sacred Heart School may have prepared her for success in the outside world, but not so much with the male species.

In this memoir, she tells the tale of her two lives: one as the non-custodial parent of her two children and the other as a rising star in the land of suits. Deemed unsuitable, except by her boss, who took a chance on her, to sell a product no one trusts, she set out to prove her naysayers wrong. But living got in the way, and she needed help. And in stepped her Delta Force — five cats and a pooch who had the power to save Mama from herself.

A summa cum laude graduate of the University of New Hampshire (bachelor's in psychology) and some thirty years later earning a master's in creative writing–nonfiction, Claire has dusted off the cobwebs of her most painful memories.

This proud Mimi of four grandchildren, two from her son (and daughter-in-law) and two from her daughter (and son-in-law), is hoping to put together a fund large enough to support the training of a working dog or comfort canine for community support.

Claire still lives in Laconia, with husband Dean and their dog, Toby.